D1267494

The Catholic
Theological Union
LIBRARY
Chicago, Ill.

KARL BARTH'S CHURCH Dogmatics

An Introductory Report
on Volumes I:1 to III:4

by OTTO WEBER

Translated by Arthur C. Cochrane

Philadelphia

THE WESTMINSTER PRESS

WITHDRAWN

The Catholic
Theological Union
LIBRARY
Chicago, Ill.

COPYRIGHT, MCMLIII, BY W. L. JENKINS

All rights reserved — no part of this book may be re-
produced in any form without permission in writing
from the publisher, except by a reviewer who wishes
to quote brief passages in connection with a review
in magazine or newspaper.

The original German edition of this work was published in 1950 by Verlag der Buchhandlung des Erzie-
hungsvereins in Neukirchen Kreis Moers. The translation into English was made with the permission of
the publisher and in agreement with Professor D. Karl
Barth in Basel and Professor D. Otto Weber in
Göttingen.

Library of Congress Catalog Card Number: 53-6528

71401

PRINTED IN THE UNITED STATES OF AMERICA

FOREWORD TO THE ENGLISH EDITION

by *Karl Barth*

The English language is undoubtedly the sacred language of the ecumenical movement — pretty much in the same way as Latin is the holy language of the Roman Catholic Church. Anyone who participates in the large or small gatherings and conferences of this movement is badly off if he is not able to read, understand, and — in a pinch — to speak at least a little English. It is inexcusable that in my youth I did not suspect this at all and that at that time I therefore neglected to acquire a knowledge of this universal and future language of the Church. When I was about forty years old I began with great difficulty, but with a good will — Principal John Mackay of Princeton, then in Bonn, was my first teacher! — to assimilate it to a certain degree. And one of the great blessings of the ecumenical movement for me, for which I am truly grateful, is that it has forced me to learn English. For if even yet I am very backward in understanding this language (especially American English!), and still more so in speaking and writing it, nevertheless, as a reader of English works I fairly soon made such progress that for a long time now books in English have been an indispensable source of instruction and pleasure for me. I must admit that I acquired the ability to acquaint myself with the theological literature, including the stack of " papers " that reach me by way of Geneva, in the course of reading innumerable detective stories, to which of course were then also added not a few books of a still higher class originating in Britain or America. (For my pleasure these evenings I am indebted to a gift by an ecumenical friend of H. Melville's *Moby Dick,* which in its way can scarcely be surpassed.) Most necessary of all, I also learned in due time how to carry on informal conversations and discussions, though not public addresses. So far, so good!

But now the fact that English is the sacred language of the ecumenical movement also means that it is not absolutely necessary for American and British theologians on their part to learn other languages, German, for example, and as a rule they do not undertake to do so. I am told that it is more difficult for them than the opposite is for us. That may well be. Moreover, they cannot feel obligated to do so when in fact the rest of us appear to be so zealous and also to be able in a certain measure to move about in their language amid their indulgent smiles. Your problem — and then indeed ours also in relation to you — actually first begins in regard to the books written by us in our other — nonsacred — tongues. It is true that what may be read in them has not been uttered from heaven. Consequently we certainly do not think that our British and American friends *must* absolutely read us. If, however, they are not able to read us at all, then that is to be regretted in the interest of mutual communication, understanding, and cooperation. That cannot come about by oral conversations alone without a knowledge of the literary foundations on both sides. Now it is just here that the kindly and deserving work of the translator intervenes who, persuaded of the importance for the English-speaking theological world of this or that book in another language, and for his part being master of both languages, jumps into the breach. He renders intelligible what would otherwise have to remain unknown, and thus assists both sides to listen carefully to each other, so that they might, with that proviso, be able to speak intelligently to each other instead of speaking past one another. Dr. Cochrane, a man who is extraordinarily competent for such work, considers Otto Weber's report on the volumes of the *Church Dogmatics* which have appeared so far to be in this sense an important book, and for that reason has undertaken to translate it into English. I am grateful to him for this assistance. I hope that his work will serve just that communication and understanding without which, in fact, even the ecumenical movement will not be able " to move " in the long run. The selection of this particular book appears to be a fortunate and timely one because even now in Scotland a group of bold, capable, and industrious men are busily engaged in a still much greater undertaking: in the translation of the *Church Dogmatics* itself and *in extenso* to which, of course, the book by Otto Weber seeks to be an introduction and, in its brevity and succinctness, naturally can be only an introduction.

But that is the very thing which reminds me now of a problem that has nothing to do with linguistic problems which in the end can be mastered through good translations. Am I in error when I have the impression that quite extensively in the world of Anglo-Saxon theology there is a definite aversion to voluminous books as such, and a certain preference for summaries that are easily understandable and may be repeated in simple catchwords? What sort of reception will be prepared for the *Church Dogmatics* there, when in view of its size it is actually not altogether unlike Moby Dick, the white whale? And will not even the translation of the book by Otto Weber, even though the number of its pages is so much smaller, be nonetheless, precisely in its conciseness, reminiscent of that unpleasant characteristic of its original, and consequently will not receive the cordial acceptance it deserves? It is certainly not the first English translation in which I have appeared. The *Epistle to the Romans,* and the collection of addresses, *The Word of God and the Word of Man,* from a very much earlier period in my life; the first half-volume of the *Church Dogmatics* itself, and not a few smaller writings, among them of course the *Credo* and *Dogmatics in Outline,* have been in existence for a long time. But now, how many have really read these translations in such a way that they are competent to speak about the content of the books? Am I deceived when I have the impression that there I exist in the phantasy of far too many — even of the best men — mainly, only in the form of certain, for the most part, hoary summations; of certain pictures hastily dashed off by some person at some time, and for the sake of convenience, just as hastily accepted, and then copied endlessly, and which, of course, can easily be dismissed? However, I could hardly recognize in them anything else than my own ghost! God as " the wholly Other "! Kierkegaard's " infinite qualitative distinction "! For me creation is nonexistent! By me culture and civilization are damned! With me ethics is impossible! According to me the Church is Noah's ark on Mount Ararat! Her task consists in preaching an otherworldly Biblicism and an inactive quietism! All in all: " neo-orthodoxy " with a faint flavor of nihilism! What else? Should I weep or laugh? Is this the only way in which I am known in the English-speaking theological world in spite of all the translations that have appeared so far? How does one read, how does one really study there, even when the opportunity and possibility for study were offered through the existence of translations? After all, I do not expect anyone to agree with me — still less that he say nice things about me. But since it now happens that there are those who have so much to say about me, without presumption I might expect that they had first informed themselves about me and therefore had read me, and moreover, had read me calmly and in some measure completely. Will the hope be fulfilled that the translation of the *Church Dogmatics,* and now the translation of this introduction, will be understood and accepted as an invitation to renounce a little the hasty theological journalism, of which up till now I have largely been a victim, and to expend approximately as much serious effort as my books have required of me and still do? And will the hope be fulfilled that then there will result a meeting of minds, a lively exchange of ideas, and a mutual advance, as all of us would ultimately like to see within the framework of the ecumenical movement? That is the question with which I accompany this publication. It is my concern for a greater, deepened, and more relevant fellowship among Christian brethren and theological colleagues, whom I think of with respect and love, but also with the desire that in the future we may be nearer to one another because we are able to understand one another better.

I have stated in the foreword to the German edition what I think about Otto Weber's book. It need not be repeated here. The reservation and the warning, which Otto Weber expressed in his own preface, may also be recommended in a friendly way to the attention of American and British readers.

Basel, November, 1952.   KARL BARTH.

FOREWORD TO THE GERMAN EDITION

by Karl Barth

May I say at once that I always have respect when I hear of anyone who has read all, yes, all, of the 4,507 pages — it actually happens! — of the six part-volumes of the *Church Dogmatics* mentioned in the preface to this book. I respect such a fellow creature because I can gauge, by the labor each of these pages actually cost me at the time I wrote them, the amount of work a person has put behind him who has read every page. And I also respect him, because anyone who has done that much has at least fulfilled an important condition for being able to judge the work I have undertaken in the *Church Dogmatics* and elsewhere. I certainly do not require anyone to speak well or ill of me; nor do I really insist that a man must read me at all. But if anyone wishes to speak about me, he should have at least read me. That is not too much to ask. Moreover (if he is a serious person and not a journalist, and therefore not a theologian who thumbs through a book), he should have read me completely. Not everyone who thinks he is able to know and say all sorts of things about me has fulfilled even this condition. Therefore, in the face of so much I hear said about me, I too may and should simply keep silent. This is the reason why I am filled with respect when I see someone who has at least taken the necessary trouble of a reader.

However, my respect turns to joy whenever I see that I have not only been read but also understood. I do not say: met with agreement. We are not here to agree with one another and to applaud one another. If there are " Barthians," then I am not one of them. We are here to learn from one another, mutually to make the best of what we present to one another in a literary way, in order then to pursue one's own way — not in a theological " school " but within the Church and thus independently. But just to that end it is necessary for us to understand one another. And in this sense I am happy when I come across people who have tried to understand the *Church Dogmatics,* and have really understood it — regardless

of what, on their part, they might then want to make of it. I am
glad when I find evidence that here and there certain things have
gotten home, and have been taken up and carried farther. Then,
indeed, I may assume that I have not simply labored in vain during the now nearly twenty years of my life which have been devoted to this work, and that it is still worth-while for me to persevere in it for the remainder of my days.

And my respect and joy become gratitude when I perceive that
someone has read and understood the *Church Dogmatics* so well
that he is in a position not only to give adequate information concerning the entire work but in addition is also able to instruct others how to read and understand it. I owe such gratitude to Otto
Weber. I do not want to extol his virtue in undertaking such a
selfless task in the writing of this book. I would simply like to say
that I am aware how his effort actually makes my burden lighter.
I look upon his work as an outline map of an area of the *Church
Dogmatics* which has already grown so large. It could also be fit-
tingly compared to the service of one of those well-made, valiant
little tugs which may be seen in the great harbors of the world tow-
ing the somewhat out of proportion and cumbersome transatlantic
steamers out into the open sea or into a safe port. For a long time
I have realized that my undertaking needs such a service. Certainly
I myself would no longer have come to write a " Compendium "
along with the " *Summa*," a " *Medulla medullae* " beside the
" *Medulla*." Otto Weber, pursuing his own methods and of his
own accord, has now ingeniously achieved something like this. I
am obliged to him for doing it, and readers will also be. The possibility of the misuse of such a book is obvious. I think of lazy people who are always in a hurry to get things done, the glib talkers
and superficial writers on this and the yon sides of the Atlantic,
who, if possible, will merely scan through even this compendium.
Otto Weber has warned them in his preface; and — following the
experience I had nearly thirty years ago with what Max Strauch
wrote about my commentary on the *Epistle to the Romans* — I
would like to emphasize his warning. But *abusus non tollit usum.*
And why should we not dare to count upon sensible readers as
well as the unreasonable ones?

Basel, January, 1950.   KARL BARTH.

AUTHOR'S PREFACE

This little book does not want to be anything else than its subtitle states: an introductory report. Certainly I am not the only one in recent years who, with ever-increasing urgency, has been impelled to write such an introduction. The monumental character of the six-volume work to date, its inaccessibility for many years to almost all theologians in our country, and, above all, the — for many people, perhaps unjustifiably — alarming magnitude of its contents have led many theological — and not only theological — contemporaries to look for such a little aid! Those who gently but firmly persuaded me in the end to write this little book must now answer for its appearance. Only I myself can take responsibility for the contents, and even that not without all sorts of inhibitions.

The inhibitions mentioned result from, among other things, also the fact that only with difficulty can so compact a survey avoid all sorts of distortions to the contents. Consequently I would not have taken upon myself such a risky enterprise if Karl Barth himself had not assured me that he could still recognize himself in this abridgment.

One cannot, however, warn too strongly against thinking that a reading of this short report might somehow take the place of Barth's work. It can only prepare the way for it. For this reason I have also quoted verbatim from the work itself as extensively as possible (but with the omission or altering of the spacing of numerous words). At all costs I did not want to get in its way. In a very special sense the purpose of this little book is rather to make itself superfluous.

In addition I call attention to the fact that the report of the last published volumes of the *Church Dogmatics* appeared in issues of the *Reformierten Kirchenzeitung* for the years 1949 and 1950.

Göttingen, January, 1950.   OTTO WEBER.

TRANSLATOR'S PREFACE

The present work is a translation of the second edition of *Karl Barth's Kirchliche Dogmatik* by Otto Weber, published by the Buchhandlung des Erziehungsverein, Neukirchen, Germany, in 1952. Professor Barth's foreword and Professor Weber's preface to the first edition remained unchanged, and a note was appended by the German publishers to the effect that in the present second edition the report covers the eight volumes, instead of six, of the *Church Dogmatics* which have appeared so far. This accounts for the discrepancy in the dates and in the number of volumes and pages mentioned.

In their forewords both Karl Barth and Otto Weber have warned against the dangers attending this introductory report, and have urged that it be looked upon as simply a useful stepping-stone to the *Church Dogmatics* itself. May I venture to add two reasons, not mentioned by these writers, why this report can in no sense replace the *Church Dogmatics?* As is well known, Calvin's major contribution to the theological literature of his day consisted in commentaries on almost all the books of the Bible. While Barth has also written several commentaries, for the most part he has embodied his exegetical work in the *Dogmatics*. No theologian in the history of the Church has so thoroughly and painstakingly grounded his theology in Holy Scripture. I cite just one example. Two hundred and seventy-four pages, of which considerably more than half are in 8-point type, are devoted to an exegesis of the first two chapters of Genesis alone! When the *Church Dogmatics* is translated, a veritable mine of homiletical material will be available to the preacher. It is my conviction that the greatness of Karl Barth consists as much in being an expositor of Holy Writ as in being a systematic theologian. And this is something the present brief cannot convey.

Although Professor Barth has made special contributions to the study of the history of Christian thought, notably his *Die protes-*

tantische Theologie im 19. Jahrhundert, it is again true that the bulk of his writings in the history of dogma is contained in the *Church Dogmatics.* By means of frequent excursuses he relates his doctrines to the stream of Christian thought, and enables us to understand the problems of our day in their historical perspective. And that too is something a brief report cannot convey.

The extreme condensation of the material in Professor Weber's book has not made the lot of a translator, striving for clarity, any easier. I have resisted the temptation to indulge in innumerable explanatory footnotes, and have kept them to a bare minimum. And I have virtually eliminated the German practice of spacing or italicizing words for emphasis.

In conclusion, I wish to express my very warm thanks to friends who have assisted me, in various ways, in the preparation of this manuscript. In particular I wish to thank Professor Emeritus F. W. Kracher, Ph.D., who read the initial draft of the translation, and Professor Otto Weber himself for the prompt and courteous way in which he answered inquiries and read the final revision.

The Presbyterian Seminary,   ARTHUR C. COCHRANE.
University of Dubuque, Iowa
January, 1953.

INTRODUCTION

Karl Barth's *Church Dogmatics* is the most voluminous presentation of its kind in a very long time. The eight volumes which have
so far appeared, with their 5,956 pages, though only half of the an-
ticipated size of the entire work, justify the common expression
that it is an evangelical " *summa* of theology." The recollection of
the " *summae* " of the Middle Ages is all the more in order since
Karl Barth shows no inclination to let himself be influenced by the
natural objection that he is practicing " scholasticism."

The physical weight of this work, however, is only the most obvious side of its real, intrinsic weight — something no one seriously disputes. For here an inquiry is made concerning the " substance " of Christian doctrine with an urgency and devotion such
that no one can disregard it, no matter what position he may take
to the whole or to particulars. In fact, this dogmatic work is at once
a document of Church history, something that has fallen to the lot
of few of its predecessors. It has not been written apart from the
life of the Church of Jesus Christ but actually in a constant reference to it. The ideas advanced in it — here we naturally first
think of " Barmen " [1] — have authoritatively influenced the decisions of the Church. But all the more deserving of attention and
respect is the fact that Barth has not allowed himself to be led
astray at all by the decisions of the " day " and to become a theological " writer of the day," but — as is shown by just those parts
which originated at the height of the Church struggle — he has
" stuck to the matter at hand."

When he started out Karl Barth did not think it should become
his task to attend to this " matter " in the form of a huge dogmatic
system. As is well known, in 1922 he urged that his " contribution
to the theological discussion " simply be taken as a kind of " mar-
ginal note or gloss," " perhaps as a corrective, as the ' pinch of

---

[1] The reference is to the Barmen Declaration of the Confessing Synod of the
German Evangelical Church in Wuppertal-Barmen, May 29-31, 1934.

spice' in the food, to use Kierkegaard's phrase." [2] He was consciously reminded of this word when he then nevertheless in the year 1927 came forward with a *Christian Dogmatics in Outline* and thereby established himself as an " ordinary theologian " who felt " neither entitled nor obligated to continue in the role of a prophet or in the attitude of a religious awakening." (So he wrote in the preface to the only volume published of that *Christian Dogmatics in Outline*, p. ix.) And one will have to acknowledge that he was right: the way out of the *Epistle to the Romans* (1919), as a " way upon earth " (*Christian Dog.*, p. ix), had to lead to Barth's applying himself to dogmatic work. It was all the more necessary because since 1921, due to his position, Barth has been obliged to deliver lectures in dogmatic theology, and because, from the very start, statements were made in his name of which he did not approve (*Christian Dog.*, p. v).

As mentioned, the *Christian Dogmatics in Outline* did not get any farther than the first volume. When its author had to begin revising his book for a second edition, he realized that the matter could not rest with a mere revision but that a new work would have to be produced, and under a new title. Thus in 1932 the first half of Vol. I of *Church Dogmatics* appeared, which, together with the second half which came out — previously in Switzerland — in 1938, corresponds roughly to the material which in 1927 was once intended for that single volume of *Christian Dogmatics*. In regard to the size the result had to be a multiplication of what had existed earlier, and as to the content, a new work.

So far three volumes of this *Church Dogmatics* have appeared. Nineteen years have elapsed between Vol. I, 1 and III, 4 (and what years they have been!). The first volume (I, 1 and I, 2) presents " The Doctrine of the Word of God " with the subtitle: " Prolegomena to Church Dogmatics." The second volume contains " The Doctrine of God "; the third, " The Doctrine of Creation." A " Doctrine of Reconciliation " as the fourth volume, and a " Doctrine of Redemption " as the fifth, are to follow.

The first volume is again divided into four chapters. The first deals with " the Word of God as the criterion of dogmatics " (I, 1,

2 *Das Wort Gottes und die Theologie*, 1924, pp. 99 f. English translation by Douglas Horton, *The Word of God and the Word of Man*, 1928.

pp. 47–310) ; the second, with " the revelation of God " (I, 1, pp. 311 ff. and I, 2, pp. 1–504. Subsections are: " The Triune God," " The Incarnation of the Word," and " The Outpouring of the Holy Spirit ") . The third chapter deals with " Holy Scripture " (I, 2, pp. 505–830) , and the fourth with " Church Proclamation " (I, 2, pp. 831 ff.) .

CONTENTS

―――――

I

THE WORD OF GOD AND DOGMATICS

[Volume I, 1, pp. 1–310]

ANYONE who is impressed by the survey of the contents just made may well ask himself whether this first volume does not constitute a complete dogmatics in itself. Does not the author in his two massive half-volumes present us already with an unusually exhaustive dogmatics? In a certain sense Barth would answer this question in the affirmative. In giving to this weighty double-volume the subtitle " Prolegomena to Church Dogmatics," he promises a detailed discussion which is to be introductory, preliminary, and basic to all that follows. However, he is not specifically concerned with speaking about certain predogmatic themes, but rather about what already belongs to dogmatics itself: " It is not a matter of things that must be said in advance, but of things that must be said first " (I, 1, 41). Hence he describes the " prolegomena " as " the preliminary part of dogmatics which deals with the comprehension of its special pathway to knowledge " (I, 1, 23). What we are allowed to hear at this point as " introductory " is already dogmatics in the fullest sense of the word! Or expressed otherwise: the " special pathway to knowledge " in dogmatics can be discussed only " in terms of dogmatics."

But what does " dogmatics " mean? Barth begins with an answer to this question. And he answers first of all with the thesis: " As a theological discipline, dogmatics is the scientific self-examination which the Christian Church makes with respect to the language about God which is peculiar to her " (I, 1, 1). In this definition it is immediately worthy of note that dogmatics, together with all other theology, is understood as " a function of the Church " (I, 1, 1). The Church speaks about God. Her speech is human speech (2).[1] Everything then depends upon whether this human speech about God agrees " with the existence of the

─────

1 Henceforth citations refer to Vol. I, 1, unless otherwise indicated.

Church." [2] The existence of the Church, however, is Jesus Christ! Δ
(2 f. and freq.). Jesus Christ — that means: " God in his gracious
revealing and reconciling approach to man " (3). Each and every
theology has the task of inquiring about this " criterion." Biblical
theology asks: " Does Christian speech proceed from Him? " Practical theology asks: " Does it lead to Him? " And dogmatics asks:
" Is it in agreement with Him? " (3).

Dogmatics is a " science " when it pursues this question " properly; that is, with a corresponding fidelity " (6). Of course, that
cannot mean that dogmatics (or theology at all) should assume an
obligation " to allow itself to be measured by standards valid for
other sciences " (8). What characterizes it as a science is first its
" effort after a particular object of knowledge "; secondly, its treading along a " particular pathway to knowledge consistent with itself "; and thirdly, its ability " to give an account of this pathway
. . . to itself and every man " (6). It is therefore not an arbitrary
activity, not an occult science, and not just idle talk. On the other
hand, it is no more than science (9). It must protest against every
" ontological exaltation " which one might like to attribute to it
over against other sciences, just as conversely it must also protest
against the " admittedly ' pagan ' general concept of science " —
without, however, taking the paganism of the latter so seriously
that it would have occasion to " separate " itself from other sciences " by using another name with an air of superiority " (9 f.).

Perhaps all that appears simple: dogmatics, pursuing scientific
methods, inquires whether Christian language corresponds to a
" criterion " which has been indisputably established for it. But
what, then, is this criterion? Barth gives a twofold answer to this
question. On the one hand, it is not necessary for dogmatics first
to discover this criterion; it exists! The question which agitates all
dogmatics has received a basic answer before there was any dogmatics: " Dogmatics presupposes that God in Jesus Christ, as he is
the existence of the Church, . . . is the truth," and indeed " is
also and precisely the truth *for us* " (11). Dogmatics occurs in the
believing knowledge and acknowledgment of this truth and a dogmatic proposition, " as a statement of faith with respect to its real
object," must therefore be " ventured in the certainty of uttering

2 " *Mit dem Sein der Kirche.*"

not human but divine truth " (11). On the other hand, just because " the truth is presupposed in faith as the accepted standard
of all things," it is also asserted that this truth " in no way is assumed to be 'present' " (13). "A human certainty cannot be
made out of a divine certainty " (11). This holds true in regard
to the dogmas formulated by the Church. They are not a " truth
of revelation." On the contrary, " the Truth of revelation is the
freely acting God himself and he alone " (15). Thus dogmatics, as
surely as it is " the science of dogma," is also " the science of dogmas . . . only in a subordinate sense and in the strictest connection with the former " (14).[3] Dogmas cannot relieve us of the necessity of making a real inquiry. Even the Bible cannot do this. To
be sure, the Church can let " her own existence, as the norm of her
language," be attested " only by the Scriptures with divine authority "! But just for that reason she is then " challenged to recognize
it herself " and " to inquire with all the earnestness of one who is
still ignorant about what Christian language may and should say
today " (15). In other words, the answer that has been given does
not exclude but demands that questions be raised ever anew!

A dogmatic proposition, we heard, looked at in the light of its
" object," is a " statement of faith." Accordingly, Barth goes on to
tell us that dogmatics is possible only in faith; that is, in a " determination of human action by the existence of the Church, and
therefore by Jesus Christ " (16). Such determination, however, is
at the disposal neither of the Church nor of an individual. " It is
God, and not we, who determines from time to time whether our
hearing is real hearing, our obedience real obedience, and whether
our dogmatics is blessed and sanctified as a knowledge of the true
content of Christian language, or is idle speculation " (18). No
matter how strongly we insist upon the conversion of the theologian (18 ff.) or upon the existential character of theological thinking (19 f.), nothing can alter the fact that what decides whether
dogmatics takes place as an act of faith is the freedom of God,

---

[3] TRANSLATOR'S NOTE: Professor Weber's treatment of Barth's distinction between
dogma and dogmas may seem unduly compressed at this point. But the same might
be said of Barth's own treatment of the subject at this particular place in his
Dogmatics. See *The Doctrine of the Word of God,* translated by G. T. Thomson.
T. & T. Clark, 1936, pp. 15 f. However, Barth later returns to a full discussion of
the subject on pp. 304–315, to which the English reader may be referred.

which — as the freedom of his grace — is honored in prayer. Accordingly, prayer is "the attitude apart from which dogmatic work is impossible" (23; there are numerous similar expressions).

Let us return to the point with which we began our reflections. We learned that "prolegomena" to dogmatics are already dogmatics itself. But why are they necessary at all? Barth replies that it is certainly not because dogmatics first has to prove or defend itself to those outside; that is, in the face of modern man's own reason. To be sure, dogmatics by its very nature will always be a kind of apologetic. But a "deliberate apologetic and polemic" has always been "an irresponsible, out-of-date, and therefore ineffectual action" (29). It takes seriously the unbelief of the one with whom it is conversing — which, in view of the "article about the forgiveness of sins," it ought not to do. It acts as if everything in dogmatics itself "had been perfectly settled," and overlooks the fact that actually all of its propositions are being constantly threatened (29).

No, dogmatic "prolegomena" are "an inner necessity, grounded in the thing itself" (30). This implies that if dogmatics must first render an account of its special pathway to knowledge, it does so in opposition to an opponent who is on the inside. It is a matter of a "conflict of faith with itself" (30), of "the paradoxical fact of heresy" (31). Heresy is a "form of Christian faith" (31), a "possibility . . . within the Church" (33). But in truth it is nothing else than a "contradiction of faith" (31). It is a contradiction which therefore represents itself as faith, which wants to be the Church, and in which faith finds itself in conflict with itself! Barth forthwith tells us the concrete heresies he has in mind: Roman Catholicism on the one side, and "pietistic-rationalistic modernism" on the other (33). This twofold heresy requires that the question which decides between it and the Church of the gospel be clarified. The question is: What is revelation, and along what lines may statements be made about revelation?

In order to show that this is really the decisive point, Barth next investigates the way in which modernism and Catholicism on their part find a point of departure for their dogmatic statements. Modernism begins outside of (Reformation-evangelical) dogmatics;

that is, with " an existential context transcending the existence of
the Church " (37), with a " general " understanding of man, his
world or his existence. (In this connection Barth also finds Bultmann going along the standard paths prepared by Schleiermacher,
36.) Whenever one proceeds in this fashion, " the existence of the
Church " and faith are understood " as a qualification of man's reality, as piety " (37). Then the possibility of doing this is always
looked upon as a human possibility. The Christian character of
such thinking has to be disputed just at this point (38). Catholicism, in contrast to modernism, begins within dogmatics; or rather,
within the sphere of divine revelation (39). It starts with the
Church. But it does so in such a way that " the existence of the
Church, Jesus Christ, is no longer the free Lord of her existence,
but is . . . bound up with the existence of the Church " (40).
But this means that here " God's action immediately vanishes and
is absorbed in the action of the man who has received grace " (40).
Revelation becomes a datum impersonally preserved, as it were,
by the Church. Or expressed otherwise: the Church bears her " existence " within herself. Actually the Church's existence is " identical with Jesus Christ " (41). (This is Barth's leading thesis,
which we have already heard expressed numerous times.) If such
is the case, however, then it is to Christ " one looks for the free
personal decision concerning what is to be the proper content of
Christian language, and also what is to be the pathway to its knowledge — the knowledge of dogma " (41). The norm of Christian
knowledge, the " criterion of dogmatics," is to be found " neither
in a universal human possibility " — as in modernism — " or in
an ecclesiastical reality " — as in Catholicism. On the contrary, the
criterion of dogmatics is " the Word of God " (43).

Barth is now ready to proceed with the theme of the first great
chapter: " God's Word as the Criterion of Dogmatics."

Before he deals with the form and nature of God's Word, he discusses Church proclamation as the event in which the Church is
the Church. It will serve to make this brief report more intelligible if we immediately have in mind the basic propositions on
which everything that follows is built.

In the first place we are to consider the thesis about the " three-

fold form " in which God's Word is addressed to us (89 ff.) . God's
Word is the " preached Word," the " written Word," and the " revealed Word," and it is all these in indissoluble unity. We may
summarize as follows: " We know God's *revealed* Word only from
the Scripture adopted by the Church's proclamation or from the
Church's proclamation grounded upon the Scripture. We know
God's *written* Word only by the revelation which realizes the proclamation or by the proclamation which is realized by revelation.
We know God's *preached* Word only as we know the revelation attested by Scripture or as we know the Scripture which bears witness to revelation " (124) .

Preached Word! This means that only God's Word makes proclamation to be proclamation, " and hence the Church to be the
Church " (89) . God's Word is the commission upon which she
rests (90 ff.) . It is the content of her proclamation which has been
promised to her. But it is not like certain other objects " given " to
preaching in the Church (93 f.) . It is " the judgment in virtue of
which proclamation can alone be real proclamation "; that is, the
" criterion " which " manages itself and is at no one's disposal "
(94 f.) . Finally, it is " the event itself, in which proclamation becomes real proclamation "; that is, " it is a miracle of revelation
and of faith . . . when for us human speech about God . . . is
primarily and decisively God's own speech " (95) . However, that
does not mean that proclamation — perhaps when it is especially
zealous, impressive, or moving — becomes God's Word. Rather
the opposite is true: God's Word *is* the proclaimed Word. To be
sure, the human word remains at the same time a responsible and
fallible word of man. But in virtue of " Jesus Christ's vicariate au-
thorization " (97) it assumes a genuinely vicarious role. In Roman Catholicism its position as a vicar has been understood in
such a way that " Christ's government " has become " identical "
with Church government (100) . Thus " proclamation . . . is de-
humanized; that is, it is drawn into a sphere . . . in which only
in appearance can it signify a humanly assailable, responsible, sur-
passable and therefore subservient action " (100) . In this way
Christ's Lordship over his Church has lost its real scope for action.
It is no longer recognizable how Christ actually still is the ruler as

a Person. However, those erroneous opinions cannot prevent the concept of the "*vicarius Christi*" (Christ's representative), applied to proclamation and to that extent to the Church, being also capable of a proper interpretation, when this representation is understood simply as subservient, a representation which acknowledges the free Lordship of Jesus Christ and permits it to rule.

Written Word! The previous remarks have stressed that the " Word " of proclamation is in no sense the Church's own Word, not even secretly, not even " at rock bottom." God's Word, which issues in proclamation, has " already been uttered," and " has already taken place " (101). And the " vicariate of Church proclamation " can only then be " genuine " and only then is grounded " in the Other who is the Lord," when in its concrete form it is a " succession "; that is, when the apostolic witness occurs in the Church's proclamation (105 ff.). We encounter this witness, however, in the canon. Moreover, it is just the " written character " of the apostolic witness which is all-important. In this written form it actually stands over against the Church, no matter how she exists at any time and no matter how she has to hear it at a given time (107). In comparison with it an oral tradition can have only relative importance. For " in an unwritten tradition the Church is not addressed, but is engaged in a conversation with herself " (107). For the same reason the Church in the last analysis is unable to restrict the exposition of Scripture: " Biblical exegesis must be emancipated in every respect; not for the sake of intellectual freedom, as liberalism insisted upon this requirement, but for the sake of a free Bible " (109). Yes, but did not the Church originally frame the canon? Later we shall have to return to Barth's stand in regard to this question. Meanwhile we must hear his basic answer: " The Bible makes itself to be the canon " (110). The Church is definitely never in possession of standards of her own by which she could decide about the canon. On the contrary, she obeys the " peremptory," " ultimate Word " which is imposed upon her in the canonical Scriptures (111). Thus it is also simultaneously asserted that when we confess in faith that the Bible " is " God's Word, it is not because a man has laid hold of the Bible, but because the Bible has laid hold of him. " In this event the Bible becomes God's Word. In the sentence, ' The Bible is God's Word,' the tiny word ' is ' refers to the Bible's existence in this becoming " (113).

The revealed Word! " The Bible is . . . not itself and as such the divine revelation which has taken place " (114). It is rather " the concrete means by which the Church is reminded of the divine revelation which has occurred, is summoned to expect revelation in the future, and is thereby challenged, empowered, and directed toward proclamation " (114). It *is* " revelation," " where the Biblical word functions as a word of witness " (116). This unity of Bible and revelation is therefore " actually an event " (116). But at the same time one may say that the revelation which in truth " produces " " Scripture attesting it " — this revelation has taken place. The event, in virtue of which the Bible is heard today as a valid witness and in virtue of which it is therefore God's Word, is the " fulfilled time," " which is identical with Jesus Christ " (119). As for Church proclamation we would have to say, " It must ever again become God's Word." The same would also have to be said about the Bible (120). But the revelation itself, the " revealed Word," has happened. It is not correct to say about revelation what must be said about proclamation and Scripture, namely, that at a given time it is God's Word by God's free grace (" *ubi et quando visum est Deo* ": " where and when God pleases " — Augsburg Conf., Art. V), but on the contrary we must say, " *Illic et tunc visum est Deo* " (" There and then God was pleased ") (121). " Whoever says ' revelation ' says: ' The Word became flesh ' " (122). But when this is said, one is speaking of an event which " in any case is only to be grounded within the Trinity itself: in the Father's will, in the sending of the Son and the Holy Spirit, in the eternal decree of the triune God; that is, not otherwise than as knowledge of God from God, as knowledge of the Light in the Light " (123). Accordingly we are here confronted with the " first " form of God's Word — the form which is determined by nothing outside itself, and which determines all the others.

God's Word encounters us in a threefold form. However, we commenced our report about what Barth has to say on the subject with his reference to the fact that in this threefold form it is the

one Word. This unique oneness in threeness and threeness in oneness " is itself the only analogy to the doctrine . . . of the divine
Trinity " (124 f.) , about which we shall hear more later.

At the conclusion of the preceding section Barth expects that
many readers will ask: What then is God's Word? Only a qualified
and indirect answer can be given: we know only this about " the
nature of God's Word," that we receive it in its threefold form.
More than this we cannot say.

Hence Barth's doctrine of the " nature " of God's Word again
lays before us the selfsame triality which we have just faced. In its
nature God's Word is, first, " speech "; second, " deed "; third,
" mystery." According to Barth this does not mean that God's
Word would be speech only in the form of the proclaimed Word,
deed only in the form of the written Word, and finally mystery as
the revealed Word. No, in each form the Word is speech, deed,
and mystery; in its very nature it bears this threefold character.

Accordingly, it is above all essentially " speech." God's Word
means " originally and invariably . . . God speaks " (138) ! What
does that mean? First, that the Word is essentially spiritual, although it is not without a " physical occurrence." It is also a " corporal and natural event " (139) . It also " possesses natural power "
(140) . " But it definitely possesses first and above all the simple
spiritual form of truth " (140) . Secondly, from this follows the
" personality " of the Word (141 ff.) . " Word " is therefore not
the same as a " doctrinal statement." " The equation: God's Word
is God's Son, renders radically impossible any doctrinaire understanding of God's Word " (142) . But this " personalizing " does
not mean that the concept of Word is " deprived of its character
as word " (143) . No, " precisely in his Word God is a Person. The
concrete significance of this is that he is the Lord of the verbal
character of his Word " (143) . Finally it follows that God's Word
as " speech " bears a " purposive " and " teleological " character
(144 ff.) . It is directed to us. Although the hearer is not absolutely
necessary to the concept of God's Word, " in practice " he is necessarily included in it (145) .

" God's speech " is " God's act," and (as we have already mentioned) this is true of God's Word " in all of its forms " (149) . It

signifies in the first instance " its contingent contemporaneity (as
an event) " (150 ff.). At this point Barth again mentions the
" three times ": the " time of Jesus Christ," the " time of proph-
ecy and the apostolate," and the " time of the Church." The difference between these times has nothing directly to do with historical disparity (which, of course, also exists). Rather it is a matter
of a qualitative difference, a " varying position in God's order "
(150). Consequently the attempt on the part of historical thinking
to make Jesus Christ or the apostles " contemporaneous " for us is
utterly futile. We do not become " contemporaneous " with Jesus
Christ as God's revealed Word by means of a historical reconstruc-
tion! [4] It is rather God's own free act when, " without an abolition of the difference," " the time of Christ becomes contemporaneous with the time of the prophets and apostles " and then again
(in proclamation) with the " time of the Church " (153 f.).

Secondly, God's Word as " deed " is equipped with " governing
power " (155 ff.). There is no escape from his claim. And just for
that reason — " not in the light of nature " but " in the light of
grace " — there is " no walled-up and self-enclosed . . . profane
area " (161). Here Barth voices his (oft-reiterated) admonition
not to take " secularism " and " worldliness " too seriously, and at
any rate not to attach as much importance to man's unbelief as to
God's grace. Thirdly and finally, the character of God's Word as a
deed denotes that it is a decision. Not that it would " first . . .
have to be understood as history and then as such also as decision."
The opposite is the case, namely, that it is " to be understood primarily and fundamentally as decision and then as such also as history " (162).

" God's speech " is " God's mystery "! The meaning is that this
speech, this divine act, is truly God's speech, God's act! (168).
Barth believes it is necessary (it was 1932 when our volume appeared!) to preface his exposition with a warning (which is truly
as timely in 1950). He finds that " on the whole we are in danger
of becoming much too positive." He is thinking of " a kind of certainty of voice, language, and attitude . . . a certainty, confidence, and sprightliness which may become all the greater as we
also learn how to incorporate such ideas as the moment of uncer-

---

[4] *" Durch historische Vergegenwärtigung."*

tainty, ' comforted despair,' ' line of death,' or the like, into our more or less intellectual calculations " (168 f.) . " To what extent is our theological conversation nothing but empty talk? " he asks (169) . For these reasons Barth now speaks about the character of the Word as mystery. By " mystery " is meant what the New Testament calls " *mysterion* "; that is, " not merely God's hiddenness, but his manifestation in a hidden way, or in a way that is unpretentious and indirectly demonstrable " (171) . Consequently the character of God's Word as mystery next implies its worldliness (171 ff.) . This worldliness is an indestructible property of God's Word because it must be true that " if God were not to speak to us in terms of our world, he would not speak to us at all " (175) . However, " worldliness, as it is peculiar to God's Word, is not in itself and as such transparent." Revelation also takes place at the same time " in spite of it " (173) . God veils himself just in order to unveil himself (175) .

Next we must speak about the " onesidedness " of God's speech (180 ff.) , which is connected with the relation of veiling and unveiling just described. In faith we are capable of grasping only the one or the other. We do not have the possibility so to speak of establishing a synthesis of both (whence would we acquire it?) . But that means that we can recognize God's unveiling only in his veiling, and God's veiling (which is more difficult to conceive but all the more important to stress) only in his unveiling. Finally, " God's speech " " is and remains " God's mystery " in its spirituality " (189 ff.) . By that we mean that the reception and hearing of the Word, as well as our readiness for the Word, stand under the sovereignty of the Word. " The Lord of speech is also the Lord of our hearing. The Lord who gives the Word is also the Lord who gives faith " (189) . Man — as a believer — is therefore neither a cognitive nor a volitional factor apart from the Lord of the Word.

We have now arrived at the second-last paragraph of our chapter: " The Knowability of God's Word." And we have reached its basic contention that knowledge of the Word can " consist only in its acknowledgment," and " this acknowledgment " can " be realized only through the Word itself and only from the Word can it be intelligible " (194) .

We are now talking about man. But not in such a way that there could be any talk about his capacity or incapacity to apprehend God's Word, but rather so that we are again speaking about God's Word itself! The fact that " the possibility of a knowledge corresponding to God's real Word has actually been given to man " is " a *novum* equally inconceivable, and it is contrary to all man's ability and capacity." It is only " understandable as pure fact, like the real Word of God itself " (202). Consequently it is impossible to take the course taught by Cartesius, namely, to advance from a certainty of the self to a certainty of God. The exact opposite is the case (205). Indeed, even our incapacity for the knowledge of God's Word may only be understood " under the presupposition " that there is a genuine knowledge of the Word (206)!

Once this has been asserted and recognized, it is then permissible, Barth teaches, to speak intelligently about an experience of God's Word. By this Barth understands the " determination " of the " experience " of men " by God's Word " (207), and this is indeed possible (210). Barth describes it as acknowledgment. He expressly calls attention to the fact that he thereby " intends to give a . . . description of Christian-religious experience or consciousness " (218). Nevertheless, as surely as such " experience " is a " genuine and humanly possible experience " (219), we must then immediately go on to ask whether it is to be conceived as man's own possibility; whether in this experience man on his own comes to realize and make possible this experience; and whether his realization thereby becomes an " independent object of interest " (223). Barth replies to this question in the negative. Rather it must be said that " the possibility of a knowledge of God's Word lies in God's Word and nowhere else " (234). Just for this reason it is to be " affirmed " " with certainty and in all human seriousness " (235), but also only for this reason!

Barth develops these basic principles as he now deals with the relation of God's Word to faith (239 ff.). Again we hear: " Faith is experience, a concretely demonstrable, temporal act of this or that man " (241 f.). However, " faith is not faith as experience " (242)! " That the faith, in which the true God is believed, is true faith, is something which is due . . . in no way and in no sense to itself, but to the fact that the true God has revealed himself to it.

That is to say, it is due to God's Word" (245). If that has been seen, Barth can again emphasize that faith is "real experience of God's Word" (250). Indeed, so radical is the overcoming of the "*homo peccator non capax verbi Domini*" ("sinful man is incapable of comprehending the Word of the Lord"), which the Word itself bears within it, that Barth does not shrink from now speaking about man's "conformity to God" which "takes place" (251) in faith, and which consists in the "possibility of hearing God's Word" (252). This does not imply an *analogia entis*. (There is no existing correspondence between God and man in the sense that "being" is peculiar to God in the same way that it is to man.) On the contrary, the conformity to God is based upon and exists solely in the Word itself. Therefore, instead of the *analogia entis* an *analogia fidei* must be asserted in agreement with Rom. 12:6 (the correspondence to God into which man is transferred by faith and therefore by the Word acknowledged in faith). Consequently, it is true of the believer that he "exists" "entirely from this object" (258).

We have been speaking about God's Word: about its threefold form, its "nature," and lastly about its knowability. God's Word then is "the criterion of dogmatics." As the Church works at dogmatics, she admits that her own language is not necessarily identical with God's Word. On the contrary, it must constantly be conformed to it. Barth shows that Protestant modernism and Roman Catholicism in quite different ways are at any rate united in the fact that they do not envisage God's Word as an "entity distinct from Church proclamation" (264). Consequently they concede to religious experience and emotion or to speculation (modernism), or to a Church left to herself and engaged in a conversation with herself (Catholicism), the rank of "criteria" of their own. But how can we then "catch sight" of God's Word "as an entity distinct from Church proclamation" (including the dogmas)? The possibility rests solely "in the fact that in the Church the Bible is read. To this fact we appeal when — not in a Catholic or modernist way but in Protestant fashion; that is, just in opposition to them — we actually reckon with this possibility" (280)! When, however, dogmatics does this, it does not inquire about dog-

mas but about dogma; that is, it asks whether " Church proclamation is really in agreement with the Bible as God's Word " (283).
Dogma is therefore not something given; it is an " eschatological
concept " (284). It always lies ahead of dogmatic work and questions, never behind them; or at any rate only in such a way that it
immediately becomes a newly posed question arising out of an answer that has been given. As a result dogmatics can never consider
itself merely as " recapitulations " of Church proclamation. On
the contrary, it has " to be concerned " . . . with its " criticism
and correction " (289). " Dogmatics is scientific not as the presentation of all sorts of material . . . but as the movement of this
material or as this material which is set in motion " (299)!

II

THE TRIUNE GOD

[Volume I, 1, pp. 311–514]

A S ALREADY mentioned, Barth entitled the second chapter of
his work: " The Revelation of God." This chapter is divided
into three parts: " The Triune God," " The Incarnation of the
Word," " The Outpouring of the Holy Spirit." We are here dealing with the first part, one of the most important of the whole
work.

Barth is conscious of how " isolated " is his position in placing
the doctrine of the Trinity at the forefront of dogmatics (316).
He refers to the widespread custom of beginning instead with the
doctrine of Holy Scripture. But he finds that it is impossible to say
" what is significant for the holiness of just this Scripture " if it has
not first been made clear — " naturally from Holy Scripture itself " — " who is the God whose revelation makes Scripture holy "
(317). Moreover, if clarity is to be achieved, the question about
" who " God is most certainly may not take second place to the
other question, namely, whether God is and what he is. On the
contrary, it is the primary and basic question, qualifying all that
follows (317). " It is the doctrine of the Trinity which fundamentally distinguishes the Christian doctrine of God as Christian, as
well as the Christian concept of revelation, from all other possible
doctrines of God and concepts of revelation " (318).

It may appear as if what we have just reported is put extremely
" abstractly." This appearance is intensified when we further hear
that the root of the doctrine of the Trinity already lies in the
Christian concept of revelation (320). However, the fact that in
this instance the " concept " is to be nothing else than the repro-
duction of the thing testified to in Scripture is immediately shown
when Barth tells us what the Christian concept of revelation essentially means. It is this: " God reveals himself as the Lord " (324).
Just this proposition, according to Barth, is " the root of the doctrine of the Trinity " (324).

Now the doctrine of the Trinity is unquestionably " a work of the Church " (325). It does not repeat statements from the Bible. It is " a translation and exegesis " of the Biblical witness to revelation. The dogma of the Trinity is therefore true because, and insofar as, it is " a suitable interpretation of the Bible " (327).

" God reveals himself as the Lord." Primarily that means that God reveals himself as one who has " structure " [1] (333). " It is not impossible for him and . . . not beneath him to be his own double in his revelation " (333) ; that is to say, the Son, in whom the revelation occurs, is other than the Revealer, the Father, and yet he is the same. " The fact of his revelation itself " declares that " it is peculiar to him to distinguish himself from himself "; " he who here reveals himself as God *can* reveal himself " (337) ! Precisely in this capacity to reveal himself God reveals himself as the Lord (337). " The Lordship which becomes visible in the Biblical revelation consists in God's freedom to distinguish himself from himself " (337) ! This distinguishing of God from himself, which is manifested in his revelation, is also revealed as a work of his Lordship in that in his unveiling he does not lose his mystery: he remains *God* in his " other " form! " God's self-unveiling remains an act of his sovereign divine freedom " (339). And thirdly, God proves that he is the Lord in his revelation, that is, in distinguishing himself from himself, in that this revelation is plainly an event. It is not a " historical " event " perceptible to a neutral observer " (343), but an event of contingent uniqueness, " a fact beyond which there is no recourse " (348). Man, however, comes to share in this simple, unique fact of God being revealed (342) ! This means that " God reveals himself as Spirit," " as the Spirit of the Father and of the Son, and therefore as the one and the same God. But now he also reveals himself as the one and same God in this way: in this unity, in this self-disclosing unity of the Father and of the Son to man " (351). We could summarize the results of this section as follows: God *reveals* himself in the Son, God reveals himself in the *Son,* God is revealed as the Father in the Son by the *Spirit!* But this tells us that God's Lordship in his revelation is manifested in the fact that, as the " Revealer," he is at once the " revelation " and the " revealedness," and yet reveals himself ever

---

1 " *Gestalt.*"

in another " form." That, in a particularly drastic abridgment, is
the root of the doctrine of the Trinity according to Barth. We can
close with the thesis (which naturally Barth had previously established) : " God's Word is God himself in his revelation. For God
reveals himself as the Lord, and according to Scripture that means,
for the concept of revelation, that God himself is the Revealer, the
Revelation and the Revealedness in indestructible unity, but also
in indestructible distinction " (311) .

Barth now develops the Church's doctrine of the Trinity " in
order to achieve a proper conceptual clarification of the question
about the Subject of revelation " (367 ff.) . Our report cannot fulfill the task of reproducing the doctrine of the Church formulated
in the fourth century and improved in succeeding centuries in
such a way that it would be rewarding for one who does not otherwise possess a more exact knowledge of the subject. We can simply try to select certain points by which Barth's elucidation of the
dogma of the Early and Medieval Church is suited to provide especially important contributions to its understanding — in the
framework of Barth's entire work.

Barth first speaks about the " oneness in threeness " and therewith argues that God's oneness " is not only not abolished by the
threeness of the ' Persons,' but on the contrary that his unity consists much more precisely in the threeness of the ' Persons ' " (369) .
Now as is well known the opponents of the doctrine of the Trinity, the " anti-Trinitarians," have constantly claimed that they are
the real champions of God's oneness. But as Barth rightly states all
anti-Trinitarianism unavoidably comes " to deny either the revelation of God or the oneness of God " (371) . That may be shown
particularly in the second " Person " of the Trinity. If only a sort
of ultimate creaturely essence (a Logos essentially unlike the Father) was manifested in Christ, then it would be either pure idolatry to worship such a being or else it would have to be admitted
that we do not receive in Christ a real revelation of God himself
but instruction about God or a guide to God. God therefore either
loses his unity in favor of a deified creature — or revelation is not
a reality.

The threeness in oneness is then dealt with. Here it becomes

clear that " God's oneness affirmed " in the doctrine of the Trinity
is not to be confused with " singularity or solitude " (373) . " We
set foot on the ground of Christian monotheism precisely with the
doctrine of the Trinity " (374) ! Now the threeness is ordinarily
conceived as a threeness of " Persons " (cf. also the Heidelberg
Cat., Ques. 25) . On account of its history Barth has misgivings
about the concept of Person. Instead he would prefer to speak
about three " modes of existence " (374 ff.) . Of course, he does not
want to surrender the concept of Person as such. But he finds that
it belongs to another context: it follows from the doctrine of the
Trinity that God is " to be understood not only as impersonal sovereignty, that is, as power, but as the Lord, and therefore not only
as an absolute spirit but as Person " (378) . Moreover, the concept
of " mode of existence " is not an innovation. Early Church theologians had spoken in this way, and Calvin, for example, used the
closely related concept of *subsistentia* in a decisive passage (*Inst.*
I, 13, 6) . Barth does not mean that God has three different attributes, or assumes three different forms of self-expression, but that
he always " exists " in a different " mode ": he is now as the one,
and now as the other (" *alius — alius — alius,*" 384) ; but he is not
now this, now that (" *aliud — aliud — aliud* ") , but ever again he
himself.

However, a reference to the three-in-oneness must immediately
follow this prominence accorded the threeness. The figure of
speech of " oneness in threeness " and " threeness in oneness " is
in itself " one-sided " and " unsatisfactory " (388) . We cannot
speak of any of God's three modes of existence by itself, for they
mutually " condition and penetrate " each other (doctrine of peri-
choresis, 390 f.) . On the other hand, we can and must " apply "
each individual Word or work of God to one of the three modes
of existence in particular (doctrine of appropriations, 393 f.) .
Both sides of these statements about God's three-in-oneness belong
together. Indeed, here we can immediately proceed by giving
Barth's summary of the " meaning of the doctrine of the Trinity "
as the conclusion of this section: " The doctrine of the Trinity declares . . . that, and how far, He who reveals himself to man according to the Scriptural witness can be our *God;* that, and how
far, he can be *our* God. He can be our *God,* because he is equal to

himself in all his modes of existence, one and the same Lord. . . .
And this Lord can be *our* God, he can encounter us and bind us to
himself because he is God in these three modes of existence as
Father, Son, and Spirit, because creation, reconciliation, and redemption — the entire being, speaking and acting in which he
wants to be our God — are grounded and prefigured in his own
nature, in his divinity" (403 f.). This sentence ought to show
most clearly what is intended in the whole section.

It almost goes without saying that Barth now proceeds to discuss each of the three divine "modes of existence" separately
(404 ff.). Basic to such a discussion is Barth's understanding of the
threeness of Father, Son, and Holy Spirit as the threeness of Creator, Reconciler, and Redeemer. It is obvious that in particular
the designation of the Holy Spirit as the "Redeemer" presents
something new in the face of a widely prevailing tradition (cf.
Heidelberg Cat., Ques. 24, for the commonest expression). But let
us first follow the prescribed order even in this brief report.

As to the first of God's modes of existence, Barth's thesis is placed
at the head of the corresponding section (§ 10): "According to
Scripture the one God reveals himself as the Creator, that is, as the
Lord of our existence. As such a God he is our Father, because he
is Father previously in himself as the Father of God the Son"
(404). The crux of the assertion evidently lies in the conclusion.
Afterward Barth repeats: "As the 'Father of Jesus Christ' God
can be our Father because — apart from the fact that he reveals
himself to us as such — he already and antecedently is as he reveals
himself to be. . . . He can be our Father because he is the Father
in himself, because fatherhood is an eternal mode of existence of
the divine nature" (411). Complete stress is therefore to be laid
upon the fact that God is Father in himself, the eternal Father of
the eternal Son. The first thing is that God in himself — as the Father — "is the author of his other modes of existence" (414), the
"fountain of divinity" (as the ancients said), and the second
thing is then his creativity. Primary is that God in himself is the
eternal Father of the eternal Son; secondary is his relation as Creator to the creature, which stands in an "affinity" to his relation
as Father to the Son. Just for this reason it is "not only permissi-

ble but mandatory to ascribe creation to God the Father as a *proprium* (as a specific work) " (418).

With the next section (§ 11: " God the Son ") we also start with Barth's thesis: " According to Scripture the one God reveals himself as the Reconciler, that is, as the Lord in the midst of our enmity to him. As such he is the Son who has come to us or God's Word spoken to us, because he is such antecedently in himself as the Son or Word of God the Father " (419). The Reconciler is therefore God the Lord in man's fallen world. He is the God who abolishes the enmity and pierces the darkness. " The work of the Son or of the Word is God's presence in which he makes himself known. In view of the fact that it is a miraculous occurrence in the midst of human darkness, and in spite of this darkness, we can only designate it as revelation. Reconciliation is another word for the same thing " (429 f.). This event constitutes something new over and beyond the event of creation. We cannot " confuse or directly identify God's Lordship in these two areas." At this point therefore we have to speak " of a second divine mode of existence " (430 f.). In this second event God's omnipotent grace is revealed. Consequently we must acknowledge " that the Subject who acts in this second event is identical with God in the fullest sense of the word " (431). This is emphasized above all by the second proposition in the thesis reported above: Jesus Christ " is the Son or Word of God for us, because he is previously so in himself " (437). Jesus does not ascend as it were to the dignity of divinity when he performs the divine work of revelation and reconciliation upon us, but " his divinity creates the revelation and reconciliation " (437). He is " the eternal Son," as the Father is the " eternal Father "! Only where this is acknowledged — in keeping with the great doctrinal decisions of the fourth century — does theology escape an " untheological, speculative understanding " of that " for us," which can be properly dealt with only on the prior ground of the " antecedently in himself " (442). That means that if we want to understand the sentence that " Jesus Christ is God's Son for us," without taking seriously the fact that he is the Son of God " antecedently in himself," the " eternal " Son, then in reality we are giving expression to a " judgment of value " for which we think we have the criterion in ourselves. Then on the basis of the crite-

ria which we have discovered, we exalt Jesus Christ to a divine dignity, or we see in him the expression or manifestation of that
which we have previously, and without him, fancied as " divinity "
or " divine Sonship." But that means that just where one does not
want to know anything about the eternal Sonship of Jesus Christ,
one is pursuing " metaphysics " (443) . Then the relationship of a
correspondence between divine revelation and human faith is arbitrarily absolutized, instead of realizing that this relationship of
a correspondence (a relationship of correlation) " is nailed to the
truth of which the dogma speaks." Because He who is God's Son
for us, the Revealer and Reconciler, is God's Son in eternity, therefore the word " faith " possesses real meaning, because it lives from
God's own eternal Word alone.

In regard to what Barth says about " God the Holy Spirit "
(§ 12) , we also propose to begin by repeating the thesis: " According to Scripture the one God reveals himself as the Redeemer, that
is, as the Lord who makes us free. As such he is the Holy Spirit,
and by receiving him we become God's children, because as the
Spirit of the love of God the Father and of God the Son, he is antecedently so in himself " (470). Its consonance with the previous
corresponding theses is striking. However, it must now be explained in what sense Barth calls God the Holy Spirit the " Redeemer." We heard above that " revelation " and " reconciliation " are synonymous terms. But Barth immediately emphasizes
that according to the New Testament " redemption " does not coincide with " revelation " and " reconciliation." " Redemption,"
" seen from the standpoint of revelation or reconciliation, is rather
God's action which is still outstanding, future, and to be consum-
mated " (430) . In this connection Barth refers to Rom. 5:10; Luke
21:28; Rom. 8:23; Eph. 4:30; Heb. 11:35 as well as I Thess. 5:8 f.;
Rom. 13:11; Phil. 1:19; 2:12; Heb. 1:14; 9:28. Now it is the work
of the Holy Spirit to guarantee to man " his personal participation in revelation " (476), to instruct and guide him (476), and
to make it possible for man to speak of Christ in such a way that
this speech becomes a " witness," and therefore " God's revelation
is actualized ever again through its speech " (477) . In all this the
Spirit accomplishes what man in no sense has the capacity to do of
himself. That means, however, that the Spirit is " the Lord, who

makes us free " and " by the reception of whom we become God's children." Consequently, in the Holy Spirit there takes place what in the sense of the New Testament can be asserted only eschatologically. It occurs! And that means that what lies absolutely before us is already a reality for us in the Holy Spirit — who is God's own Spirit and who never becomes our spirit. Precisely this is what Barth means when he ascribes the work of redemption to God the Holy Spirit. However, once again everything depends upon the fact that the Holy Spirit does not first become the Holy Spirit in the event of revelation, in the occurrence of his special work (489). No, " the event of revelation also has on its subjective side clarity and reality, because even the Holy Spirit, the subjective element in this event, is the essence of God himself " (489). Strenuous reflection upon this " antecedently in himself " (see also above) leads Barth to an energetic defense of the addition of the " filioque " advocated in the Western Church, according to which the Holy Spirit has " proceeded " from the Father and from the Son. The Eastern Church acknowledges that in revelation the gift of the Spirit from the Father actually takes place through the Son. But she " reaches out beyond revelation " (503), when she explains that in the eternal, inner-trinitarian being of God it is otherwise: there the Holy Spirit proceeds directly from the Father. Such a distinction actually contradicts all that Barth has shown in his doctrine of the Trinity. For here everything depends upon the fact that God in his revelation is none other than he is in his eternal reality. In all this Barth continually wants to call attention to the truth that in God's revelation we have to do with God himself and with the whole of God, and that apart from revelation we are unable to conceive any thoughts about God. It is made sufficiently clear that thereby the mystery of God is not attacked. However, it is really God's mystery: the mystery of God revealing himself as the Lord.

III

THE INCARNATION OF THE WORD

[*Volume I, 2, pp. 1–221*]

———

THE SECOND chapter (" The Revelation of God ") began with the doctrine of the Trinity, which supplied an answer " to the question concerning the Subject of revelation as attested in Holy Scripture." The second half-volume of Vol. I begins with the second part of the chapter, which we are now to discuss.

In order to understand Barth's meaning we must realize that we still find ourselves in the realm of " prolegomena " and thus in the context of the doctrine of God's revelation. Barth commences with the statement that the triune God is the " Subject " of revelation (1).[1] And he always remains the Subject; he never becomes the predicate or object (1). He is always the same One who reveals himself. He is free. But he is " free for us " and also " free in us " (2). The meaning is that in God's freedom it is a reality that " his revelation comes to man " (3). The " objective reality " of God's revelation for us is Jesus Christ. It is the incarnate Word. Only on the basis of this reality can it then be said that Jesus Christ is the " objective " possibility of revelation. (Later on the Holy Spirit is said to be the " subjective " reality and possibility of revelation.)

Now according to the New Testament witness the " simple and unique reality, Jesus Christ," is to be defined in this way: " The Word or Son of God became a man, and was called Jesus of Nazareth; therefore this man, Jesus of Nazareth, was God's Word or God's Son " (15). Or: " God's Son means Jesus of Nazareth; Jesus of Nazareth is God's Son " (17). It is a declaration about oneness, although it evidently embraces a twofold knowledge. In the New Testament the emphasis is laid now on the one, now on the other. The first half of the two sentences mentioned above renders the Johannine type of New Testament witness to Christ, and the second half the Synoptic type, whereas Paul refers equally now to the one and now to the other (18, etc.).

[1] Quotations now refer to Vol. I, 2, unless otherwise indicated.

However, the first (the Johannine) type may certainly not be so understood as if its advocates "first had a particular idea of God, or of a Son or Word of God, of a Christ, and then had found this idea confirmed and fulfilled in Jesus" (18). Where this opinion prevails in theology notwithstanding, we have a "docetic" Christology: the man Jesus is of no consequence in what is of decisive importance; important is only the preconceived "concept of a Christ, logos or mediator" (18). On the other hand, one certainly may not interpret the second (the Synoptic) type as if it were a matter of the "idealizing and apotheosis of a man" (22), as if Jesus of Nazareth were somehow raised to the status of deity. This would be "ebionite" Christology. Starting from either of these positions the way to a knowledge of the divinity of Jesus Christ is absolutely blocked.

A rational synthesis of those two Biblical types also is impossible. They do have a unity, but they have it in the name of Jesus Christ and thus in the essential content of the New Testament itself, not, however, in a human assertion of it. (We must pay attention to this when here — p. 27 — and later on we hear about the opposition between Luther's and Calvin's Christology; Luther follows the Johannine, Calvin the Synoptic, type.)

Only on the ground of the reality of revelation can — and must! — its possibility also be discussed (an insight which Barth repeatedly inculcates throughout his entire work). This possibility lies primarily in God's freedom to "traverse the boundary between him and us" (34 f.), that is, in his "condescension" (35), his abasement. More precisely, it consists in the fact that "in the mode of existence of the Son" the one God became man (37); that is, God's condescension occurred "just in his Son" (38). Men can be like him, as his "adopted sons" (38), in him who is the eternal Son. (In this connection Barth again emphasizes that such an assertion is to be made only as a "commentary" on the "revelational text." Therefore, it is never made abstractly and absolutely, but always in such a way that in making it we "do not place ourselves above the reality of revelation but beneath it"; 39.) Therefore, when God in his Son "assumes a form known . . . to us" and enters the cosmos (39), there can be no talk of an *analogia entis,* of a correspondence between the Creator and the creature already existing from the side of creation. Nor can there be any talk of an already existing " adaptability " of the world " for God's revelation " (41). On the contrary, revelation is to be spoken of as utterly free grace occurring in the world (41), in which God, veiling himself, encounters us there where we are, and encounters us in such a way that we can " understand " him (43). Finally, the fact that God's Son became man does not imply any acknowledgment of a previously existing adaptability of man to be a bearer of God's revelation, but rather first of all the execution of the judgment that we are " flesh " (44). It is therefore a confirmation, not of our judgment about ourselves, but of God's judgment upon us. To be sure, once that has been seen, it must also be said (subsequently, that is, on the ground of the reality of revelation) that God's revelation " had " to be an incarnation (48). Man's adaptability to be the bearer of God's revelation rests basically upon the fact that " only Jesus Christ " is " the man who is flesh "; " flesh as the possibility of God's revelation " is therefore " entirely the possibility of Jesus Christ himself " (49). It could be summed up as follows: The " true God and true man " want to be understood as being in and with one another. Consequently nothing approaching a doctrine of man which looks at man apart from the incarnation of Jesus Christ follows from it.

In a second paragraph of the same part of the chapter (§ 14 of the whole work: pp. 50 ff.), Barth deals with the " time of revelation." As we shall return later to Barth's explanations about " time " mentioned above, we shall confine ourselves here to what is most essential.[2]

As we learn what man is only from revelation, likewise we can only let revelation tell us what time is (50) and above all what the " time of revelation " is. Or we might put it in another way: " As humanity in general became something new and different in that God's Son adopted it and took it up into a unity with his divinity . . . so time became another new time when it became the time of Jesus Christ, although and while it belonged to our lost time " (57). But exactly in this way did it first become " real, fulfilled time " (57). It becomes immediately evident that thereby a posi-

[2] Cf. Chapter XI, pp. 159 ff.

tion has been taken in regard to the much discussed problem of
"revelation and history." Barth offers a condensation of what is to
be said in this regard: "Revelation is never a predicate of history;
on the contrary, history is a predicate of revelation" (64). But
really history! Really time! It is precisely revelation (and the fulfillment of time accomplished with it) which enables us to recognize time as *finite,* as directed to an end: "There is infinite time
. . . only for a time consciousness which, in regard to revelation,
is ignorant or forgetful" (76). Time is limited only because God
in his revelation has reached into our time!

Now Barth distinguishes not merely between our divinely created lost time and the time fulfilled in God's revelation (especially
p. 54), but he connects the "time of expectation" with the fulfilled time as the "time which precedes" it, and the "time of recollection" with the fulfilled time as the "time which follows" it.
Thus, at the same time, he arrives at the relation of the Old Covenant to the New. For the "time of the witness to the expectation
of revelation" is "the time of the Old Testament" (77), and the
time of the New Testament is correspondingly "the time of the
witness to the recollection of revelation" (112). In this formulation we are immediately struck by the fact that, unlike the view
which has been by far the most common, the time of the New
Testament itself is not characterized as the time of fulfillment or
as fulfilled time. Barth emphasizes the opposite, namely, that "Jesus Christ as the expected One is actually manifest in the Old
Testament as well" (79 and freq.). In support of his position he
is able to appeal, not only to Augustine or Calvin among others,
but also to Luther (83 ff.) and Lutheran orthodoxy (85 f.). Thus
both Testaments are genuinely and essentially related to the one
revelation. And Barth is able to give a parallel arrangement to his
statements about the "time of expectation" and of "recollection": in both cases the "covenant" is attested as God's revelation; in both cases God is a hidden God in his revelation; in both
cases God is known as the One "who is present, as the One who
is coming." The "covenant" is fulfilled in that God has revealed
himself in the incarnation of the Word. The "hiddenness" of the
revealed God is fulfilled in the crucifixion, in which God "has become a hidden God to himself" (98). The presence of God, as

the presence of the coming One, is fulfilled in the resurrection, which, itself not to be thought of eschatologically, now allows everything else (in the Old as well as in the New Testament) to be " thought of eschatologically " (129). But what then is the difference between the Old and the New Testament? Here we are informed that it consists in the fact " that the coming Christ, about whom the New Testament witness speaks, is already the object of recollection as the One who has come " (132. This subject is dealt with further in Vol. II, 2, especially; cf. Chapter VIII, pp. 9 f. of this book). " That cannot be said of the Messiah who is awaited in the Old Testament " (132). Expressed otherwise: there is the same relation to the one revelation but viewed from a different direction. Hence it follows at once that the Old Testament, looked at by itself, is a " Jewish abstraction " (98). The reality of revelation and with it the reality of the " fulfilled time " standing before, between, and as it were, over both Testaments, prevents any isolation of the Old Testament. That is especially true of the testimony to God's hiddenness in the Old Testament. " It is not a testimony to any sort of divine hiddenness, but the prelude to God's hiddenness in the stable at Bethlehem and on the cross of Golgotha " (98) !

Barth concludes his preliminary discussion of Christology — it is still just a part of the " prolegomena " — with a section that deals with the " mystery of revelation " (§ 15; pp. 134–221). The title serves to indicate that he is about to develop Christology proper; for " Christology deals with God's revelation as mystery " (144). The threat of dissolving this mystery has always existed. A " physical understanding of salvation," " sacramental mysticism," and a " magical objectivism " have exhibited one side of this threat; a " spiritualistic moralism " the other (143; in 1938 Barth could still be of the opinion that this was the only fallacy still existing at that time). At any rate the Christology of the Early Church, in contrast to modern Christology, did not dissolve the mystery. " And therefore, in one's approach and in principle, one must decidedly be on its side " (145).

" Who is Jesus Christ? " That is the question to which an answer is now to be sought. And Barth answers with the Early

Church: He is " true God and true man " (145).

This, however, must " always be understood as an equation of unequals " (150). For the Word, which becomes flesh, remains subject (147). It remains " God's free, sovereign Word." Hence the " equation " can never be reversed: the flesh does not become Word, man does not become God. (For this reason " the modern Protestant faith in Jesus the religious hero," as well as " the Catholic devotion to the heart of Jesus," " is to be rejected as a deification of the creature "; 151). A critical discussion of Mariology is provided as a " test case." Not that it errs in designating Mary " the Mother of God." (To deny this would mean rather that " He whom Mary bore " had been some second thing " besides being God's Son "; 152). But it is false to set up an independent Mariology, and naturally the accompanying doctrine of the immaculate conception is even more false. For here Mary, as a creature that receives grace on the strength of the creature's own assent, is straightway thought of as the most concentrated expression of the *analogia entis* and of natural theology. Here the creature that receives grace is a creature that in itself is equipped to be an intermediate step between the Creator and the creature, and is qualified to receive the God-man (153–160).

But that irreversible equation is a reality. The Word became *flesh*. That not only means it became man; it means that the Word became man " who stands under the divine sentence and judgment" (165). " The nature which God adopted in Christ " is " identical . . . with our nature under the presupposition of the Fall " (167). To be sure, in such a way that Christ is " the same as we are but in a quite different way than we," in that " now in the flesh he does not do what all flesh does " (170). However, the sinlessness of Jesus is not to be understood as a sort of superhuman quality. Rather it " manifestly consists in his acknowledgment of the meaning of the incarnation, namely, that unlike Adam . . . he does not want to be like God . . . but . . . bears the wrath of God . . ." (172).

But how are we to understand that the Word " *became* " flesh? In other words, how are we to paraphrase the unity of divinity and humanity? To use the language of early theology: what about the *unio hypostatica?* Here Barth considers the old Lutheran-Reformed differences in Christology. The principle from which he proceeds is this: the *unio hypostatica,* the " event of the incarnation of the Word, . . . is to be understood as a *completed* event, but also as a completed *event* " (180). Lutheran Christology stresses the first, the " accomplished fact " (180) , the " objective facts of the case," which the " reality of Jesus Christ " represents. While agreeing with the starting point of this Christology, Barth raises the question in relation to it whether " it does justice to the freedom, majesty, and glory of God's Word . . . so that they are not almost destroyed and lost in his having become flesh " (182) . Reformed Christology emphasizes the second half of the above sentence. Its concern is that the incarnation, as surely as it is a completed event, nevertheless is just as surely an event. It wants to underline the truth that the Word, while being flesh, nevertheless also is and remains " what it is in itself," and consequently also exists " outside of the flesh " (the familiar " *extra Calvinisticum* "; cf. Ques. 48 of the Heidelberg Cat.) . While also agreeing here with the starting point, Barth asks, however, whether with this insistence upon the "dynamics of the *egeneto* " sufficient justice has really been done to its " static character " (185) . No synthesis of these two Christological tendencies (and of further deductions from them) can be found (186) . The second of these " concerns " (the Reformed) is an expression of the " necessity of faith," whereas the first concern (the Lutheran) contains solely a — highly legitimate — " demand for faith." Barth obviously believes that when the Reformed position is thought through in a way that would make the Lutheran concern its own a synthesis would then be possible. In itself it would be quite adaptable to such reinterpretation (186 f.) . But he also regards it as possible that the question cannot and may not come to rest. In any case he is of the opinion that it is a matter here of an opposition of theological schools within the one Church. It is to be taken seriously. It demands a decision (187; cf. 27 and 177) . But he does not therefore call for a " union theology," but the acknowledgment that the one mystery is " reflected " in this duplicity of theological schools.

A discussion of " the miracle of Christmas " forms the conclusion of the Christological project (187 ff.) . Its most obvious char-

acteristic is Barth's vigorous defense of the Virgin birth within the
framework of his interpretation of the Early Church dogma. In referring to the " miracle " of Christmas the essential " mystery " of
Christmas is " designated," not dissolved. This " miracle " is " the
conception of Jesus Christ by the Holy Spirit or his birth from the
Virgin Mary " (189). Special attention should again be called to
the fact that the reference to this " miracle " does not dissolve the
mystery but rather designates it as such. " The dogma of the Virgin birth is . . . a confession of the unlimited hiddenness of the
vere Deus vere homo. . . . It obliterates the last possibility, which
perhaps still remains, of understanding the *vere Deus vere homo*
intellectually as an idea or as an arbitrary interpretation, somewhat in the sense of docetic or ebionite Christology. There remains
only the spiritual understanding of the *vere Deus vere homo*,
namely, that understanding in which God's own work is seen in
God's own light " (194). In its special and unique character of a
sign the Virgin birth is paralleled only by the empty grave (195
and freq.). Both miracles denote " the existence of Jesus Christ
. . . as that human-historical existence in which God himself, and
God alone, is directly the Subject, whose temporal reality is not
only called forth, created, conditioned, and upheld by God's eternal reality, but which is identical with this reality " (199).

The " quite unmiraculous reality of man " (203) is also a factor
involved in the miracle of Christmas. Mary, the human being, and
the only human being to " co-operate " in this instance, is " an object of sovereign, divine action ": the Virgin birth erases absolutely each and every " synergism " and " monism " (203). Mary
" cannot be God's fellow worker " (205). And yet grace befalls
this member of disobedient mankind (206). It is " the mystery
. . . that she receives a capacity for God she does not possess "
(206). The forgiveness of sins is " the thing designated " (207), a
new beginning wrought by God. The exclusion of sexuality, to
which the Virgin birth points as a sign, signifies man's limitation
and condemnation; it is God's " gracious judgment " (209). And
so " man indeed also has a part to play," " but only just in this
way: only in the form of the *virgo Maria* . . . , only in the form
of the man who does not will, accomplish, or create, not the sovereign man, but the man who can merely receive, merely be pre-

pared, merely let something happen to him and with him " (209).
The " conceived by the Holy Ghost " serves to testify that " the
empty space," to which the " born of the Virgin Mary " points,
has been filled (215). Even in the divine incarnation what is at
stake is the " freedom of the Holy Ghost and in the Holy Ghost "
(217). " Consequently, right at this point where revelation begins,
the Word of God is not without the Spirit of God " (217).

Barth concludes this section with a reference to the fact that
" the positive element which occupies the space singled out by the
natus ex virgine " is God himself " in the inconceivable deed of
creative omnipotence . . . in the inconceivable deed of reconciling love . . . in the inconceivable deed of redemptive wisdom, in
which he completely adopts the creature, and in such a way that
he imparts and grants to him nothing less than his own existence " (220).

IV

THE OUTPOURING OF THE HOLY SPIRIT

[Volume I, 2, pp. 222–504]

REVELATION has taken place. The Word has become flesh. God has revealed himself as the One who is free for us. Revelation is an "objective" reality, and hence a possibility. But what about the "subjective," about what is usually called the "reception of salvation"? This question does not find — but has found — its answer in the Holy Spirit. The Holy Spirit is the "subjective reality" of revelation and thereby also its "subjective possibility." As the title of the first section of this part of the chapter states, the "freedom of man for God," corresponding to God's freedom for man, consists in the Holy Spirit.

Now Barth first inquires about the "area" "in which God's revelation is subjectively real." This "area" is the Church; that is, it lies "in the twofold togetherness of those whom God acknowledges in Christ and those who acknowledge God in Christ" (241). However, the Church herself also has her "objective side"; that is, that without which God's revelation does not come to man at all (242). It consists in definite signs of the "objective reality" of revelation (243 f.). "In her objective side" she is "sacramental; that is, she is to be understood analogically from baptism and the Lord's Supper" (253). As a "sacramental area" the Church is "the area in which man has to understand himself as one who is on the way from the baptism which has been administered to him to the Supper which is to be administered to him. She is the area in which he begins with faith in order in this way to come to faith: *ek pisteōs, eis pistin* (Rom. 1:17)" (253). For those acquainted with the subject it hardly needs to be mentioned that this is not meant to establish a "sacred human domain" but "God's domain" (248). The "signs" are therefore signs of God's Lordship over men and the world.

But on the other hand God's revelation in its subjective reality consists "in the existence of men, who have been persuaded by

God himself that the objective reality of revelation is present precisely for them, and indeed in such a way . . . that they can no longer understand their own existence from themselves but only continually from that reality. . . . Therefore, they can understand themselves only as brothers of the Son, as hearers and doers of the Word " (253). Barth is quite conscious that he is ignoring the question how the existence of such men comes to be. He argues that what was valid in Christology is just as applicable here; namely, that one can speak of such a possibility only on the ground of its reality. However, this reality is not that of this or that type of qualification of men but a reality of the Holy Spirit. For this reason the " subjective " can never become a theme on its own (262). " The subjective reality of revelation . . . is included in its objective reality " (262). If, therefore, those divinely persuaded men, as distinguished from those " signs " we mentioned, constitute the " subjective side of the Church's reality " (262), then we are not speaking of an independent subjectivity of her own, but once again of God's revelation.

Only now can Barth also speak about the " subjective possibility " of revelation. Only now can the " how " of man's freedom for God be discussed (264 ff.). First of all, the negative statement: " Except in the Holy Spirit " we are " not free for God " (266). Positively it may be summarized in Barth's following propositions: 1. " By the outpouring of the Holy Spirit it becomes possible in the freedom of man for God's revelation to befall him, because in it he is enabled to hear God's Word " (269); 2. . . . . " because in it he is dissuaded by God's Word from thinking of any possibility of his own for such an event " (280); 3. . . . . " because in it God's Word inescapably becomes his Master " (289).

As these propositions give an answer to the question about the " how," at every step they point away from man's own possibilities to God's Word. In retrospect Barth states, " We were prevented from establishing the reality of revelation in God, and then its possibility in man " (305). But now what about man's religion? Barth devotes a special section to this subject under the significant title: " God's Revelation as the Abolition [1] of Religion " (pp. 304 ff.).

---

[1] " Aufhebung " — a word for which there is no precise equivalent in English.

Barth does not dispute that God's revelation has something to do with religion. The reality of revelation would be denied if we were not willing to say that it " is also just that: it is Christianity " (306). Or it would be more accurate to say that " God's revelation is actually God's presence, and therefore God's hiddenness, in the world of human religion " (307). However, this means that God's revelation " at all events also finds itself in a position in which it can then, among other things, be denied as *God's* revelation " (308). That is to say, insofar as God's revelation is a reality within the religious world, it is exposed to the misunderstanding of being for its part a religion, perhaps its peak or culmination. Where this misunderstanding takes root — and according to Barth's richly informative references it has already happened in orthodoxy — there " religion is not seen and explained in terms of revelation but revelation in terms of religion " (309). It is useless to think of explaining the relation of revelation and religion in the sense of a " systematic co-ordination "; one cannot analyze one and then the other, because the other, namely, religion, is to be seen or defined only from revelation (323).

Wherefore, religion is to be defined as " unbelief," as " an " affair, indeed, as " *the* affair of the godless man " (327). This is developed from two sides. First of all, in religion " an image of God which man has obstinately and arbitrarily devised for himself " takes the place of the divine reality (329). Stated concretely: " If man would believe, then he would listen; but in religion he does the talking. If he would believe, he would let something be granted to him; but in religion he takes something. If he would believe, he would let God act for Himself; but in religion he dares to reach out after God. Because religion is this snatching at God, it is opposed to revelation " (330). Moreover, in religion man tries " to manage his own existence, to justify and sanctify himself " (338). But that is what God does not tolerate in His revelation (338). Even the witness of the Old Testament is sharply opposed to it (339 ff.).

Barth definitely guards against seeing these theological judgments confused with the value-judgments of the science of religion (327). Accordingly he carefully distinguishes the real crisis of religion which occurs in revelation from the " immanent questionableness of religion " (343) which grows out of the knowledge that religion is always a " reflection " of what man himself " is and has " (345). Where this insight is awakened, man is driven inward in his religion and there emerges the " relatively new way of religion " which manifests itself concretely as the " twofold way of mysticism and atheism." Of these, mysticism is the more conservative; atheism is " thoughtless," " puerile," but " ultimately the stronger " (351). Meanwhile these two ways are at bottom only " opposed " to the religion they combat " as a fountain is to a stream or as a root is to a tree." Precisely the essential thing in religion is very much alive in mysticism and atheism, namely, the exercise of a supposed " capacity to be in the world and to be a man " (354), the assertion of man's ability to dispose of his own existence. And therefore the " real crisis of religion must befall this capacity as well — at the very first and decisively " (355). Consequently, theology can in no respect align itself with mysticism and atheism in their critique of religion.

The statement that religion is " unbelief " also pertains to the " Christian religion as such " (357). Nevertheless it may be said: " The Christian religion is the true religion " (357). How is that? " Not otherwise," Barth answers (356, 360), than " in the context of the doctrine of the *justificatio impii*," of the justification of the ungodly! She does not bear her " truth " in herself, not in her character as a religion, certainly not in being linked with the history of the Western world (and therefore not in the " proud and yet so deceptive idea of the *corpus christianum* ") (366), and above all not in certain " symptoms." [2] On the contrary, she is to be compared to that " Peniel " of Gen., ch. 32, to that place " where man stands absolutely against God and just as such . . . becomes a man marked by God, and who can do nothing else but pray: I will

[2] TRANSLATOR'S NOTE: A " symptom " or sign that the Christian religion is the true religion would be the renunciation of the claim to be so in virtue of any inherent merits. But that would not make it the true religion. Not the fact that Protestantism is a religion of grace, but grace itself, the justifying and sanctifying truth in the name of Jesus, makes Christianity to be the true religion. Consequently Barth considers it a singular dispensation of Providence that among the heathen religions of the Far East we find almost exact parallels — not to the Greek or Roman Catholic — but to the Reformation form of Christianity as a religion of grace. The Jodo-Shin and the Jodo-Shin-Shu religions in Japan and the Bhakti religion of grace in India prove that the truth and reality of the Christian religion is not found in its historical structure as such but in the grace of Jesus Christ.

not let thee go, except thou bless me . . ." (371) . The truth itself is " the ground of the symptoms " (372) , and only one thing — " the name of Jesus Christ " — decides " about truth or falsehood among religions " (376) . " The Christian religion is a predicate for the Subject of the name of Jesus Christ " (381) and the adjective " Christian " does not signify a " laying hold of a possession of our own but only a reaching out after a divine possession decreed in this name. It is therefore an inquiry about our election " (384) . Christ is not the king chosen by us; on the contrary, we are the people chosen by him — and this relationship is irreversible (384) ! However, if that has been seen, it can also be said that the relationship between the name of Jesus Christ and the Christian religion is an " act of divine justification " (387) and " sanctification " (393) . Then it can also be stated that " the divine fact of the name of Jesus Christ " " establishes," " beyond all dialectic," the " creation and election of precisely her religion (namely, the Church's) as the one and only true religion " (391) .

Barth's doctrine of the " Outpouring of the Holy Spirit " closes with a detailed section on " The Life of God's Children " (§ 18, pp. 397–504) . We are now concerned about the " Christian man," and that means about the man who " in his self-determination, without which he would not be a man," . . . is " an object of the divine predetermination " (400) . This man is " therefore the free man upon whom God guarantees and establishes his freedom " (403) . Consequently, as little as the " grace of revelation is limited by his humanity," just as little is his humanity " limited by the grace of revelation " (400) . The mystery of the Holy Spirit is that man attains his freedom just where he recognizes God's freedom for him and where he is determined by it.

The " Christian life, the life of God's children " consists " in these two concepts: in the love and praise of God " (408) . With these two terms Barth wants to repeat what is expressed as the substance of the Christian life in the " twofold commandment to love " (according to Mark 12:29–31) . Thus the " love of the neighbor " is understood as praise of God.

Love for God can be nothing else than the human answer to God's love for us; that is, to " God's sacrifice of himself in his

Son " (416). As such it can be nothing else than an " act of obedience " (424). To that extent it can actually be required " of one
who . . . belongs to God " (423). Still more clearly: " To love
means to become what we already are as those who are beloved of
this (Lord). To love means to choose God as the Lord who is our
Lord in that he takes our part and acts as security for us . . ."
(429). Love is therefore not the pursuit of a natural tendency
found in ourselves but " a seeking for God " (430). It is not an
achievement, but gratitude (441). And (according to Scriptural
passages cited) it is complete, because God completely takes our
part. Herein lies " a similarity " between God's love for us and the
love for him required of us (435).

Now the love of God and the love of the neighbor are not to be
divorced, but neither are they identical (443). The neighbor is
not God! Otherwise " humanity " as such would be divine, and
therefore grounded in itself (445), or the " orders," in which the
neighbor is to encounter me, would immediately pass as God's creation (445 ff.). No, says Barth: " Neither conceptions of humanity nor ideas about the orders but only Holy Scripture must and
can . . . establish what the neighbor is " (447). Scripture, however, also forbids us in any way giving the commandment to love
one's neighbor a secondary or subordinate position to the commandment to love God (448). Rather, the former is also given " in
and with " the latter (452). Love for God lives from and in the
fact that God " loved the world." And at the same time the commandment to erect a " sign " of this love in the " present, transitory world " (453 f.), which is none the less God's world, is contained in that fact. The erection of this sign is the praise of God
in this his world.

But who is the neighbor? His " original and intrinsic form " is
that of one who " is a bearer and representative of divine mercy
for us " (459). Barth explains this by the parable of the merciful
Samaritan who was a neighbor to the man who fell among thieves
because he showed mercy to him; moreover, he became " the merciful neighbor " to him while receiving mercy himself (462).
Therefore, the law directs us to the neighbor only insofar as it " is
first of all the gospel "; that is, a proclamation of mercy in the
mouth and in the person of him who utters the parable (462).

Hence it is also understandable when Barth formulates the following sentence: " My neighbor is the fellow man who deals with me
in the role of my benefactor " (463). The kindness he renders me
" consists in the fact that I am directed by the neighbor into an
order in which I . . . may and must offer my praise to God, whom
I love because he first loved me, in a manner suitable and pleasing
to him " (463). Such a " commissioned and authorized appearance of a fellow man " is to be found, however, only " insofar as
there is a Church in the midst of this world " (465). If we may
recognize " in the prophets and apostles men for whom Jesus
Christ has become the neighbor," then for us there has thereby
" opened up the possibility of men being able to have this function," and to have it also outside of the visible Church. The chal-
lenge to praise God can come to us from a fellow man even " where
at first we think that no matter where we look, nothing of the
Church is to be seen " (469). When this neighbor is for us a representative of God's mercy, he is not a being distinguished by any
positive virtues, but " a sinful fellow man punished because of his
sins " (475).

What is the testimony I owe my neighbor in praise of God?
Barth answers that in the first place it is the fact " that, with respect
to helping him in his need and mine, I do not begrudge him
the Word " (488). Secondly, that I " lend him a helping hand as
a sign of God's help which is also promised to him " (492).
Thirdly, that in relation to him " I authenticate by my attitude
what I have to say to him by Word and deed " (495). But what
then does it mean — finally — " to love as thyself "? Self-love is
not required of us! If I love my neighbor " as myself," then my self-
love is not thereby perhaps indirectly justified; on the contrary,
it is condemned (499). Therefore I am reminded of the fact
that I, even while I love, am a sinner. However, that I am called
upon at all "to intervene and offer myself as a sinner " (500) ; that
I am counted worthy to receive such a commandment, and thus,
as I am, to praise God, enables the commandment to become
knowable as grace, and it should encourage me to put my trust in
this grace (501 ff.).

V

HOLY SCRIPTURE AND THE CHURCH

[*Volume I, 2, pp. 505–990*]

WITH THIS part of our report we are summarizing two chapters of Barth's *Dogmatics:* the third, " Holy Scripture," and the fourth, " The Proclamation of the Church." For our brief survey this summary commends itself because even the third chapter speaks at the same time about the Church in each of its three sections (§§ 19–21). The titles run as follows: " God's Word for the Church," " Authority in the Church," and " Freedom in the Church." The doctrine of Scripture is, therefore, at once a doctrine of the Church.

We recall that Barth refused to begin with the doctrine of Scripture. He made his start with the doctrine of God's revelation, and that meant with the doctrine of the Trinity. But naturally this was not done by reflecting at random — and how often we find this stressed! — but rather in a hearing of the Scriptural witness. Therefore he did not proceed from the question about the possibility of revelation but from its reality. Likewise, the doctrine of Scripture does not begin again with a discussion about whether Scripture might really have this or that validity. On the contrary, his present basic proposition, " The Bible is the witness to revelation," is for its part grounded in the fact " that the Bible has actually given an answer to our question about God's revelation, in that it has placed God's sovereignty before our eyes " (511).

The Bible is a witness. Consequently it, itself, is not the thing that is attested. It is to be distinguished from revelation " insofar as it is only a human word about it " (512). However, it is also united with it " insofar as revelation is the ground, object, and content of this word " (512). It is therefore " to be understood as a human word from the standpoint of what it specifically says," and " it is to be expounded in its connection with what it specifically says " (516). Only this understanding, this exposition, and a hermeneutics constructed on it, is pertinent. According to Barth

there is no special Biblical hermeneutics (515, 521, 812). The special thing about the Bible is the "majesty" of God's Word testified in it (522). When we seek to understand the Bible otherwise
than in view of what it specifically and simply says, it is surely an
incongruous kind of hearing, and therefore a thoroughly unhis-
toric procedure as well (516). In view of this special element in its
case, Biblical hermeneutics cannot let itself be dictated to by a
general hermeneutics, and indeed — "just for the sake of a better
general hermeneutics" (523).

Now the Bible meets us in the form of the canon, that is, "of
Scripture . . . discovered and acknowledged by the Church as
Holy Scripture" (524). If we attach ourselves to this ecclesiastical
decision, we, however, are thereby being obedient "in and with
the Church to a judgment which had already been pronounced before the Church could pronounce her judgment," and "which the
Church . . . could only confirm" (525).

The decision about the canon, however, is a decision by the man
who hears. Consequently in principle it is not absolutely withdrawn from error. As a result the canon can only be designated as
"relatively" closed (527). This is also shown by the fact that at
the time of the Reformation, at any rate — by the exclusion of the
so-called Apocrypha, and somewhat by the preparatory distinction
between the protocanonical and deuterocanonical writings as well
— changes in the canon still occurred (527 ff.). However, such a
change would be possible only as an act of the Church (530) and
thus as a daring act of faith. "For the sake of the real authority of
the Biblical canon we must again learn to understand its establishment as a testimony of faith, and its acknowledgment as obedience
of faith. Therefore we must understand its actual existence as indefinite, even when we should have no occasion at all to object to
it" (532)!

The Bible is the witness of men. What — according to its own
declarations — gives it then such a patently distinguished position? The answer first of all is to the effect that it is the content of
this witness. Hence it is the fact "that in its decisive center it attests the resurrection of Jesus Christ from the dead" (538), and
the fact that its witness awakens faith and just therein proves to be
God's self-attestation. However, those who here bear witness are

also really " special men " (539) : men who " had the unique and contingent function of the first witnesses " (539), and whose existence is " the existence of Christ for us and for all men " (539)! They have " seen and heard in a way that happens but once " (543). As Barth remarks a little later, there is no possibility of going back behind this proclamation of the authorized witnesses to an actuality independent of it. " The historical truth, which even Biblical science in its way actually has to ascertain, is the true meaning and context of the Biblical texts as such " (548).

Therefore: a binding witness! So very much so that later on we read the sentence " that Holy Scripture, as the original and legitimate witness to God's revelation, is God's Word itself " (557). In what sense is that true? It is true in the sense of a " divine decree, deed, and decision, to which . . . we . . . on the one hand look back as to something that has already happened and to which we on the other hand look forward as to something in the future " (557). That statement, therefore, does not denote " a state of affairs which is immediately obvious to us or which is at our disposal " (557). With that we have arrived at the doctrine of theopneusty, of the " inspiration " of Scripture.

As is well known, the standard Biblical passage in this connection is II Tim. 3:14–17, and here especially the sentence in v. 16: All Scripture is " divinely spiritual " — as Barth now renders it. That is, it is " impregnated, filled, and governed by God's Spirit . . . God's Spirit breathing, diffusing, illuminating it " (559). However, in addition to this Barth notices, among other things, that " in the middle of the passage an assertion is made about a relation between God and the Scripture which can be understood only as a decree, deed, and decision of God himself. Consequently, as such, it cannot be further explained. Rather, it can only be referred to — and not for nothing so curtly " (559). It is the mystery of " free grace " which here rises resplendent over Scripture. The situation is quite similar in the case of the " decisive middle " of the other principal passage: II Peter 1:19–21. What is important is that in both instances there is no occasion to think of special experiences of the authors or of the godly men who speak (in speaking as in writing). The important thing is that theopneusty " within the circumference of Biblical thought "

can only signify the "special attitude of obedience of the men
elected and called to this admittedly special service" (560). Both
texts, together with the concept of theopneusty, refer us to the
present, "to the event which takes place in ourselves." But they
only refer us to it. Theopneusty has in view what Scripture "was"
and "will be," and "indirectly" also what it is (561). It is to be
understood as "the act of revelation in which the prophets and
apostles in their humanity become what they were, and in which
alone they in their humanity can also become for us what they
are" (563). Moreover, Barth emphasizes that in such an understanding of inspiration the human imperfection of the Biblical
witnesses, yes, even the "assailability" of their theological statements, is to be soberly acknowledged — just as Israel, from whom
the Biblical witness stems, is also "the one natural proof of the
existence of God he has given" and is a living witness of the freely
electing God in, and in spite of, the fact that she is open to attack
(563 ff.). Applying this to Scripture we can say that the human
word we hear in it is not in every case appropriate, but it is an
elected, and, in this election, an authoritative human word. The
essential thing in the concept of theopneusty is that God acts upon
the witnesses and upon the hearers of the witness, and, what is
more, upon both in the revelation of his mystery (cf. I Cor.
2:6–16). God's "self-disclosure in its totality is theopneusty, the
inspiration of the prophetic, apostolic word" (573). The Church's
doctrine of inspiration in itself was rightly conceived to be a
verbal inspiration and not simply an inspiration of its content
(575, 592). However, in the interest of a misconstrued certainty
(581), it made inspiration into a "completed and static state of inspiration," [1] a datum (575). It made itself guilty of a "seculariz-
ing of the concept of revelation" (576). When it looked upon inspiration as a "marvel," it allowed free grace to become a supernatural work (580, etc.), and thereby at the same time (even very
early in the history of the doctrine) the "real humanity" of the
Scriptural word was called in question (575, 584 f.). These objec-
tions do not apply to the Reformers, whose doctrine of inspiration
is in "praise of God, and extols God's free grace" (579). But they
certainly do apply (in addition to the Early Church doctrine) to

---

[1] "Verbal*inspiriertheit*," which Barth contrasts with "verbalinspiration."

orthodoxy, whose doctrine of inspiration reveals an " obvious secularism " and therefore must be attacked and rejected " as an
error " (583). Its supernaturalism was "not grounded deeply
enough," and its aim was an exceedingly " naturalistic " postulate;
namely, that the Bible should afford a divine, infallible history
(583). A marvel takes the place of miracle! Thus the mystery of
the Holy Spirit is dissolved. The Bible becomes " a self-sufficient
paper pope which, in contrast to the one at Rome, who after all
is a living pope, was now delivered into the hands of its exposi-
tors . . ." (583)!

The propositions, with which Barth continues, develop what
was already indirectly recognizable in outline. He closes with the
admission that, looked at humanly, the " weakest spot " in all
evangelical theology is the question about who actually guarantees
the divinity of the Scriptural witness (598). Here most certainly
no universally obvious answer can be given. Indeed, here one can
only say: " Scripture is recognized as God's Word by the fact that
it *is* God's Word " (597). There is no means in this world by
which that fact can be proved. It can only be confessed — but even
then not haphazardly. And just because this confession has its
ground and truth in God's Holy Spirit, theology's weakest spot
is also the place at which it " possesses all its imperishable
strength " (598).

The theme " Scripture and Church " is expounded in two sections (§§ 20 and 21). Their presupposed theses make it clear that
they correspond to each other. The thesis for " Authority in the
Church " (§ 20) begins with the sentence: " The Church does not
claim direct, absolute, and material authority for herself but solely
for Holy Scripture as God's Word." The corresponding sentence
in regard to " Freedom in the Church " (§ 21) is: " A member of
the Church does not claim a direct, absolute, and material freedom for himself, but solely for Holy Scripture as God's Word "
(741). So then a parallelism runs through all the sentences of both
theses and through their subsequent amplification as well.

According to the wording of the thesis rendered above in its
opening sentence, it is logical that § 20 begins with a discussion
about the "Authority of the Word " (as correspondingly § 21 be-

gins with a discussion about the " Freedom of the Word ") and only then speaks about " Authority Under the Word " (as § 21 speaks of " Freedom Under the Word ") .

In the first place the " authority " of the Word as a Scriptural word could be described generally in terms of the Bible being undoubtedly the " oldest document " the Church possesses. But with that, the subject is by no means exhausted (601) . It is the question whether the Church possesses in the authority of Scripture a genuine counterpart, that is, an ultimate counterpart. If, of course, Scripture were only a sort of expression for something lying back of it, for a higher court as it were, for a truth which we also could somehow find beside it, then for this inquiry the Church would be thrown back upon her own resources. Then she would actually be " in herself a direct, absolute, and material authority " (603) . Then she would have no counterpart. Or expressed in a different way: If the promise, given to the first witnesses, of Christ's presence in and with their testimony is not valid, then there can be, it is true, a memorial society, or a society with common ideals and sentiments in line with the modern Protestant understanding of the Church. Yes, then there can also be the Catholic Church with her own capacity for knowledge, but there certainly cannot be an evangelical Church. And vice versa! If that promise is valid, " then the revelation is sheltered in the word of the prophets and apostles so far above the Church . . . that she will do well to refrain from laying hold of it to make it her own possession . . ." (607) . Therefore the Church here faces a decision, and, what is more, she faces it " time and again " (607) . At any rate, the fact remains: " The evangelical Church — and with her the true Church — stands or falls by her understanding the statement, ' The Bible is God's Word,' exclusively . . . and therefore does not claim a direct, absolute, and material authority either for some third court of appeal, or for herself " (607) .

From this standpoint Barth now furnishes a penetrating criticism of the Roman Catholic understanding of tradition. However, the foregoing observations enable him at the same time to expose the concealed traditionalism in modern Protestantism as well; namely, the " enthusiastic faith," with which it is imbued, " in a direct access to revelation granted the Church." (Thus, passing

Scripture by, it resorts to this or that handy court of appeal.) At
the same time Barth is able to show how men like Hugo Grotius
or Georgius Calixtus (incidentally just like Schleiermacher; cf.
602) arrived in fact at a traditionalism of their own from a " syn-
thetic theology " (619).[2]

The decision is between an " obedient Church " and a " self-
governing Church " (640). In this connection it should be remem-
bered that self-government is the prerogative of God (639). A self-
governing Church, which desires to have direct access to Christ
apart from or alongside of the witness of the apostles and prophets (646), inevitably finds herself engaged in a monologue (651).
(Only now and then is the monologue seemingly disturbed.)

" Genuine authority " is exercised " precisely by the Church under the Word and thus under Holy Scripture " (653). With this
statement we are at the second part of our section: " Authority
Under the Word." It is defined quite specifically as a human authority, comparable to that of a father and a mother, but in an
opposite sense: " because there is revelation and Church " (and
hence the rule of God's Word among us men), " therefore there is
family and state, not the reverse of this " (654). This genuine human authority of the Church is constituted " in a common hearing and accepting of God's Word " (655), and this communion
" becomes . . . concrete in a Church confession " (655).

What are we to think about the Church's confession? Barth declares in a summary: " Ecclesiastical authority consists in a Church
confession . . . , that is, the voice of others in the Church accost-
ing me in particular agreements and common declarations, and, as
such, preceding my own faith and its confession " (662). Church
authority in its concrete form (and consequently the confession in
all forms) is always a " decision " (662), and " a decision, moreover, with respect to Holy Scripture " (666). It is thus a " spiritual
authority." Those who speak and hear in such a decision concur
" in obedience to God's Word " (666). From this it follows at the
same time that Church authority (and a Church confession) cannot be " raised to a principle "; as a court of appeal it remains
" under the Word " (666). This truth is now further elucidated
by the different forms in which the Church's authority is exercised.

2 " *Theologie des ' und,'* " lit., " a theology of the ' and.' "

First of all, there is the decision about the canon, about which we
have already spoken, and to which Barth returns. Next he mentions the peculiar authority of certain " teachers of the Church "
(673 ff.) , the " Church Fathers." He calls attention to the fact that
the authority of the Reformers in the evangelical Church is " analogous " to that of the early Church Fathers in the Roman Catholic
Church (677). In a legitimate sense the concept of a teacher of
the Church " includes " that of an " elder and more experienced
fellow pupil " (678). His authority cannot possibly be ultimately
binding. It is nonetheless a " regulative principle " in the Church.
Consequently the Church is referred to the — thoroughly relative — authority of the Reformers, unless she is perchance " led
out beyond the Reformation by a new contingency " (681). This
is, indeed, by no means unthinkable. But it would " require very
weighty matters " for it " to eventuate " (684). However, the relative authority of the Reformers cannot possibly come to mean
that we are bound to the " *exousia* ' Lutheranism ' " or the " *exousia* ' Calvinism.' " Neither Lutheranism nor Calvinism may become for us " hypostases," or angelic powers in the sense of Gal.
4:8 f. or Col. 2:8, 20 f. (689). On the contrary, the very thing that
concerned the teachers of the Church plainly demands that we
take a critical attitude toward them (691).

Barth then cites a Confession of Faith as a third example of the
Church's authority " under the Word." By a Confession of Faith
he understands " a formulation and proclamation of an insight
into the revelation attested by Scripture. It is an insight granted
to the Church within a definite circumference. Its formulation
and proclamation come to pass on the basis of common delibera-
tion and resolution " (693). This definition is then further developed in detail. It is noteworthy that according to Barth every Confession of Faith possesses a definite " geographical circumference "
and an equally definite " temporal character " (700 f.). It is by
nature concrete; otherwise it would become a principle. Furthermore, the " *damnamus*," the specific denial of false doctrine, is essential to a Confession of Faith. To be sure, in it " the whole risk
involved in a Confession of Faith . . . becomes apparent " (705).
It claims for itself concrete authority just in its momentous deni-
als. Yet it remains " a document of a human and therefore limited

insight." Indeed, its authority rests " quite definitely in its limitation." It rests in the fact that a Confession of Faith can never be
anything else than an asseveration of an understanding of Scripture and a testimony to the authority of Scripture (709). If all
these restricting considerations are kept in view, then of course it
can and must be said that a Confession of Faith " does possess ecclesiastical authority; that is, it may and must be heard in the
Church as the voice of our fathers and brethren in the faith having become audible in an extraordinary way " (725). It is not
thereby infallible. " The infallible and so unsurpassable and unchangeable Confession of Faith " is rather solely " the praise which
the Church, as the body eternally united with its Lord, will render
to her Lord in this her own eternal consummation. It is therefore
an eschatological concept, to which there is no corresponding realization here and now " (737).

As already mentioned, the same is true of the " freedom in the
Church," with which the next section (§ 21) deals, as of " authority." As there is no arbitrary authority in the Church, so there is
no arbitrary freedom; that is, a freedom claimed by an individual
for himself. The freedom that matters in the Church is " the freedom of the Word," and only then in this freedom is there also " a
freedom under the Word " (thus the two parts of this section).
Now Barth was writing in the year 1938, at a time in which " authority " has become a " favorite slogan," and " freedom " a " term
of abuse in the world " (743). All the greater is the danger of representing the Church's authority in terms of a secular authoritarian
principle and so at the same time treating secular freedom with
abuse. The Church must withstand both of these. The authenticity
of her struggle " against false ideas of freedom " can therefore be
maintained only when at the same time she interests herself " in the
freedom which is suppressed and persecuted in the worldly realm "
(745). Only when she takes such an attitude can she then give cred-
ible assurance that authority and freedom, as authority and freedom of the Word and under the Word, are always to be differentiated and yet presented together.

The theological basis for this statement is to be found again in
pneumatology: " As God in his revelation is no less the Holy
Spirit than the Son, so God's Word in Scripture is no less Spirit

than it is Word " (746). And " as the Son can be revealed only by
the Spirit and only the Son in the Spirit," so " authority must necessarily be interpreted by freedom and freedom by authority "
(746). Seen in this light Roman Catholicism with its arbitrary authority is just " rebellion against the authority of God's Word "
(747). Modern Protestantism, in handing us over to the " God in
our own hearts," is simply the erection of a tyrannical authority
and not the freedom proclaimed by it (748 f.). " Who can be a
worse tyrant for us than the God in our own hearts? " (749).

The freedom of the Word definitely consists in the " power "
that meets us in Holy Scripture, and which exposes " the essentially problematic character of all other subjects " in the world. Indeed, " the whole truth is that Holy Scripture in its utterly insignificant appearance has more power than all the rest of the world
together " (760). It is, to be sure, a hidden power (761), but it
signifies an assault upon the actual world. Moreover, it is an assault by a " superior " power (762), because it is the assault of one
risen from the dead (767). But now this power has " a special
sphere and place for its operation: the Church " (768). And moreover — in contrast to the Roman doctrine of a " *depositum* " — it
is true in such a way that the Word not only had the power and
freedom to create the Church but so that it continually creates the
Church in this its power and freedom. There is also a *creatio continua,* a constant creation of the Church (771 f.). Consequently it
should also be said that Holy Scripture is the " concrete bearer of
Church government " (777), and that therefore human Church
government cannot very well claim to let Christ be the highest authority in the Church if in a clerical or sectarian fashion it " hur-
ries past " the concrete dominion of Scripture (777).

" Freedom under the Word " is really man's freedom, and the
freedom of the individual in the Church at that. It is not a matter
of a freedom which we had in virtue of our humanity or perhaps in
virtue of a " direct relationship to God " grounded in our individuality (789), but a freedom which God's Word in the Church
gives to us. That the Word also comes to the individual is not due
to his character as an individual. Nor is it based upon special
things that have happened to him. (In this regard one must guard
against any arbitrary optimism or even pessimism) (792). The

" really special events in our life . . . are not those we can affirm as being humanly demonstrable in this way." On the contrary, they are " absolutely identical with our participation in the great deeds of God in his revelation " (794). Believers do not know by themselves. Neither are they " ignorant." They are " co-knowers — *conscientes* " (796).[3]

But what does this freedom mean in actual practice? Barth explains first of all that it should be designated " as the assumption of a responsibility for the exposition and application of Holy Scripture " (797). With our own word we are somehow " included " in the sphere of the revelational event (798). It is in keeping with the human form of God's Word that it has " even surrendered itself to this necessity for an explanation " (799). However, the freedom granted us here is not entrusted solely to a " body of Biblical scholars," but " the whole Church " is " the organization for this mediating service " (801). A congregation that is like a child who has not reached the age of responsibility is a rebellious congregation (801)! Furthermore, freedom under the Word consists in a " voluntary act of subordination " to Scripture (802) and in the manifold acts of Scriptural exegesis: observation, reflection, and appropriation. In this context Barth now comes to speak — more fully than previously — about questions of hermeneutics which today are such a burning issue. He begins by repeating his earlier thesis that there is no " special " Biblical hermeneutics (812 f.). He then develops his very significant ideas about what today are usually referred to as " presuppositions " which in one way or another we " bring along with " us. Barth admits that every reader of the Bible, consciously or unconsciously, brings with him " some philosophy or other " (816). It is a fact beyond discussion. The problem arises first " in connection with how " it is to be " used " (818). And in this regard it is certainly important that we be " thoroughly conscious " of the " thought patterns we have brought with us " (818). Then, further, they acquire the character of an " experiment," of a " hypothesis " already assumed beforehand, but even now to be tried out upon Scripture (819 f.). They cannot therefore " claim any independent interest for themselves " (820). " Every absolutely posited philosophy must lead to

---

[3] " *Selbstwissende . . . Unwissende . . . Mitwissende* " — a play upon words.

the falsification of Scripture " (821)! For the absolutizing of philosophy is "an act of unbelief" (821)! Consequently no pre-eminence can be given to one philosophy over another (822). Each
has its importance solely in the service it renders to "reflection"
upon Scripture (823). In each and every exegesis of Scripture it is
a question of the obedience of faith. Only in the actual work of
exegesis is the reader and hearer led "out of the system of his own
interests and questions" to "focus his attention" upon the Scriptural word itself (828 f.).

The "Proclamation of the Church," to which Barth now de-
votes the fourth chapter of his work (831 ff.), was already charac-
terized as a form of God's Word. In the thesis at the head of § 22
("The Church's Commission") it is stated quite precisely: "God's
Word is God himself in the proclamation of the Church of Jesus
Christ" (831).

God's Word in the mouths of men! The enigmas and the abundance of "human complications" springing up here are obvious,
and Barth does not overlook them at all. But preceding all that "is
the divine simplicity," and "above all the misery of the Church is
the glory of the commission she has received" (836)! God "acknowledges" the Church's proclamation "in virtue of the grace
of revelation and its attestation" in such a way that it "is not
only an announcement of human ideas and convictions but . . .
God's announcement of himself" (834). This is the first thing
that must be seen! Only then can it be kept in mind that it is quite
impossible for man to effect such proclamation, and in truth, because the attempt "to speak about God" is an impossible one
(838). God is not an object! But this impossibility "has already
been removed in Jesus Christ" (837), in that he gave himself into
the hands of men, rose from the dead, and elected men to be his
witnesses! As had always been the case hitherto, so also in this connection, the possibility follows only from the reality. "The knowledge of its humanity, which in itself is lost, follows from nothing
else than from faith in the true divinity of Church proclamation.
And from it also follows the knowledge that it can live in its humanity only from its divinity, that is, however, from the grace of
God's Word" (841). The human word has been attacked and it

is open to attack. So only in virtue of God's promise can it stand in an " indirect identity " with God's Word (849), in an identity which does not abolish its human character but adopts it.

However, with that, we are faced with the problem of " pure doctrine," in which Church proclamation emerges in its character as a dependent and therefore authorized ministry. And at the same time we are thus faced anew with the task of dogmatics, whose problem is that of pure doctrine. The task of dogmatics is not identical with the task of proclamation (861), and vice versa (862). Rather, dogmatics effects " the transition from Bible to sermon " (865). At the same time it must necessarily take a " critical " attitude to the sermon. But it certainly cannot possibly be a " skeptical and negative " attitude (867). It is not an undertaking which professes to know the answers but — as " an auxiliary service of the Church " (861) — is a special inquiry about the substance of proclamation. And it can engage in this inquiry only in the trust " that God's Word has never left itself without a witness in his Church, and never will " (867).

Before Barth goes on to describe dogmatics more precisely — in two sections — as a function of the " hearing " (§ 23) and of the " teaching " Church (§ 24), he again critically discusses the fact that for a long time ethics has been separated from dogmatics (875 ff.). For the theology of the Reformers such an independency of the two would have to be characterized as " impossible according to its presuppositions " (876). It has become possible only since it was thought that the " holiness of the Christian " is somehow " directly perceptible " (in contrast to Col. 3:3). When it was looked at in this way, then dogmatics naturally had to become suspect as now " being an idle intellectual game " (881). For ethics, on the other hand, " an exchange of subjects, namely, of God and of man," had to become " the real constituent principle," and so ethics at bottom ceased to be a theological discipline. Barth comes to the conclusion that at any rate ethics substantially belongs to dogmatics. " Dogmatics cannot be anything else: it must also be ethics. Its dialectic and its whole attitude must be ' existential '; that is, it must also be related to human existence because it is related to God's Word " (888).

The thought of both of the following sections is again quite

parallel. It will be appropriate to give in full the wording of the
theses at the head of them. For § 23: " Dogmatics challenges the
teaching Church to a new hearing of God's Word in the revelation attested in Scripture. But dogmatics can do this only when it,
on its part, takes the position of the hearing Church, and therefore
hearkens to God's Word as the norm to which the hearing Church
as such knows herself to be subject " (890) . For § 24: " Dogmatics
challenges the hearing Church to a new teaching of God's Word
in the revelation attested in Scripture. But dogmatics can do this
only when it, on its part, takes the position of the teaching Church,
and therefore is itself claimed by God's Word as by a subject which
has been given to the teaching Church as such " (943) . Even the
subsections of both sections correspond to each other. In § 23 the
" formal " task of dogmatics is discussed, in § 24 the " material ";
and in § 23 the " dogmatic norm " is dealt with, and in § 24 the
" dogmatic method."

First of all, it is important that the Church should be considered specifically as a hearing Church. It is not enough that she has
heard: she needs to hear ever again (898) . For the Church's proclamation is never really safe against backsliding. Heresy lies at the
end of such backsliding. However, it is regularly preceded by the
Church forgetting; that is, forgetting " that even the correctly
teaching Church cannot teach in her own cause and therefore not
on her own authority, not in her own power, nor according to her
own directives " (902) . Just such " preheretical deviations " are
the concern of the " formal task of dogmatics " (903) . Dogmatics
does not have the task of establishing or " proscribing " accomplished heresies. That is a matter for the whole Church (906) . But
dogmatics has to issue a warning " where it sees the obedience,
which proclamation has to render, threatened " (908) .

The " norm " established for dogmatics, and of which it has to
remind the teaching Church, is in itself a single one. Yet it becomes concrete in three demands for a " Biblical, confessional,
and ecclesiastical attitude." Here special prominence should be
given to what is said about the " confessional attitude " (919 ff.) .
" The dogmatic theologian . . . must have his relatively defined
homeland with its relatively defined horizon within the Church "

(919)! Yet just relatively! "In a confessionalism thought of mor-
phologically . . . there slumbers somewhere always an animistic
paganism with its fear and veneration in the face of certain field,
forest, or mountain demons . . ." (920)! However, on the other
hand it remains true: a dogmatic theologian cannot, for example,
be Roman Catholic and evangelical at the same time (921). What
positively is to be understood as the "confessional attitude" of
dogmatics is defined by Barth in this way: it is a matter of "the
faithfulness required by God's Word to the Fathers, and to the
Church's confession as to the voice of those who were in the Church
before us. . . . But we are being obedient to the Word and not to
them when we remain faithful to them" (926). Barth bluntly declares that when he says "Church" he means the "evangelical Reformed Church" (927). But his dogmatics cannot thereby become
a "Reformed" dogmatics. Dogmatics is rather Church dogmatics
(not even "evangelical" dogmatics). Otherwise it would not be
understood that the dogmatic question and answer has in view the
one and whole Church (924 f., 929). In addition the relation of
the three evangelical Confessions of Faith (the Lutheran, the Reformed, and the Anglican; 929) is indeed also such that the dogmatic theologian is faced with a decision; but the decision is of another kind than in regard, say, to Roman Catholicism. What separates them is "not heresies, but . . . particular errors, particular
faulty and misleading theologoumena, erroneously and arbitrarily
constructed, such as can also arise within the Reformed Church
itself, without, for that reason, making a schism necessary" (929).
Precisely in a fidelity to the confession, the dogmatic theologian
will have to look beyond the "confessional status." The "establishing" of "conflicting schools and movements" within the evangelical Church can "ultimately be only for the sake of overcoming
them" (933). Therefore neither veneration of "field, forest, and
mountain demons" nor "ancestral worship" is the answer (936)!

Wherein does the "material" task of dogmatics now consist?
(And with this we come to § 24.) The "formal" task, as we saw,
lay in warning against heresies possible at any time. The "material" task, that is, the interpretation of the contents of "pure doctrine," serves "to call the Church which is hearing God's Word to
the remembrance and to the consciousness of *what* she hears when

she hears God's Word " (951). The " what," however, in virtue
of its own " dynamic," will then oppress and disquiet the Church.
It will demand from her that she fail not in the responsibility required of her. And it will prevent her from becoming not only
" heretical " but also a " dead Church."

The particular motif of the dogmatic " method " will consist in
the " paradigmatic achievement of the necessary relation of hearing to speaking " (955). Like the " norm " of dogmatics it is " the-
onomous " (958; cf. 911). But here, where it is now a matter of the
subjective possibility of pure doctrine, dogmatics must seek to preserve a theonomy in the " relative and concrete form of auton-
omy." The dogmatic method is therefore free; but its freedom is
the " freedom of obedience " (963). However, both of these, freedom and obedience, would perish if in its method dogmatics were
to assume the form of a closed system (963). Dogmatics must be
as it were an open structure: open because it is free in obedience;
open also for the reason that the dogma, at which it aims, is " an
eschatological concept " (967); open above all because " the content of God's Word is now just God's work and action, and therefore God's free grace, which as such is withdrawn from our grasp
and our disposal " (971).

VI

THE KNOWLEDGE OF GOD

[Volume II, 1, pp. 1–287]

A NYONE with the slightest acquaintance with Barth will not expect from him a discussion of the question whether "there is" a God, nor a proof that "there is" one. In fact Barth even begins by establishing that neither the "whether" nor even the "possibility" of knowing God is open to debate (2 ff.). This is not a comfortable dismissal of a problem, for there are sound reasons for it. For only because God is actually known in the Church, can we speak of the possibility of such knowledge. This possibility does not have its roots in whatever reasons may lie outside God's own reality. The meaning is that one cannot prove to any man that there might be a knowledge of God except by testifying to its reality for him. We could express it in another way. The ground of the possibility of the knowledge of God is not in man or in the world, therefore not in the creature but in the Creator himself. God would not be the Creator if the possibility of knowing him were to follow from anything else than from himself and his revelation. However, it is to be admitted that in view of the real knowledge of God the question concerning the possibility that emerges in it is then also meaningful. Barth spends a whole section on the "knowability" of God, on the "possibility of the knowledge of God" (67 ff.). Only this is really a secondary thing; it can never become primary.

Knowledge of God occurs, it has its "consummation," in that God's Word places man before God (8 ff.). "Man knows God as he stands before God" (8). We are therefore not speaking about God "in himself" but about "God in his relation to man." However, that also means: "in his distinction to man" (9). Knowledge of God is not "to be understood as man's oneness with God" (9), but in it, on the contrary, an objective comprehension is posited, as Barth emphasizes over and over again. "Objective" — what does that mean? Naturally not that God were or would be an "ob-

ject " like other objects. It is a question of an " absolutely unique
objectivity " (13) . " We do not have him (God) in the way we
have other objects " (21) . And yet God becomes an object for us!
This means first of all that in the faith, in which alone we have a
knowledge of God, we make a firm distinction between God and
ourselves. God is not our faith. Neither is he our knowledge of God
nor even our experience of God. He is not our religious feeling.
If this were misunderstood, there would be no more talk of Christian faith. " God speaks, he makes demands, he promises, he acts,
he is angry, he is gracious. Remove the objectivity of this ' he,' and
faith as love, trust, and obedience also collapses " (13) !

This " objectivity " of God, as it is given to faith, has its original
ground in the divine Trinity. " Objectivity is in his triune life as
such, and with it knowledge is a divine reality before there is a
creaturely objectivity and knowledge " (15) . Expressed in a different way, as the triune God, as Father, Son, and Holy Spirit, God
is not an undifferentiated " being " to himself and in himself, but
he " confronts " himself. And above all he reveals himself to us as
the triune God. He makes himself to be an " object " for us in his
revelation, to be our " counterpart." For he does not meet us as an
eternal idea we could appropriate, as it were, to ourselves, but as
an active " I " and insofar as an absolutely unique " object."

" Absolutely unique "! How very true this is may be shown
when further consideration is now paid to the opposite side of
what has been said hitherto: " God before man " (33 ff.) . Here it
is first clearly shown why it is important that God's " primary objectivity " be trinitarian. God is the " object " of which we in no
wise take possession in the act of knowing. From God's objectivity,
as it is granted to us in faith, we are continually directed to that
other trinitarian objectivity. " But that means that his unveiling
in his works and signs always implies for us his veiling as well; his
revealedness also always implies his hiddenness; and love for him
can never be without fear of him. . . . We cannot celebrate and
receive the sacrament he instituted without seeking and finding him just in the sacrament over and above the sacrament as
such . . ." (54) . God is never that kind of " object " that we could
think of ourselves as an independent subject over against him. All
other " objects " we " do have," " because we already have our-

selves " (22), but this is not true in relation to God. Whoever
knows him loses himself. " The fact that we know God is his work
and not ours " (43). " He is and remains the One whom we only
know because he makes himself known; he is and remains the light
that is visible and seen only in his own light " (43 f.). Precisely
this means that he is also a mystery just in his becoming known!
He " remains " so " because he himself makes himself so clear and
certain to us " (46).

God's objectivity, as we heard, is " primarily " trinitarian. What
we receive in contrast to it is a " second objectivity " (55); namely,
that " of his works and signs in our creaturely sphere, before our
eyes and ears, and in our hearts. As such, and of themselves, they
are not capable of yielding a knowledge of him " (55). Barth can
forthwith designate as a " sacrament " this objectivity in which
God lets us " participate " in his truth, in short, this his " revelation " (56). And just from that standpoint he explains how our
knowledge of God is " limited " (" knowing in part," " mirror,"
" riddle "; cf. I Cor. 13:8 ff.). " The real basis and essence of the
sacramental reality of his revelation is the existence of the human
nature of Jesus Christ " (58). " The humanity of Jesus Christ as
such is the first sacrament, the foundation of all that has been
instituted and used by him even before and after the epiphany
(appearance) of Jesus Christ as God's secondary objectivity in his
revelation " (58)! It signifies that in the humanity of Jesus Christ
there takes place, on the one hand, the special, unique " eminence
of a creature " (59). But, on the other hand, it is also " God's
self-abasement and self-estrangement " (59). Both in one! And
this " is true . . . of the whole sacramental reality which has
been instituted and used to attest his revelation, and to that extent, as the means to the knowledge of himself " (59 f.). " As
such " it is " neither identical with revelation nor with the real
knowledge of God." Rather, the sacramental reality " serves "
revelation " when God reveals himself and is known." Also, however, it can " not serve . . . indeed, it can hinder and prevent it "
(the offense) (60). Or seen from another side, precisely in this
" sacramental reality " God's " I " becomes for us a " Thou and
He " (62 ff.), but yet in such a way that we no doubt " really and
truly," but nevertheless only " indirectly," participate in his own

self-knowledge (as I) (64). Thus God's revelation is quite genuinely his own revelation. But it certainly does not become immediately perceptible to us, something we could manage as it
were. God remains the Lord in his revelation (65) !

Only on the ground of the reality of such a valid and yet indirect
knowledge of God can we ask about its possibility (67 ff.). And
here we come to speak about " God's readiness " (68 ff.) and of
" man's readiness " (141 ff.).

" God's readiness " — what does that mean? First of all Barth answers: " He is in his nature, and as he confronts us in his action,
so constituted that he can be known by us " (70). Or to put it dif-
ferently and more concretely: " God is the truth," and just therein
lies his readiness, his " knowability " (73). But this cannot be expressed at all — we need only to think of John 1:14 — without immediately adding: " We are mindful of God's grace when we say
that God is knowable " (74). If we do not pay sharp attention to
that, then we inevitably fall into a speculative truth, in virtue of
which we transcend our own nature and being into the infinite
and call this ultimate transcendence " God " and " God's truth."
Barth now wishes to show by a detailed proof (82 ff.) that actually
we have " no analogy " (no corresponding magnitude), on the
basis of which we somehow could make intelligible to ourselves
God's Lordship (83 f.), his being the Reconciler (84 f.) and the
Redeemer (85 f.).

Whoever is familiar with theological discussion will notice that
we have here reached the point at which Barth must come to terms
with the Roman Catholic doctrine of the *analogia entis* (86 ff.).
According to it there exists, for all their disparity, nevertheless
something basically in common between man and God: " the idea
of being, in which God and man at all events are comprehended
. . ." (89). Insofar as man is able to know what being is, he can
then also know God's being as the most real being, and, at least in
general, can gain a knowledge of God apart from his revelation. (It
is the official dogma of the Roman Church since the Vatican Council.) In a detailed and carefully reasoned argument Barth protests
against this interpretation, chiefly because a cleavage in God's nature is basic to it. Quite generally and quite abstractly God's being is said to be " naturally " knowable, and God's action upon us

is said then to exhibit another second thing, which of course may
be known only on the basis of revelation. This " splitting up of the
thought of God, and, connected with it, the abstraction of God's
real work and action in favor of a being of God in general," is, according to Barth, " not to be forgiven " Roman Catholic theology
(91 f.) . The purport of this is that we know about God exclusively
as the One who acts upon us as the triune God. We have to look
exclusively to this God who acts upon us. And every confusion of
this point of view is a fundamental perversion of the theological
point of departure.

It stands to reason that in pursuance of the debate with the doctrine of *analogia entis* Barth again declares " every ' natural theology ' " to be " incontrovertibly impossible." But he goes on to ask
why it is that notoriously the problem of " natural theology "
" cannot come to rest " (93) . The explanations of this problem are
arranged strictly in a critical and in a, so to speak, positive part.
(However, the " positive " part is none too gratifying for the champions of " natural theology.") The first is still to be found under
the subject of " God's Readiness," the second under the other subject of " Man's Readiness."

In the first part — partly taking up again in detail what was said
earlier, and in part going considerably farther — Barth critically
enters into the reasons usually advanced in favor of " natural theology." First, there is the assertion that a natural knowledge of
God actually exists (93 f.) . But is it the real God who is " known "
in this way? " What God is for the natural man, and whatever man
may then call his God, is an idol, which of course he knows . . .
but which, as an idol, can in no way lead him to a knowledge of
the real God. . . . Rather, it will . . . keep him away from it "
(94) ! Secondly, there are pedagogical and pastoral points of view
as, for example, effecting a basis for discussion between Christians
and non-Christians, establishing a " point of contact," indicating
man's responsibility. But even the best of intentions is of no avail,
if along the well-trodden paths one nevertheless does not once arrive at a real knowledge of the real God (99) . And in addition —
is it really a sound practice, is it at all honest and permissible to
encounter the " natural " man, as it were in a mask, since the theologian in such a case takes the position of unbelief, even when it is

only assumed (100 ff.) ? Is it not the only expedient thing when
" unbelief " . . . is " immediately occupied with faith itself and
as such " (105) ? Thirdly, there are Scriptural passages that do refer to a natural knowledge of God. Now in fact there are many
texts compelling us to raise the question (109). A line runs
through the whole of Scripture, by which it is evident that God appears not only himself as a witness to his revelation, but " also man
. . . and with man the whole created cosmos, challenging man for
his part to be a witness " (109) ! But it is not man " independent "
of God's revelation (113), not man as the counterpart to some divinity or other (118 f.). The co-witnessing word of man always
points " to the Word which God as his Lord has already uttered
and will utter again " (128). From this standpoint, Rom. 1:18 ff.;
2:12 ff., as well as Acts, ch. 17, are discussed in detail, in which it is
forcefully brought out that all three passages are closely connected
with the judgment announced and the gospel proclaimed.

At the conclusion of the critical expositions Barth asks himself
how it is that in spite of all counterarguments " natural theology "
throughout the centuries of Church history has proved and still
proves to have such a persistent vitality. He gives an answer to this
in the beginning of the next section (" Man's Readiness," pp.
141 ff.).

" Man's readiness," his " openness for grace," would also include, besides his neediness, a definite knowledge (of this neediness as of the reality of grace) and a willingness (to accept grace)
(143). But it should be stated that certainly " nowhere does the reality of the Christian, of the Christian in the Church, of even the
good Protestant Church Christian " (not to speak of others), give
evidence of " an openness of man for grace." " Natural theology "
is " the unavoidable theological expression " for just *this* fact
(150) ! It bears witness to man being closed (to grace). It attests
man's religious self-sufficiency and enmity to grace. And after all
there is nothing remarkable about that. But what is remarkable is
the circumstance that natural theology " can nevertheless tolerate
beside it in the area of the Church (as also by the way in the area
of other religions), at least apparently, another theology, a theology

of revelation " (152). However, this last fact proves nothing else than that actually " even revelation . . . is absorbed and domesticated by man; he changes a question put to him into an answer given by himself — by himself once again " (154). Hence the judgment is understandable: " The triumph of natural theology in the area of the Church, described as the absorption and domestication of revelation, is very simply the process of civilizing the gospel " (157). Natural theology, the perfect expression of man's enmity to grace — that, then, is Barth's positive answer to the question cited above!

But is there then no man at all who is open for God, for God's revelation and grace? If this were to prove true, then indeed " natural theology " would be the only one still remaining. It " would doubtless be the proper theology within the reach of the man not knowing the true God " (160). But we repeat our question: Does that man exist? Looking at man himself, Barth answers in the negative: " God's knowability . . . cannot be made intelligible as a predicate of man as such " (162). However, there is an " other aspect "! " The man who is ready for God is truth and life; but he is not identical with man as such " (165)! We can speak of *this* man only Christologically (166). In Christ " man is ready for God " (169). " Our flesh is also present when he knows God, as the Son knows the Father when God knows himself " (169). Jesus Christ is " the real man " (171), and he alone " sees to it that in and through him we are not outside but within " (174).

But now " as a rule " the Bible " expressly " describes " our participation in the existence and work of Jesus Christ " by " calling it a work of the Holy Spirit " (175). And " as a work of the Holy Spirit faith is man's new birth from God, on the basis of which even here man may already live from what he is there in Jesus Christ and so in truth " (177). It is therefore the true " readiness of man," in opposition to which " natural theology " (to which Barth now returns again) seeks to maintain the " illusion " of " man's independent existence as such " — and it does so with conspicuous vitality (185). As little as it is worth-while to fight against it outside the Church, just as surely it is " destined " for nothing else " than to disappear in the area of the Church " (190). With

that Barth closes with an exhaustive evaluation of the first article
of the Barmen Declaration (194 ff.) .[1]

Barth brings the doctrine of the knowledge of God to a close
with a section that deals with its " limits " (§ 27, 200 ff.) . In this it
is not for him really a matter of the limitation of our knowledge
of God, to which attention has already been called. It is rather the
answering of the question about where the knowledge of God orig-
inates and what is its goal. From what has already been reported,
we can easily understand Barth's main premise: " God is known
only by God." (That is the point of departure — and inasmuch,
the boundary continually to be respected: just in his revelation
God is the hidden, incomprehensible One.) Nevertheless we are
empowered and commissioned to know him in our perceptions
and conceptions. The " genuineness " of our knowledge of God
consists, therefore, in " our perceiving and conceiving being
adopted and destined for participation in the truth of God by God
himself in his grace " (200). After we have already referred to
Barth's emphasis upon God's hiddenness, we may now confine ourselves to the second thing: we may and ought to apply our perceptions and conceptions! In the repudiation of " natural theology "
there is already the knowledge that our conceptions as such are not
suitable; indeed, that in themselves they are not " true." " They
become true " (218) ! But just for that reason it may be stated:
" We can, may, and must speak of the God who awakens us to
faith in himself by his revelation; we can, may, and must therefore
perceive and conceive this God " (220). For in Jesus Christ " the
hidden God has truly made himself comprehensible " (223).

From this standpoint Barth now no longer merely contends
against the self-sufficiency of human perceiving and conceiving
which wants to find the truth in itself. But — in view of the truth
of God's self-condescension — Barth contends all the more against
a skepticism and resignation which also, in light of the revelation

<hr/>

1 TRANSLATOR'S NOTE: The Barmen Declaration is the Confession of Faith of the
Confessing Synod of the German Evangelical Church, drawn up in Wuppertal-
Barmen, May 29–31, 1934, in opposition to the German " Nazi " Christians. The first
article reads: " Jesus Christ, as he is testified to in Holy Scripture, is the one Word
of God which we have to hear, and which we have to trust and obey in life and in
death. We reject the false doctrine that the Church might and must acknowledge,
apart from and beside this one Word of God, still other events and powers, forms
and truths as sources of her proclamation, (and) as God's revelation."

that has taken place, does not furnish the humility and obedience to venture assertions. " Resignation is not humility, but the pride which does not want to accept God's grace . . . as such. And humility is not resignation . . ." (240) ! Resignation would be to abandon the place at which God's revelation puts us. For this place is characterized first of all by the fact that we must offer our gratitude (243 ff.). We have to acknowledge that God has revealed himself and how he has revealed himself (244), and we have to do so joyfully (246). Secondly, our position is determined by the fact that we have every reason to be filled with " awe and amazement " (247 ff.). It expresses itself also in our gaining the courage actually to speak, instead of keeping silent because of the utter frailty of our ideas. In this reverence we shall certainly always have in view the " distance " between our work and its " object," but yet in astonishment, mindful that it is a distance which has truly been " overcome " — in the incarnation of the Word (251). As surely as there is no " analogy " to God's revelation in our conceptions, perceptions, and words as such, just as surely can we now, in view of revelation, speak of a " real fellowship " " between the knower and his knowing on the one hand " and " the One known on the other " (252). In this way, as it were retrogressively, the concept of " analogy " becomes thoroughly applicable, yes, " inevitable " (254). It now rests upon the fact " that God's genuine revelation radically approaches what we are able to say with our human words, and chooses from among them — a choice with which we may then in obedience associate ourselves " (256). Thus human words are now actually able to say something that they, as it were " by nature," would not be able to say. The truth we therewith utter is never our own; it is always God's truth. For that reason we can never make any of our assertions except in humility. And yet in the midst of every temptation we may be sure that God's truth is also now the truth of our words and sentences. Hence it is entirely appropriate for Barth to end this whole section with statements about " temptation " and " comfort " (286 f.).

VII

GOD'S REALITY

[*Volume II, 1, pp. 288–664*]

W̲E̲ FOLLOW in our report farther along the way Vol. II, 1, of
the *Church Dogmatics* takes us. With the above title we
have given the substance of the second part of this volume (the
sixth chapter of the entire work). Who and what is God, as he lets
us share his knowledge in his revelation?

If we ask who or what God is, then it is evident that we have
therewith asked about God's being. Anyone acquainted with the
subject immediately sees looming up before him the whole doctrine of being, particularly that of the Middle Ages, and many a
man will shudder at the abyss of philosophical abstractions which
for centuries have been linked with the doctrine of God. Now
Barth does not do for his readers the favor young Melanchthon
once did for his, when in the first edition of his *Loci* he simply declared in regard to the doctrine of God that " it would be more
proper for us to adore the mysteries of God than to investigate
them." Instead he alludes to the fact that the same Melanchthon
at a later period even more thoughtlessly reintroduced the traditional doctrine of being, together with the " natural theology " involved in it (290 f.). Barth regards this " second error " of Melanchthon as much " worse " than the first. But he wants to avoid
" both of them." Hence in a certain sense he is quite able to speak
of God's " being."

But of what " being "? In the course of answering this question
Barth once more returns to the doctrine of the Trinity. The reason
that so much that is alien and confusing has forced its way into the
doctrine of God is, in his judgment, because the doctrine of the
Trinity was usually first dealt with after the doctrine of God. But
how should one be able to say anything about God's being apart
from the Trinity? Or how should what is then said not become
philosophy, speculation about being, and " natural theology "?
But after the Trinity has been discussed, and God's being has been

seen as God's-being-in-revelation, one can then speak of his " reality "; that is, of the unity of God's being and act (293).

The doctrine of God speaks about the living God (294 f.). He is
the God who does not meet us as act in itself (*actus purus*) but —
as must necessarily be supplemented (296) — as this quite definite, unique " act," as the living, active One in his revelation
(*actus singularis*). God's being is " being in Person " (300)! But
this definitely does not mean that he is a " personified being " (300).
Rather, it means " the being who in the reality of his Person realizes and unites the fullness of all being in himself " (300). This —
in essence — is what Barth means when he speaks about " God's
being in an act " (288 ff.).

By this, a logical decision has been made which has perhaps not
yet been immediately perceived. What is denied is just a " pure
spirituality " of God, which thinks of God, as it were, without a
nature, a so-called philosophical spiritualism. " Acts occur only in
the unity of spirit and nature " (299), and if God is the active
agent, he cannot then be " that chemically purified absolute spirit,"
as theological and philosophical speculation is so fond of regard-
ing him (299). He is spirit, " but just the divine Spirit." And he
is " certainly also nature, but just the divine nature " (304).
Therefore, we cannot comprehend his nature either by elevating
to the uttermost our conception of spirit or of nature, and even
less by erasing spirit or nature.

But what kind of " act " is God's being? Barth gives a twofold
answer which meanwhile is nevertheless a single one. God's being
is his " being as the One who loves " (306 ff.), and it is " being in
freedom " (334 ff.). This twofoldness of the statement is of great
consequence: it determines hereafter Barth's whole doctrine of
God's " attributes " or, as he expresses it more appropriately, of
God's " perfections." They are those of the " divine loving "
(394 ff.) or those of the " divine freedom " (495 ff.).

So first of all God's being is that of the One who loves. " God is
love! " But take care: God is not the essence of what we could
have perhaps ascertained as " love " apart from his act. Perhaps we
could briefly sum up Barth's view as follows: God is his love. How
could it be anything else? This love is first " a seeking and creating
of fellowship for its own sake " (310 ff.). It is this, in the second

place, " without regard for an already present qualification or worthiness in the one loved " (312 f.) . God's love is — thirdly — " an
end in itself " (313 f.) . And fourthly, God's loving is " necessary "
on account of himself (because it is just his own being) . Yet for
that very reason it is " free of every necessity with respect to its
object " (314 ff.) . So it is not at all as Angelus Silesius thought:
" I know that without me God cannot live for a single moment . . ." (316) !

In this connection Barth inevitably comes to speak of the fact
that God as the loving God is a Person. In so doing he reaches into
what is notoriously a veritable thicket bristling with theological
problems. He first establishes that it is impossible to construct
God's existence as a Person [1] out of our (somehow experienced or
thought of) human existence as a person.[1] Why not? " Man is not
a person but becomes one on the ground that he is loved by God
and in turn may love God " (319) ! God alone is a person (320) .
The only person whom we know as a human person is Jesus Christ,
and " even he is, in fact, the Person of God the Son, in whom humanity, without itself being a person, was adopted into fellowship
with God's personal being " (321; the assertion is related to the
doctrine of the anhypostasis or enhypostasis of the human nature
of Christ; cf. *Kirchliche Dogmatik,* I, 2, 178 ff.) . In this connection Barth then provides a penetrating survey of the theological
discussion about the question of the " personality of God." In conclusion he first states that the concept of " God's personality " is
" too pallid " to warrant " basing " anything on it. The essential
thing is " not that God is a person but what particular person he
is " (333) . Then he states that once again the decisive thing in
the concept of " God's personality " has already been settled in the
doctrine of the Trinity. The fact that we are aware of the divine
" Thou " has its origin in God being eternally I and Thou in himself. God is " the personal God, if at all," as the trinitarian
God (334) .

But now what about God's " being in freedom "? We have already indicated that God's love, as *his* love, is free. In his turning
toward the creature God is constantly altogether himself and of
himself. Hence the concept of freedom, according to Barth, pur-

---

[1] *" Personsein."*

ports " what in the theology of the Early Church was called the *aseitas Dei* " (340) .[2] God's freedom has no kind of conceivable limits. In fact, he " does not even need his own being " (344) , because he indeed always " already has " it; " nay, he himself is " it. But on the other hand Barth attacks (even more emphatically) a conception of God's " absoluteness " which ultimately shuts the creation off from him and thereby seeks to pare down his freedom from below, as it were. Rather, God's freedom must " also mean his freedom to be immanent. Moreover, it is an immanence such as does not exist at all among other creatures " (352) . Or we might state it this way: " God is free enough to be immanent to another creature in the most diverse ways in view of his own differentiation " (353) ! God is free to be with his creature, and what is more, in the most multifarious vivacity, and, at the same time, in a " holy orderliness " (357) . Is this speculation? According to Barth it is rather " Christology which must constitute and remain the presupposition and criterion for the knowledge and understanding of God's freedom in its immanence " (360) . God has not lost his freedom in Christ, but as the loving One he confirms it!

According to the usual sequence of dogmatic material (and to which Barth now adheres) , a section would now come which — if we may be permitted to say so — is usually, alas, thoroughly boring: The doctrine of God's " attributes." It would repay us to reflect upon what is the real cause for the customary boredom at this point. What we usually find in most works is an enumeration of single " attributes." To be sure, it is richly supplied (often merely embellished) with Biblical quotations. Very frequently they are taken in a purely figurative sense. To many it appears difficult to speak about God's " attributes " at all. Barth rightly calls attention to the merits of a little book by Hermann Cremer (*Die christliche Lehre von den Eigenschaften Gottes,* 1897) , which appeared half a century ago. In spite of everything it injected some life into the wasteland of an earlier period. Since Cremer, and going beyond him, the first dogmatic theologian to give special attention to this area is Barth. At any rate, he treats it as a place for sprightly, that

[2] Doctrine of the divine self-existence or that God has the ground or source of his existence in himself.

is, theological, inquiry and propositions. The defect of traditional presentations was the lack of a true theological sprightliness, and here it is overcome. So a good four hundred pages devoted to this part of the *Dogmatics* do not become sour for the reader. Meanwhile this report at this point will have to proceed with a bare summary.

Barth does not like to speak of God's "attributes." Instead he prefers the — likewise traditional — concept of God's "perfections." The reason is "that God's nature possesses 'attributes' in common with the nature of other creatures. That it is identical with a fullness of perfections is — if this concept is taken strictly — a 'property' (attribute) of God and of God alone" (362 f.). So God is identical with his perfections. (He *is* mercy, righteousness, etc.) If he is called "the Lord of glory" (I Cor. 2:8), then this glory has no existence of itself. But again, even the "Lord" is never to be thought of without this, his glory. He is with his glory; his glory is *one* with himself. The doctrine of God's perfections has to exhibit this unity (365, 367). Thus it is also understandable why Barth is willing to allow the question about the "how of God to be merely a repetition of the question: Who is God?" (372). This last statement has, indeed, already directed us exclusively to God in his revelation — to what God, if otherwise? And in keeping with the already customary practice we will certainly have nowhere else to inquire about God's perfection.

As mentioned above Barth distinguishes between two series of divine "perfections," namely, those of the "divine loving" and those of the "divine freedom." Now a surprising feature of Barth's work is that he presents grace and holiness, mercy and righteousness, patience and wisdom as "perfections of the divine loving." And scarcely less surprising is the other series, that of the "perfections of God's freedom: unity and omnipresence, immutability and omnipotence, eternity and glory. Thus righteousness, among others, is a perfection of the divine love! Immutability a perfection of divine freedom! However, let it be immediately stressed that Barth always presents two perfections together. He co-ordinates grace and holiness, to take as just one example, so that in his mind he ensures that grace continues to be taken seriously as God's

grace, holiness as God's holiness (475). As for the rest, it is clear
to Barth that love and freedom are never to be thought of as separated from one another. " There is no love of God in itself and as
such, just as there is also no freedom of God in itself and as such "
(395). Our thinking in this whole field can only make cautious distinctions, but it can never separate.

We can call attention only to a few things out of a tremendous
abundance of what is offered. It includes whole special inquiries,
as for example, into the Molinistic concept of the *scientia media*.
We are confining ourselves to frequently discussed or particularly
characteristic points.

The discussion of the idea of grace inevitably leads again to a
debate with the familiar Roman Catholic view. According to
Barth grace in the Scriptural sense is " an inner being and self-
conduct of God himself " (397). If he is gracious, then it always
means that he himself condescends to one utterly unworthy of such
an act. " Grace is not only a gift of God which he could give or not
give, not simply an attribute which could belong or not belong to
him. No, God himself is gracious. And grace itself is actually and
essentially divine " (400). " As we sin against God himself, so
God himself takes our part when he is gracious to us " (400). Of
course, contrariwise the Roman Catholic conception of grace as a
" supernatural gift " incurs rejection.

We already have heard that Barth links the concept of God's
holiness with that of grace. By that it should become evident that
grace is really God's grace, and hence " we cannot and may not
cling to our concept of grace " (403). What is signified by the
statement that God is holy as the one who loves? This — that God
in his love " is and remains the Lord. Consequently he distinguishes his own will from every other. He asserts his own will over
against every other. He condemns, excludes, and destroys every
contradiction and resistance to his will. And so in this fellowship
he consents to and allows only his own good will as such " (403).
The " Holy One of Israel " is the Redeemer (Isa. 41:14; 43:3,
etc.) ! As the law does not stand beside the gospel, no more does
God's holiness stand beside his grace (407). Directed against Albrecht Ritschl's celebrated thesis concerning God's wrath, Barth

asserts that God's wrath occurs *in* his love, and the reverse: God's forgiveness occurs *in* his anger and judging (407, 408 ff.) .

In our general survey above, especially striking has been Barth's characterizing of God's righteousness, together with his mercy, as perfections of the divine loving. " God's loving is divine, a doing and being distinct from all other loving, in that it is righteous " (423) . God's love is characterized as righteous thereby " that God, in wanting and creating fellowship, accomplishes and does what is worthy of himself. Thus in this fellowship he brings his weight to bear against all opposition and resistance, and so in his fellowship allows his dignity to triumph and reign alone " (423) . Now admittedly a danger might suggest itself here, especially in view of certain Reformation warnings, that all reference to God's law and judgeship would disappear from the idea of righteousness (429) . In opposition to this it has to be made clear that precisely in his forgiving, in his grace, God " attests and confirms " his righteousness, " his law, as being truly and properly his very own revelation " (420) . " He is righteous just when he is merciful " (431) . For " God's righteousness, the faithfulness in which he is faithful to himself, is revealed as succor and redemption, as a saving divine intervention for men, in the poor, the wretched and the helpless as such and only in them . . ." (435) . This last is said by Barth directly in view of the relation of justification and justice which he worked out for the first time in the well-known publication of 1938 by that title.[3] Justification, God's righteousness in general, is misunderstood, if it pushes justice aside as an auxiliary power. It robs it of its earnestness. Thence, it is also understandable that Barth — here again quite sharply opposed to " modern " theology — sets forth God's righteousness as *justitia distributiva*. It is a " judging righteousness, and thus an absolving as well as a condemning righteousness, a rewarding as well as a punitive righteousness " (439) .

But what is his source for saying all this? Where does God reveal that he is righteousness when he punishes *and* forgives? Where is God's " retributive righteousness " nevertheless the righteousness which saves the lost — and only them? Where is God's anger truly an anger-in-love, so that God's righteousness is truly a " perfection

[3] *Church and State.* Student Christian Movement Press, London, 1939.

of the divine loving," as Barth so strongly insists? Here Barth
comes to speak about the event of Good Friday. The elucidation
of the death of Jesus Christ, which is the sole basis for all those assertions, is among the most important in Barth's whole book (443–
457). What takes place on Good Friday? There occurs what could
happen only to God's own Son; namely, that " God's condemna-
tory and punitive righteousness against human sin" takes " its
course " (450). God's righteousness is carried out, and so in God's
Son " man incurs what he deserves." (451). The Son of God, " as
the authorized representative of the divine Judge," is " likewise
the representative of the judged " (451)! (At which, by the way,
the disputed association of ideas in Ques. 12–18 of the Heidelberg
Catechism comes to mind and by the line of reasoning is affirmed.) Finally, on Good Friday it happens that God's Son " effectively " takes our place, and " with him our reconciliation with
the righteous God " is " realized, and also the triumph of God's
righteousness as well as our own righteousness before him " (453).
In this way Barth's theology of the cross actually shows what at
first appeared so strange: God's righteousness is a perfection of his
loving, because it occurred particularly in Jesus Christ.

God's patience! Anyone who has read Barth's utterances in recent years will have noticed how frequently he speaks of it. What
does he mean? He means that " for the sake of his grace and
mercy " God grants " to another . . . time and space for his own
existence." In so doing he " does not annul or destroy this other
one, but accompanies, bears, and gives him a free rein " (461).
God's grace is a judgment upon nature, but " not its catastrophe "
(463). In this sense, meaning is to be found even in the familiar
Thomistic sentence, *gratia non tollit, sed perficit naturam* (463).
Biblical examples are Cain and the little book of Jonah. In the
light of God's patience even God's " judgments and punishments "
do not contradict the truth that " actually he wants to preserve his
creature and does not want it to perish "; they are " altogether temporal and, as such, symbolical judgments and punishments " (472).

Foremost among the " perfections of the divine freedom " are
God's oneness and omnipresence (495 ff.). " Oneness " signifies
God's singleness (and with it a radical stripping of the world of its
gods; 499 f.), and God's simplicity: " In all that he is and does, he

is wholly and indivisibly he himself" (501). God's oneness has nothing to do with the "monotheism" of a philosophy of religion; the highest conceived unity is not God (504 f.). God's oneness is not to be understood without considering that "election is the character of revelation" (507) : Israel's God possesses "oneness in the love in which he acts toward Israel . . ." (509). The mono-theism of the New Testament is grounded "in the messianic self-witness of Jesus" (513).

Especially surprising to many will, again, be what Barth now says about God's omnipresence. He begins anew with the theology of the Trinity: " God not only exists but coexists in himself. Therefore he can also coexist with another" (521). And at the same time we are reminded of what we heard about God's pa-tience: God grants space and time to another (523). However, the meaning is that there is no theological justice at all for thinking of God as spaceless (or timeless). " At any rate the Christian con-cept of God is exploded and dissolved if absolute spacelessness is ascribed to God. Spacelessness means an absence of distance. And an absence of distance means identity" (527)! " There is indeed nowhere where God is not, but ' nowhere ' is not God; on the con-trary . . . he is somewhere" (530). Seen from this standpoint omnipresence does not mean God's spacelessness but his freedom to be in space. His freedom! He is not " forthwith " wherever one wants to have him. His presence is ever *his* presence. His presence in creation (which is not a " general truth "; 537) is manifested in his special presence at any time: " It is only the One who is pres-ent here and now who is the God who is present in the world generally" (538). However, we are thereby referred back again to God's presence which is given to us in Jesus. " The opposite to Jerusalem and Gerizim, and the opposite to the temple made with hands . . . and also . . . the opposite to Rome, Wittenberg, Ge-neva, and Canterbury is not (as a liberal shallowness understands this matter) the universe, but just Jesus " (541). " The spatiality of Jesus Christ in heaven and upon earth " is what abides, and " therefore, according to the witness of the New Testament, the relativity, but also the reality of God's special presence, is re-vealed " (543). In this connection the Lutheran-Reformed oppo-sition in the question of Christ's presence — " an unfortunate con-

flict " — comes up for discussion (548). Barth ("in agreement
with the Reformers ") wishes " to make a distinction and say that
He is present there [4] intrinsically and originally and here symboli-
cally, sacramentally and spiritually." But at the same time ("in
agreement with the Lutherans ") he wants " to hold them together
and say that He is present here no less than there, but there and
here he is really present: there and here the whole Christ according
to his divine and according to his human nature " (551). — One
wonders whether certain reproaches against the supposed "absolute transcendence " of Barth's concept of God will not gradually
subside now?

From what Barth says about God's " immutability and omnipotence " special prominence should be given to what he says about
answers to prayer. He does not understand God's immutability as
inflexibility — something no one will any longer find surprising.
That which is purely motionless " is death " (555)! God's immutability is truly his, and hence that " of his knowing, willing, and
doing and therefore of his Person " (557). Therefore it can be seriously said that he repents of something (558 ff.). Therefore God
has " a real history in and with the world he has created " (565).
And therefore there is " an influencing of God by the prayer of
faith on the ground of God's own freedom " (574), and to that extent a " coregency " of believers (575)!

Everywhere Barth is intent upon showing that God's " perfections " are those of the trinitarian, of the revealed God, and therefore of the God who acts concretely. This is also true of God's omnipotence. As his total efficacy, it is not a materially " empty but a
full capacity, not a nondescript but a completely concrete capacity " (598). " It is omnipotence precisely in that . . . He cannot
do all things " (599). God cannot do what has no foundation in
himself (600 ff.). (He cannot do something which perhaps has its
basis in our conception of what is possible.) It is even true of
God's knowing that it limits itself, " since that which is not its object is just therewith declared to be absolutely void " (622).

In the same context, discussed repeatedly already, belongs the
fact that Barth refuses to regard God's eternity as timelessness.
" God has time just because and while he has eternity " (689)!

4 TRANSLATOR'S NOTE: I.e., at the right hand of God.

" Nothing less than the certainty of faith, the possibility of trust-
ing in an abiding God, depends upon the fact that time is not excluded from his duration but is included by it so that we in our
time may know and respect his time — the time he has given us "
(690) . But as surely as God is not timeless, just as surely is he pre-
temporal, supratemporal and posttemporal (698 ff.) , as the Lord
of time eternally! But this means concretely nothing else than:
" Jesus Christ the same yesterday, and today, and forever "! " The
past is that from which he has set us free, and the future is that for
which he has set us free " (708) .

This first volume, about which we were to report in this chapter,
ends with explanations of God's glory. Here Barth may be said to
have summarized his thoughts. And some people, who would be
only too glad to take Barth for a gloomy zealot, might just for example be given to read what (alas, for the Reformed Churchman!) he is able to say about God's beauty (773 ff.) , in order that
they might be relieved of some prejudices. In any case our whole
report, even in view of the five further volumes yet to be reviewed,
could be furnished with the title " The Glory of God."

VIII

GOD'S GRACIOUS ELECTION

[Volume II, 2, pp. 1–563]

————

Toward the end of the preceding volume (II, 1, 740) Barth had called theology a beautiful science. Indeed, " it may be candidly said to be even the most beautiful among all sciences." " One can be a theologian only gladly and joyfully, or basically one is not a theologian at all. Just in this science there cannot possibly be any patience with sour looks, peevish thoughts, and tedious phrases "!

It may be said that the volume we are now to consider does much to dispel the theological unpleasantness that has been incurred. It enables us to comprehend a doctrine, which causes many a theologian understandable hardship, as the " sum of the gospel " (1). By a complete change in the approach Barth sets the whole difficult and complex doctrine in motion in a new and fruitful way. If in the foregoing Barth has already many times opposed the " Fathers " in details, while respectfully taking into consideration the dogmatic tradition (that is demonstrated by a veritable wealth of valuable citations), so he is also conscious of treading utterly new and hazardous paths with his version of the doctrine of predestination. By it the Church is asked whether she on her part thinks she is able to move along these paths.

To be sure, the traditional view does not dispute that the doctrine of election by grace has something to do with the gospel. That is apparent, for example, in the position Calvin gives to his doctrine of predestination (Book III of the *Institutes!*) . However, Barth declares: " The election by grace is the whole gospel, the gospel *in nuce* " (13) . Any reduction, any reservation, any murkiness which could arise at this point and (let us say the idea of the *decretum horribile*) shall have arisen, is utterly contrary to it. He does not take credit for being the very first to assume this position. For example, he even lauds the canons of Dort because " in its presentation the doctrine of predestination again acquired the character of evangelical proclamation " (17). Actually, however, he goes far beyond all comparable predecessors.

The doctrine of predestination has a long history. It also possesses a traditional basic tendency. A definite consensus obtains among its serious advocates. Barth mentions three things. All serious advocates of this doctrine see God's freedom, God's mystery, and God's righteousness authenticated in election by grace (18 ff.). These three must now be understood, however, in a theological, Christian sense (something the serious advocates referred to also certainly wanted to do). Above all, it means that it must remain evident that God's electing is really not an empty, absolute act, as it were, but, as God's act, an act of his free grace (25 ff.). And it is questionable whether this was always observed.

The contrasts become apparent right in the question about the basis for the doctrine of election (36 ff.). It is not grounded in a doctrinal tradition itself (37 f.), nor in its practical and pastoral " usefulness " (38 f.), nor even in experience. This last would mean that it is grounded in an abstract view of man and in his so puzzlingly diverse decisions (39 ff.). Nor is it finally a matter of basing it " simply," that is, abstractly, upon God's " omnipotent will " (46 ff.). Who, then, is the electing God? He is definitely not some thought of absolute world ruler (52)! He is much rather exactly he who reveals himself in his concrete electing which has actually taken place; and he does not reveal himself apart from it.

With that we now face Barth's basic premise. When we speak about God's election, we are not speaking about some sort of darkness beside, behind, or above the revealed God, but we are looking exclusively " at the name of Jesus Christ and at the existence and history of the people realized in him, and whose beginning and end is decided in the mystery of his name " (63). We are not speaking about an abstract God but about God in Christ! And we are not speaking about an abstract man-in-himself, but about the man Jesus Christ! And we do this because in the name of Jesus Christ " the electing God and the elected man coincide " (63). Or as we read later on: " Jesus Christ is the electing God " (111); " Jesus Christ is the elected man " (124). It may be said that the whole of Barth's doctrine of predestination is summarized in this twofold proposition. To anyone familiar with the preceding volume, and especially with Barth's teaching about God's " perfections," this will now no longer be so surprising as it certainly otherwise would be.

Barth's reiterated and basic premise rests chiefly upon Eph. 1:4: chosen *in him!* Barth is anxious to show that in connection with this particular passage a " Christological explanation of predestination " definitely had been attempted earlier, among others, even by Calvin (65 ff.). He is also anxious to show how in any debate with the orthodox-Lutheran doctrine of predestination it must be emphasized that if one were " faced with the choice, one could still regard the doctrine of the *decretum absolutum* on the Reformed side as better calculated to secure the Reformation, the Christian cause in this whole matter " (77). More, however, Barth does not say. On the contrary, he finds in the Lutheran doctrine the " intention " to " set forth a Christological basis for election " (81). At all events he makes this intention his own. Precisely the doctrine of the *decretum absolutum,* of God's absolute decision in advance, points as such in the opposite direction: to a darkness beside or behind God's revelation, to an " empty spot," where just the name of Jesus Christ belonged (111). So Barth can object to the classical Reformed doctrine point-blank: " There is no *decretum absolutum.* There is no will of God different from the will of Jesus Christ " (124).

When Barth now places the positive development of his doctrine of election under the title " The Election of Jesus Christ " (101 ff.), this idea has two sides. The election is that which has been executed by and through Jesus Christ, and it is that which has happened to him. He is truly " the electing God " and " the elected man."

" The electing God." An exegesis of John 1:1, 2, shows that God's ways are his ways in Christ from the very beginning. God's electing (and all his action is an electing) is an electing in Christ, and insofar an electing of man on the strength of it. If there can be any talk of a *decretum,* then it has to be characterized as a *decretum concretum.* " From eternity God has destined himself to be the bearer of this name in free, unconditional self-determina-

tion " (108). And for this reason we do not lay hold of God's gracious election by brooding over a *decretum absolutum,* but instead
we are " to lay hold of . . . and affirm . . . the manifest grace of
God in God's electing " (113). In Jesus Christ we are " concerned
directly with the electing God himself " (115). When we keep that
in mind, it becomes evident that in election we do not have to do
with an unrevealed will of God, but with God's revelation. Here
lies Barth's most serious objection to Calvin: " that in the last
analysis he tore God and Jesus Christ asunder." Hence, " his electing God (is) . . . not the *Deus revelatus* who, as such, is also
the *Deus absconditus,* the eternal God " (119). Accordingly, in
the orthodox doctrine as well, it could then " not become, and remain clear, that the complement of election is faith; it had to result
in experiments with other complements. They always lie near at
hand when one imagines he is able to have intercourse with God
and pass Jesus Christ by . . ." (121; examples are Tersteegen's
mysticism, or an " inner-worldly " asceticism, and an industrious-
ness perhaps like that of Benjamin Franklin). Johannes Coccejus
constitutes the only exception in the orthodox-Reformed camp,
but without material effect in this matter (122 f.).

" Jesus Christ, the elected man." If, according to Eph. 1:4, we
are elected " in him," then the meaning is that we are elected " in
his person, in his will," and moreover, " in and with his being
elected " (125). The absolutely unique thing in Jesus Christ is
precisely this unity of the one who elects and of the one who is
elected, this unity of God and of man. John 17:24 and Luke 9:35;
23:35 show especially that he is " the elected man," at which the
latter passages show even more clearly that he is elected as the suffering One and for suffering (126). He is " God's Son solely
through God's grace " (129), and " as he became Christ, so we become Christians " (127). But above all, in Jesus Christ it happens
that " God — in that he himself becomes this man — makes himself responsible and answerable for the man who has become his
enemy, and that he makes the whole consequence of his action —
his rejection and his death — to be his own concern " (133). Thus
man, " even as a sinner " has truly died " in him " (134). Yet God
has also raised him from the dead, and " thereby God affirms his
elected man as his own Son . . ." (135). The election of those

who are elected " in him " consists concretely " in their faith in Him " (135). Barth is able to sum up what that means: " To believe in Jesus means to have his resurrection and his intercession in mind and at heart. And that is just what it means to be elected. The man who does that is, ' in him,' the object of God's gracious election " (136).

Let us call attention to the fact that from the above standpoint Barth takes a position in regard to the old controversy between supralapsarianism (election " before " the Fall, the latter being included under it) and infralapsarianism (election " after " the Fall). He denies the presuppositions of both systems. But he finds that supralapsarianism is more correct insofar as it permits the necessarily decisive factor to be built into it (namely, " the knowledge of the elected man Jesus Christ," 154), while conversely the idea of a *decretum absolutum* also can be avoided in it " without removing its basic principle."

But what about rejection? What about " double predestination " (*praedestinatio gemina*)? Barth's reply to this question in the section on " The Election of Jesus Christ " is of such a nature that it can be enlarged upon in further explanations. He affirms a " double predestination "; in fact, God's eternal will is " twofold." It contains " a Yes and a No " (176). But — " in the election of Jesus Christ, which is the eternal will of God, God has intended the first — namely, election, blessedness, and life for man; but the second — rejection, damnation, and death for himself " (177). God " chose our rejection " (179). So far as a " No " is uttered in predestination, it is " in no case a ' No' that befalls man " (181). " Therefore faith in God's predestination in itself and per se means faith in man's nonrejection, not faith in his rejection " (182). Sentences of tremendous consequences! From them it follows that evil — looked at " in Christ " — will be able to have " only the possibility of existing as the impossible, only the reality of existing as the unreal, only the independent power of impotence " (185). In, and in virtue of, God's choice, evil is simply a power that has been overcome, and Satan is not God's ultimately real adversary.

Evil, the evil one, has been beaten, condemned to impotency. With this thought, which Barth unswervingly inculcates through-

out his whole book, is combined a further one, namely, that God's
electing and rejecting bears in itself nothing fixed and static at all,
nothing of a universal law settled in advance. On the contrary, it
possesses the " character of actuality." We are certainly and delib-
erately speaking of God's eternal will. But we are speaking with
equal deliberateness " of an eternal occurrence, when we speak of
the divine predestination " (202) . We recall that in the preceding
volume Barth spoke about God's history with his creation. Here it
is made plain. " The mystery of all that happens in the world is
God's decision which eternally precedes it " (203) !

The doctrine of election, because it points us to Christ, turns
our attention to his congregation. Only to that extent does it also
have the individual in mind. But in the case of the latter, Holy
Scripture is " not in such a hurry " as the classical doctrine of predestination was (215) . Consequently Barth next develops a doctrine of the " Election of the Congregation " in a separate section
(215 ff.) . He appropriately cites Rom., chs. 9 to 11, in this connection, and frankly lets this section consist preponderantly in an exegesis of these chapters. But then in that way the subject is also
already illustrated in a special way: when we speak about the election of the congregation, it is a matter of the ever special election
of Israel and of the Church.

What is the congregation? It is " that human fellowship which
provisionally forms in a special way the natural and historical en-
vironment of the man Jesus " (216) . In what does its special character consist? In its witness to the world! And its provisional character? In that it " points beyond itself to the fellowship of all
men . . ." (216) . It is important to keep this last constantly in
mind; later sections in the entire work will return to it.

But now as to the inner dichotomy of the congregation: Israel
and the Church! It scarcely needs to be mentioned that Barth does
not arrange them simply in a historical succession. But neither
does he by any means equate them. They have their unity and di-
versity in Christ. As " Israel's crucified Messiah " he is also " the
secret Lord of the Church," and conversely " as the Church's risen
Lord " he is " also Israel's revealed Messiah " (218) . As Christ is
one, so the congregation is one. It is " irrevocably both: Israel and
the Church " (218 f.) . Hence it follows that Israel is " the Jewish

people which opposes its divine election." But it is nevertheless " at the same time the secret origin of the Church." " The Church is the assembly of Jews and Gentiles convoked on the ground of election." But at the same time she is " Israel's manifest destiny " (219). In Israel it " becomes apparent what God elects for himself," namely, " not an obedient but a refractory people " (227). Over against it the Church is destined now from the other side to be " the mirror " of God's " mercy " (231). Or again we might express it in a different way: " The Church form of the congregation is to its Israelitish form as Jesus' resurrection is to his crucifixion, as God's mercy is to his judgment " (233). Only once again one may not think of a rigid juxtaposition of " Israel " and " Church." Romans, ch. 9, in particular, teaches how God ever again has made the " Church " out of " Israel " by his effective choice. It teaches how there is thus plainly a " pre-existent life of the Church in Israel." Of course, it is only like the " light," which, streaming from him who is to come, already falls " provisionally " upon Israel's history (234). And conversely even the Israel which rejects its Messiah still belongs (to the congregation) as an indirect witness to the gospel. It " cannot make itself sterile for God. Ahasuerus in his way is also a witness of Jesus Christ " (260). God's promise is not invalidated.

In the middle, as it were, between Israel and the Church, uniting and distinguishing both of them, stands the " eternal election of the one man Jesus of Nazareth " (286). Assembled around him, so to speak, Israel's destiny is " to praise God's mercy in the passing away, in the death and in the removal of the old man — of the man who opposes his election and therefore God " (286). The Church for her part exists in order to proclaim " what in God's hands should and may become of the man he adopts and accepts " (291). Christ, the elect, triumphs in the " gracious end " which Israel manifests, as in the " gracious beginning " which the Church attests and exhibits (cf. 286). Indeed, " in the resurrection of Jesus Christ . . . God has canceled the finality of the Jews' rejection of Christ. At the same time, however, he nevertheless also put an end to the finality of the rejection of the Jews themselves when, against Israel's will, he asserted his will with Israel . . . yet just at the same time . . . he acknowledged Israel." And so " this ac-

knowledgment by God of his will with Israel . . . created the
Church " (320) ! At this point we again hear resounding what has
already been called to our attention above: the ultimate powerless-
ness of evil, of the " No." It is the rejection of rejection. Our last
quotation comes from Barth's exegesis of Rom., ch. 11 (in which
he acknowledges the merits of E. F. Ströter's exposition, in spite of
its " serious errors "; 294). Before we raise this or that obvious
scruple, will we not first have to make sure whether such sentences
as the one we have just cited do not express in their way, imita-
tively and reflectively, that " depth " and that " unsearchableness,"
about which Paul testifies in Rom. 11:33 ff. as in a hymn?

But in the light of such tremendous aspects, how do matters now
stand with the individual and his election? Barth devotes the most
exhaustive section of the present volume to this question (pp.
336–563).

" The individual " — certainly he is also involved! But there is
also " an individuality of man which has been negated in Jesus
Christ " (346). The individual who separates himself from God is
none other than the godless man (347). And yet Jesus Christ has
taken just the godless man's place! And there are those " who are
isolated from God," " godless men," who are not only elect in
Christ but who " live " " as God's elect " in virtue of the promise
which is also valid for them. They are the ones who " hear " and
" believe " God's promise (352) ! It is true that " not everyone
who is elected lives as one elected " (353). But thus the decisive
thing depends upon the congregation comforting each individual
with the promise: " In Jesus Christ you too are not rejected — he
has assuredly borne your rejection! — but in him you are elected "
(354). Now everything really depends upon people being " addressed directly " (355) ; the congregation always speaks " in the
second person " (357).

Ever and ever again Barth drives home what has already
emerged from the last quotations: the congregation may not take
unbelief too seriously, at least not so seriously as she takes God's
promise. One may say that here is to be found the very point of
all that Barth has expounded. " If the divine decree is identical
with Jesus Christ (thus taking up again all that has been said hith-

erto), then the commission of the elect congregation, in relation
to the many, consists exclusively in the proclamation of the gospel . . ." (358). " Precisely the believer cannot possibly recognize
a final datum in the unbelief of others " (360). The true separa-
tion is not between the elect and the reprobate, but " between the
ungodly and believers " (362). But must not believers recognize
themselves as the ungodly in themselves? And does not the ungodly man also stand under the promise (362)? " There is reason
to see the elect and the others together in their entire opposition
to one another, in any case, not to understand their opposition as
absolute " (386). Even believers are indeed " potentially the rejected — only in Christ are they not the rejected "! Hence they
have grounds for knowing and confessing their " solidarity " with
the ungodly (383).

But does not this admonition, together with its significant dogmatic principles, lead now to a doctrine of *apokatastasis,* of " universal atonement "? It may be that perhaps this doctrine could be
so construed from Barth's statements. Yet then it would be done
against his express opposition. It is true that in view of the univer-
salism of God's love he guards against " making a closed number,
according to the method of the classical doctrine of predestination,
out of the open number of the elect in Jesus Christ, over against
whom all other men would then stand as the rejected " (466). But
then he also declares: " On the other hand, it would manifestly not
be admissible to make the open number of the elect in Jesus Christ
to be the totality of all men " (467). The first assumption " runs
foul of the homogeneity of God's real and revealed will in Jesus
Christ. . . ." The second will not do " because precisely in Jesus
Christ we have to do with the personal, living, and therefore free
will of God with respect to the world and every man " (467).
" The New Testament nowhere says that the world is elected "
(468). He explicitly states: " The Church is . . . not to preach an
apokatastasis . . . but neither should she preach an inferior grace
of Jesus Christ, nor a wickedness of man superior to grace. On the
contrary, without a weakening of the contradiction, but also without a dualistic independence, she should preach the supremacy of
grace and the impotence of human wickedness in the face of it "
(529). We shall be able to appreciate this all the more as a particu-

larly pregnant utterance, clarifying the dogmatic relations, now
that Barth has expressed himself in almost the same way in his letter to the 1949 meeting of the Convention of Reformed Ministers.
He wrote that it is much more advisable " to preach a quickening
gospel " at the " risk " (of the error relative to *apokatastasis*) " than
to preach a law that kills without this risk " (*Ref. Kirchenzeitung*,
1949, p. 150) . It is quite obvious that for Barth it is a matter of the
freedom of grace and by no means of a law of universal atonement.
In the face of this tendency it will be out of place — especially
here — to criticize details. Let it be sufficient on the part of the
reporter to observe that also according to Barth it is nevertheless
true that in opposition to the " in Christ " of election there is an
" outside of Christ " of nonelection. The Bible gives us neither the
right to look upon God and Satan as if they were ultimately equivalent, in the way dualism does; nor on the other hand, to deduce as
a logical consequence the cessation of evil from the fact that it has
been overcome. At this point there remains a final question, an
ultimate mystery.

Barth brings his presentation of the doctrine of predestination
to a close with a section on " the destiny of the rejected," and so of
the man " who opposes his election which has taken place in Jesus
Christ " (498) . As the destiny of the elect in its very nature consists in the witness with which he is charged, so the rejected man is
also in his way a witness; that is, a witness on the left, as it were, a
witness of what in Jesus Christ has been overcome and is destined
to pass away. Now the problem of the rejected converges upon the
most enigmatic figure in the Bible, upon Judas Iscariot (508) ,
upon the disciple who " delivers up " Jesus. He delivers him up to
the enemies. But in doing so he also " delivers him over " to the
heathen! But then just in this very respect he is " replaced *de facto*
. . . by Paul " (530 ff.) ! And is it not so that this " handing over "
points to a still deeper mystery: to what God " gave up," to God's
" delivering up " of man, which is his judgment upon us, and
which as judgment — not without the co-operation even of Judas
— was executed in Jesus Christ? In fact, still keeping to the New
Testament concept of " paradosis " (delivering over, delivering
up) , Barth pursues the thought to a final consequence: this " delivering up " of God, which befell man in Jesus Christ, is again the

basis of the — apostolic " tradition " [1] (554). Does not Judas actually fulfill in the end what was positively and negatively the destiny of the Jews as a whole in the history of salvation, namely, this twofold " delivering over," in which God's own " delivering up " came to pass (561 ff.) ?

Perhaps these last thoughts expect too much of us. It is as if we found ourselves at the peak of a high chain of mountains: the air is thin, and clefts and precipices are all around us. Only with the greatest hesitation will many a reader want to make this last ascent with the party. Many may also find that the rope is not fastened on tight enough; that is, the peculiarly manifold meaning of the Greek New Testament word, " deliver over, deliver up." And yet: when in such a manner we are led to dizzy heights, are we not able to get a closer view of many things at once which otherwise seem to us to lie far apart? Are we not able at least to suspect that there are connections which are otherwise invisible? In any case it is well that in a final conclusion Barth again conducts us on down nearer to the valley region of the Church's task. What is to be done with the " rejected "? The gospel is to be preached to him! God " wills that the rejected man should believe, and as a believer should become an elect reprobate " (563) !

---

[1] If the word " tradition " were rendered " delivery," it would bring out the play on words in the German.

IX

GOD'S COMMANDMENT

[Volume II, 2, pp. 564–875]

⸻

BARTH's doctrine of God departs considerably from what may be said to be traditional in this regard. When he immediately included the doctrine of election in it, it became especially evident. (Cf. the preceding section of this report.) He gave full reasons for doing so. He wishes to avoid at all costs the possibility of " speaking of creation and sin without having first considered the decisive word and mystery of the doctrine of reconciliation (and that means of election) " (96) . When we speak of God's creation, of his providence and of sin, then, as has been shown, the mystery of the election by grace already surrounds and determines all such utterance. For this reason and in this sense the doctrine of election must be discussed within the doctrine of God. How should we even be able to speak about God's grace abstractly, as it were, without specifically mentioning the election by grace? " There is no created nature which does not have its existence, being and continuance from grace. . . ." In fact, " here even sin and death, the devil and hell . . ." form " no exception. For God's knowing and willing is gracious even where it operates as negation (and in this sense is permissive) " (99) . Thus it is understandable why Barth takes up the doctrine of election before the doctrine of creation and in connection with the (now no longer " abstract ") doctrine of God, and why he, to that extent, deviated from the usual practice (quite apart from all the radical divergences in details which we have partially discussed) .

No less novel is the fact that Barth now treats *ethics* also " as a task of the doctrine of God " (564 ff.) .

To be sure, a misconception, which is readily understandable, must be eliminated immediately at this point. Of course, since the time of Kant and those under his influence, there was nothing particularly novel in bringing ethics into the closest connection with the " idea of God." Consequently, one might be tempted — provided one did not know Barth — to see shades of Marburg suddenly arising here. However, such a thing could only really happen to the degree in which one was ignorant of Barth! For with him it is really not a question of God being the essence of the " morally good " (ascertained elsewhere than from His own work) !

What is the question then? How, in Barth's view, does ethics belong to the doctrine of God? Barth devotes the first section on the subject to answering this question (§ 36, II, 2, pp. 564–612). And his answer is given in a presupposed thesis: " As the doctrine of God's commandment, ethics explains the law as the form of the Gospel. . . . It is grounded in the knowledge of Jesus Christ because He is the sanctifying God and the sanctified man in one. It belongs to the doctrine of God because the God who claims man for himself, at the same time . . . assumes responsibility for this man . . ." (564).

" The law as the form of the gospel "! Many will here recall Barth's earlier pamphlet, " Gospel and Law " (1935). And actually this whole section only repeats in an extended form what Barth then set forth — much to the displeasure of many of his readers. The point in question may be clarified very simply in the familiar structure of the Ten Commandments. They do not begin at all with a " Thou shalt not. . . ." They begin, on the contrary, with the announcement of inconceivable grace: " I am Yahweh, thy God, who hath brought thee out of the land of Egypt, out of the house of bondage. . . ." The law, Barth tells us, is the " form and structure " in which the gospel meets us (567). There is no law in and for itself, and no gospel in and for itself; there is only " the one Word of God " (567) ! Or in our context: The concrete form of election is sanctification!

Theological ethics discovers, however, that a " general " ethics already exists. Man asks about the good in one form or another. Actually there are two facets to this fact. On the one hand, it " confirms " the " truth that God's grace has been bestowed upon man, by which the question about the good has been, from the very beginning, so posed that man . . . cannot escape . . . it " (574). But on the other hand, strange to say, precisely " that general concept of ethics exactly coincides with the concept of sin " (574) ! For with his own question about the good, man actually wants to

"shun . . . God's grace" (574). Thus, what is involved in theological ethics, as an ethics of grace, amounts to "an annexation of
a kind like that which took place in the entrance of the children of
Israel into Palestine" (575). Here a protest is registered; a humanly erected ethics is "vigorously refuted." Nevertheless, it is a
positive refutation. It is a refutation in view of the fact that "the
man Jesus, who fulfills God's commandment," does not "give,"
but "by God's grace, is the answer to the ethical question which
God's grace had posed" (573).

Hence it is impossible for theological ethics to try to justify its
position over against a general ethics ("apologetics"), as if the
latter now really represented a criterion of its own as opposed to
God's grace (577 ff.). However, it is also impossible to isolate theological ethics from "general" ethics. For this would also again
presuppose that the one or the other would let itself be restricted
to its own special "sphere" (582 ff.). And finally, the Roman
Catholic demarcation and synthesis of natural ethics and an ethics
of grace (moral philosophy and moral theology) is also impossible. The chief reason here is that grace is now no longer God's free
grace. "From the first it has to share its power with a capacity of
nature" (589).

No, theological ethics is concerned purely, originally, and exclusively with God's grace which has been accomplished in election.
"It is an ethics of grace or it is not theological ethics" (598). It
does not first inquire about man in and for himself, and about his
ethics, or about his "nature." Rather, it starts from the fact that
the man "to whom God's Word is addressed and for whom God's
work has taken place," that is, every man, whether he is already or
not yet a believer, in no way exists for himself and belongs to himself, but rather "exists because and as Christ exists" (599). The
basic idea in Calvin's ethics re-echoes in our ears when, at this
juncture, we repeatedly hear: we do not belong to ourselves, we
are not from or for ourselves (cf. *Inst.* III, 7, 1). If, then, man exists only in Christ, only "as a predicate of this Subject" (599),
then he has been therewith disposed of. For as Christ is the electing
God and the elected man in one, so he is also "the sanctifying God
and the sanctified man in one" (598).

Thus, in ethics, no new theme is introduced, as if man's own questions and activity were now perhaps to occupy the foreground. Whatever is to be said about man in ethics must be said in virtue of Christ. " In a Church dogmatics the ethical problem can consist only in the question whether, and in how far, human action is in praise of the grace of Jesus Christ " (600). Even humanity is there included. " There is no humanity outside of the humanity of Jesus Christ and outside of the voluntary or involuntary praise of the grace of God which has been realized in him " (601). Hence we cannot distinguish dogmatics and ethics from each other in such a way that " dogmatics would perforce have to do with God and faith in him, but ethics would be concerned with man and his life " (604). The question about the good is to be answered along these lines: " The goodness of human action consists in the goodness in which God acts upon man " (607). Or we might put it this way: " Man's action is good to the extent that his action is Christian "; that is, to the extent that he acts " as a man who knows that God has adopted him in Jesus Christ; that in Jesus Christ . . . a decree has been made concerning him; and that by Jesus Christ . . . he has been called into a covenant with Him " (607).

Man's destiny has been decreed! God's grace in Jesus Christ, which has been bestowed upon him, is at the same time God's reaching out after him; it is at once God's commandment. Thus, when we inquire about God's commandment, our inquiry does not bypass grace, election, and Jesus Christ. We do not ask about something else. Rather we receive the commandment because God in his grace makes himself our commander. Therefore, Barth can bluntly say: " ' There is ' no commandment of God "; on the contrary, " this is the fact of the matter: God gives his commandment " (609). When we speak about God's commandment, we are concerned with an event!

The last sentence confronts us again with Barth's basic premise; the law does not exist as something independent over against the gospel. It is " enclosed in the gospel " (619). This sentence appears in a new section (§ 37), which discusses the commandment as " God's claim " (612–701).

Who, according to this, is the God who raises his claim upon us?

He is none other than he " in whom we are permitted to believe "
(617)! His claim does not depend upon his superior power. Nor
does it depend upon a divine goodness subsisting in itself. Instead
it rests upon the fact that, in virtue of his grace, " our human existence is no longer left alone, no longer left to itself, but . . . has
been adopted and included in God's divine existence in Jesus
Christ " (619). It means precisely that the commandment is " enclosed in the gospel " and is encompassed by it.

Where, then, is God's commandment to be gleaned? How can
we know it? What does it look like? We will understand why Barth
does not now immediately refer to the Decalogue or to the Sermon
on the Mount. (That will come later!) Both of these could too
easily be conceived " in themselves " as collections of independent
ethical principles, loosed from the person who is speaking and
without regard for the one to whom they are addressed. No —
even in the question about the content of the commandment Barth
directs us to Christ. And, moreover (naturally), not to Christ as
an " ideal," but to God's will which he obediently fulfills in us
and for us. However, it again means that he directs us to the work
of grace which results in the " establishment of the law " (624)!
The law meets us in a binding way precisely as a fulfilled law, and
not as an ideal (625). God " spoke about the good when he did it;
he spoke about himself when he offered up himself for us " (627).

However, God's grace, God's will, which is accomplished in the
work of Jesus Christ, possesses " teleological force " (629); that
is, it is directed toward a goal. " The goal of grace, which has been
accomplished and revealed in God's covenant with man, is man's
restoration to his image, and thus to a fellowship with him in eternal life " (629). From this standpoint God's claim is concretely
the claim which is known among his people and in his Church.
Nevertheless it also applies to the whole world (634). And its
purpose is " that man's action become, be, and remain the action
of one who accepts God's action " (638). Or expressed in another
way: man is required to be " in conformity to divine grace and to
that extent, in conformity to Jesus Christ and his people " (641).
The man who hears this also hears, and should admit, that he does
not belong to himself (645), but that " God is our righteousness "
(646). In a word, he is called to faith (647). After all, God's com-

mandment does not want anything except the faith in which we
let Christ be our Lord, our righteousness, and our sanctification.

Consequently the " form taken by God's claim " is essentially
that of " permission," the " granting of a quite definite freedom "
(650). God wants us to do his will joyfully, gladly, and gratefully.
It certainly does not mean that God now condones the many kinds
of license we had previously given ourselves (659). God's commandment is a protest against such license, because, in reality, it is
nothing but a " disguised slavery " (660). Just because of the freedom which he grants us, God puts an end to our being our own
judges of what is good and evil (662). Man is now " relieved of all
the anxiety and fear of existing for himself " (663). And this is
based upon the fact that God exists for man. Just because God
takes our existence upon himself he sets us free from all that. And
now " the sum and substance " of everything that is " required "
of man consists in " abiding " and " persevering " with, and in,
what has been prepared for him in and through Christ. (So it is in
keeping with a paraphrase of the New Testament use of the words.
See pp. 667 ff.) However, with that, we are again at the central
theme of Christian teaching and Christian dogmatics. If we lose
sight of this, it becomes incomprehensible how we actually stand
under an obligation and a permission at the same time. Then there
arises either a legalism — an " obligation which is not a permission," or a lawlessness — a " permission which is not an obligation " (671). Either of these must be the result when we reduce
God's commandment, that is, his permission, to a principle (670).
However, things will be different once we see that the unity of the
obligation and the permission is grounded " in the fulfillment " of
the commandment " which has taken place in Jesus Christ " (672).
Then, at any rate, God's commandment ceases to be an " ideal "
for us (674), and obedience now actually becomes an obedience
" in the Lord," no matter how it may manifest itself. (For an ideal
torments us or fosters illusions; at all events it plainly intensifies
our arbitrariness, our anxiety, and our fear.)

God's commandment is not only a claim. A claim, as such, could
accost us purely from without. In any case it could be an empty
claim, a mere " imperative," a mere " obligation." God's com-

mandment, however, is at once " God's decision ": in the commandment it already has been decided what in our life and action
is the good. Barth discusses this now in the ensuing section (§ 38;
pp. 701–818).

What, then, is God's concrete commandment for us? Now the
question is raised from a new side, and even more meaningfully
than before. However, before it is raised specifically, Barth discusses the " sovereignty " of the divine decision; namely, that in
this decision, solely in view of God's grace and God's covenant,
man has an absolute counterpart (714), so absolute that here, and
only here, is he truly challenged to be responsible. In this situation man cannot fall back upon preconceived ideas. He cannot find
in them what may be right in any particular instance. Rather, he
is actually engaged in an " encounter with God " as " our Judge."
Then all " ethical reflection " can only be an act of the deepest sincere humility on our part, which does not know what is right, but
which honestly and tirelessly asks, " What must we do? " (718).

Yes, but what now? We repeat the question: What then, to put
the question concretely, is God's commandment for us? Barth answers in the first place that it is definitely not a " general rule "
(740 ff.). If it were, then, " in the exact sense of the word," it
would " actually not be a commandment at all " (741). An " idea
of the good " is not a commandment! The " categorical imperative " is not a commandment (and it is to " Kant's credit " that he
too saw that it ought not to be) (743). Even conscience is not
an instance of the commandment. Strictly speaking, " conscience "
does " not " belong " to anthropological concepts, but within the
category of eschatological ideas " (744).[1] God's commandment is
certainly concrete. But that does not mean that it has not been
given to us in a " completeness, clarity, and definiteness " which
requires obedience (746). The quandary as to how we should obey

----

1 TRANSLATOR'S NOTE: Barth's meaning might be misunderstood here. He states:
" Conscience is the totality of our self-consciousness insofar as it can be the receiver,
and then also the knower of the Word, and so also of God's commandment which
befalls us; insofar as we (provided God wants to speak to us) can become God's
co-knower. . . . The concept of conscience (like that of the human 'spirit' in its
distinction to body and soul corresponding to the Holy Spirit) belongs, strictly
speaking, not to anthropological, but within the category of eschatological concepts. . . . It is not an independent 'voice of God.' . . . It knows about God's
commandment, when it hears God's commandment " (Dogmatik, II, 2, 744).

is not due to God's commandment, and its supposed obscurity, but to our own unwillingness (747).

God's commandment is attested for us in Holy Scripture. But where? Barth's answer is that it is attested absolutely everywhere in Scripture! Naturally, Scripture by no means produces " general principles " everywhere. No, on the contrary, it does not do that at all. Taking the Pentateuch and Matthew's Gospel as examples, Barth shows how God's commanding or Jesus' demand are meant to be " nothing but highly accidental acts and modes of conduct. They are understood to be necessary only in their historical contingency." They are " nothing but acts of obedience to be performed in their proper place in this or that way. They are merely decisions about whose meaning no discussion is possible at all. For in no way do they refer to a higher law . . ." (751). Yes, but then how are all these " accidental " commandments united? The answer is to be found in the One who issues them! " God is faithful and unchanging " (755). God's commandment, therefore, may be " as little abstracted " from the history in which it meets us, " as from the Person of the commanding God " (756). In the Bible, in keeping with its proper theme, it is not a matter of the " proclamation of ethical principles " (759), but of the actualization of God's gracious election (756) !

Only when this has been clearly recognized can we also turn to those Biblical passages in which are to be found something like " collections " and " summaries of God's commandments " (760), such as the Decalogue and the Sermon on the Mount in particular (762 ff.). They are, " so to speak, God's solemnly promulgated self-qualifications, and at the same time . . . the . . . solemnly promulgated qualifications for his people " (762). They are strictly of a historical character. The Ten Commandments " belong in the context of the social, legal, and religious order revealed to Moses and delivered by Moses to the people " (763). They " manifestly stake off the sphere within which God's dealings with his people are to be enacted, as well as the actions of his people before him and with him " (764). But precisely this fact then establishes them as " the basic statute of the divine covenant of grace," " valid for all times " (765). The Sermon on the Mount, on the other hand, is a document testifying that " the order governing the life of God's

people . . . now appears in the light of the fact " that it has been
" fulfilled for man's salvation and blessedness " (767) . " If the
Ten Commandments tell where man may and ought to stand before and with God, then the Sermon on the Mount tells us that he
has really been placed there by God's act " (768) . It is an " announcement of the Kingdom of Heaven " (768) . It is " Jesus' self-
announcement " (770) . It is the " announcement of the new man "
(774) . But the Decalogue and the Sermon on the Mount are merely
a proclamation, a documentation of what is, as such, primarily and
truly basic: God's election of Israel, God's creation of the Church.
The Bible does not know " God's commandments as general moral
principles " (781) , but all such summaries themselves belong " to
the history of the covenant of grace " (781) .

But then, what have these " summaries," what have the Ten
Commandments and the Sermon on the Mount to do with us? The
answer is that " the Bible wants us to become contemporaneous
and homogeneous with those other men " (that is, with those who
heard these summaries at a particular time in history) " with respect to God's commandment, the publication and understanding
of it, as well as our situation over against it. It wants us to be every
bit the companions of those men in relation to God's commandment " (783) . But how are we to do it? Are we therefore to derive
abstract morals, as it were, from what has been delivered to us here
as a witness? Certainly not! We will be like those men when
" God's commandment is, also for us, always a concretely definite
and plenary demand " (784) . The " goodness required by God's
commandment " is never some " abstract good-in-itself "; it is " the
goodness of God's eternal election by grace, the goodness which
bears the name of Jesus Christ " (785) . In regard to this matter,
however, we will not now simply be " instructed " in a general way
by that witness. On the contrary, " its revelation " will be " medi-
ated " to us in it (786) ! That is to say, we find ourselves, in virtue
of the Biblical witness, not merely analogous " to the Biblical situation and happening between God and man "; but " the God who
spoke and acted with them (the witnesses) is also, in virtue of
their testimony, directly our God " (788) . Thus, the Ten Commandments and the Sermon on the Mount concern us not only indirectly, but directly (788) . God's commandment, even in its tem-

poral form, is "also for us an eternally valid standard" (789).
Therefore, we are jointly affected!

Who? We? We Church people? Let us remember what has already been indicated above, and also what was communicated in
the preceding section of this report! Certainly God's commandment is heard in the Church; in the Church God's justice is acknowledged in faith. But "even the man who does not accept it
actually stands under the truth of the Word — be it then with
head unbowed" (787). For God is "the Lord of the whole world
and . . . the Lord of every man . . ." (787)! Consequently the
validity of the commandment in the congregation may be characterized as exemplary and representative, but not as exclusive.

This point of view proves important, especially in view of what
Barth subsequently designates as the "political service of God."
(The expression is found on p. 807.) He speaks of it in connection with a section he entitles "The Goodness of the Divine Decision," and in which he discusses Rom., chs. 12 to 15, from various
points of view. He mentions it, first of all, when he tells us that the
goodness of God and his commandment must prevent us "atomiz-
ing" his commandment, and, as it were, staking off a sphere outside of the commandment, possibly a sphere of "natural orders."
Right here Rom. 13:1–7 is also broached. Moreover, but from a
further viewpoint, God's goodness signifies the "unification" of
men "among themselves." That is to say, in regard to the State,
the circumstance that its order is not that of the congregation but
represents an "order of the sword, of coercion, and of fear," indeed "an order devoid of grace," does not imply the exclusion of
its sphere from the congregation's responsibility (806). For even
this "graceless order," as surely as it is destined to pass away, has
nevertheless been placed under God's grace, under God's patience;
in it God's opposition to despotism takes effect. And therefore the
"reasonable service to God" of Christians can and should also
"have the form of political service to God; it can and should also
consist in their participation in the existence and life of that provisional and graceless order of human affairs" (807). The State
does not in this way become the Church. The congregation lives
its own life (808); but this life "also has a political dimension"
(808). However, the political sphere is only an illustration of the

fact that God's commandment does not place the congregation in a pious (and then legalistic) isolation (cf. also 804 and 814 ff.). God's goodness, apprehended by faith in the congregation, is indeed actually and plainly turned toward man, and what happens in the congregation points, "in prophetic anticipation," to the life of man in general (814).

Barth ends his doctrine of God's commandment, and with it the entire doctrine of God, with a section on "the commandment as God's judgment" (§ 39, pp. 819–875). What he says here, naturally touches in part upon his discussions of God's righteousness (II, 1, 423 ff.; cf. Chapter VII of this report). But here Barth goes even farther than he did then. It may be said that both sections, taken together, trace in outline what we may expect as Barth's version of the doctrine of justification and reconciliation. At any rate the idea of "reconciliation" occurs right at the beginning of this section. God's judgment in his commandment, the "essence of all temporal realization of his decree," is "essentially identical with reconciliation." (819). That immediately points to a leading thought: God's judgment is "the proof of his . . . love for man" (821). For God accomplishes this judgment in Jesus Christ (823, 826, etc.). Thus, even when we speak about God's judgment, we must look to Him, and not beyond Him!

It means, in regard to man, that Christ's death is an "actual demonstration by God" (836), in which the claim which the commandment lays upon us, and the decision which is passed upon us in it — together with our failure on both counts — are finally revealed. Christ's death bears this import because it exhibits the judgment which "is our actual encounter with God" (838). Our guilt becomes manifest in the cross of Christ. But now, nevertheless, in such a way that the "condemnation undoubtedly befalls us just in the Person of Jesus Christ, and therefore in such a way that what remains for us is the forgiveness of our sins" (841). This implies that God certainly does not want us to stare bewitched at our load of guilt, although it assuredly brought Christ to the cross. God "asserts . . . his title to us. He maintains it against the claim Satan would like to make upon us . . . and God thereby provides for our justice in his sight against Satan's injustice . . ."

(844). As certain as it is true of us that we are always sinners, so it is nevertheless even more certain that we are always righteous. " The forgiveness of sins means that these two predications do not exclude one another, nor confront one another in a dialectical balance, but in a preponderance of the second over against the first . . ." (846)! That such is the case could by no means be invented. Its proof is to be found rather in its " actual demonstration by God " in the resurrection of Jesus Christ (848).

Several times in the last paragraph " justice " was mentioned. We recall that this was also the case earlier. God's mercy is not just " cheap grace," but " is accomplished in the form of a legal action . . ." (850), in which God proves himself to be " an extremely just judge " (850). It might now be asked whether man then goes scot-free " so easily," now that Christ has borne the judgment of the divine commandment. Barth replies that God's " No " certainly remains upon a man when he " does not live from the forgiveness he has been granted; . . . when he does not let God's Son speak for himself, but still wants to be his own spokesman; when he does not want to confess his sin, but wants to excuse and justify himself " (851).

" Righteous in Him " — that is what we are told there. In ourselves, without Christ and without the Holy Spirit, we simply have nothing to show. Everything depends upon this strict relationship. But it causes all theology " to remain powerless in itself " unless it " becomes prayer " (853). What was said previously (and indicated in this report) is real and " true " only in prayer (854).

Thus, as the doctrine of God discusses " the purpose of the divine judgment," it ends with a summons to faith. For it is " the exact correspondence to God's judgment and grace " (857). Sin (and the sin " of the whole world " at that) is unbelief (858). Faith means, on the other hand, " to affirm in practice that our pardoned sin is recognized as sin, and that our recognized sin, as such, is pardoned " (860). With this last insight, which is to be explained further to the effect that man knows only from pardoned sin that it is sin (860 ff.), it has already been made clear that faith and repentance are two sides of the same act. And hence the way has again been prepared for the concluding insight that God's purpose in his judgment is our sanctification; that is, man's " equipment,

preparation, and training for the eternal life which has been destined for him and promised to him " (865). Sanctification is an
accomplished fact: it is Jesus Christ! It is our sanctification solely
by faith in him, in repentance, and in prayer. (It is characteristic
for Barth to close on this note.)

X

THE WORK OF CREATION

[Volume III, 1, pp. 1–476]

———

T HE THIRD volume of *Church Dogmatics* embraces the " doctrine of creation " in four parts. From the first the reader approaches this part of the mammoth work with special interest. One
can understand when Barth assures us in the foreword to Vol. III,
1, that in it he has " set foot upon a territory " with which he feels
" considerably less familiar and sure of himself." Perhaps many
may ask themselves whether Barth could have anything of importance to contribute at this point at all, after everything he had
said and written against " natural theology "? How could one expect a " theology of the first article " from Barth? As it is, we are
not going to get one either — in the usual sense of the word. However, it appears that because of his approach to the subject, Barth
is now able to develop a doctrine of creation, which is not isolated
from the rest of the contents of theology and neither is it sub-
merged in them. For this reason every reader has cause to be grateful that Barth set to work " with a will," " but also with anxious
sighs."

The first part of the third volume now to be discussed contains
only a single chapter: " The Work of Creation " (1945). The second part appeared in 1948, and again comprised only a single
chapter, running to eight hundred pages: " The Creature " — a
doctrine of man. Then the third and fourth parts contained the
doctrine of God's providence (1950) and of the commandment of
God the Creator (1951).

Barth devotes a whole section (§ 40: " Faith in God the Creator," pp. 1–44) to explain the nature of the statements now to
follow. There is ample need for it. For the doctrine of creation is
to a large extent a sphere in which both " reason " and " faith " in
turn (and together) act as spokesman. In fact, the doctrine of creation is the most important source for all " natural theology." It is
all the more important for Barth — having the wording of the first

article of the Creed at hand — to proceed immediately from its statement: " I believe . . ." " The doctrine of creation is an article of faith no less than all the rest of the Christian confession . . ." (cf. Heb. 11:3; p. 1). This proposition, as it stands, needs to be established. In other words, it should be shown that the content of the first article is a " mystery " (3). To that end Barth, first of all, points out that it is by no means " self-evident " that the created reality has a " nature of its own over against God's nature " (3). " If the world has not been created by God, then it does not exist. If we do not know it as created by God, then we do not know that it is " (5). Secondly, neither is it " self-evident " that " this whole sphere is from God," and that God is therefore " *before* the world " (5). And thirdly, when the Creed speaks of the Creator, it does not mean some " supreme being," but the " Lord of Israel's history " (12). By creation is to be understood a completed deed, an " accomplished fact without parallel " (13), namely, that " God founds creaturely history as the history of salvation he has decreed " (14), and thereby proves that " the reality of history " is " not originally foreign " to him (14). Finally, both " heaven and earth," the two together being the " sum total of reality different from God " (17), appear simply and solely as created reality in the mystery of creation. Even heaven, the " upper, greater, invisible reality " (20), is created even as the " earth "! And so it is true: " There is no more sweeping secularization of that which now belongs to the *saeculum,* at its highest and lowest levels, than the knowledge that God has created heaven and earth (really heaven too!) " (20). Indeed, there is not a word in the first article which does not point to a mystery!

But where now does the doctrine of creation — as a doctrine of faith — have its starting point? Not forthwith in the fact that it stands " at the beginning of the Bible " (24)! To tie up to this hitching post, without taking other aspects into account, would be a " diffused," " scattered," and " peripheral " Biblicism, rather than one that is " necessary," and gets at the " center " of Scripture (25). The starting point also of the doctrine of creation can lie only " in the fact attested in the heart of the Bible " (26). That means (and here we now come upon the dominant theme of this whole part) that the approach to the doctrine of creation is to be found in the Person of Jesus Christ. The "unity of God with man" has been accomplished in him, and therewith it has been revealed that God is "really not alone" (26). God created the world, "as surely as his eternal Word, without ceasing to be God, became something else, namely, flesh — and therefore not Nothing" (27)! And on the other hand, in the unity of God with man which was accomplished in Christ, it has also been revealed that man is "not alone" (27). In the Person of Jesus Christ God is disclosed to us as the Creator, and therewith also the creatureliness of man and the world. "He who has discovered man as God's creature here, in Jesus Christ, has thereby immediately discovered heaven and earth too, as an object of the divine creative act" (29). Moreover, this is true not merely "noetically" (in the sense of knowing) but also "ontically" (according to being). Jesus Christ is truly "the Word," "by which God has accomplished creation" (29)! However, once again the meaning and effect of this is that we not only know the Creator in him but that in him "the Creator" is "present." "The man who believes in Jesus Christ is concerned *ipso facto* with the Lord of heaven and earth with or without signs" (37). The faith, in which this takes place, as "a life in the Creator's presence," is at the same time "a life in the factual experience and acknowledgment of his power over all things and circumstances" (37). But with this it is also a life "in the experience and acknowledgment of his right to his creature" (which Jesus established in the reconciliation of the world; 38). Finally, it is "a life in the acknowledgment and experience of His benevolence" (41). It may be said of the believer that "for him God the Creator has become trustworthy . . ." (42). It now becomes apparent that creation is grace (44)!

After what we have seen hitherto, no one will any longer expect to find a doctrine of creation "by itself," an exposition of the first article "for itself." The work of creation is not the "sum of all God's works" (51), but neither is it an isolated work. Rather, "as God's first work" it is, as it were, the "model" or "shell" of God's second work. Creation belongs within the whole of God's one work, which Barth calls the "accomplishment of the covenant of grace" (46). And, moreover, it may be said "the creation is the establishment of a place for the history of the covenant of grace"

(46). So we understand why the most exhaustive section in this chapter (§ 41) bears the title: " Creation and Covenant " (44–377).

Anyone who speaks about the covenant of grace (and it cannot be done without recalling in particular the theology of Johannes Coccejus), speaks of the " history of salvation " (*Heilsgeschichte*). Barth also appropriates this concept throughout, in a conscious relation here to the " conservative theology of the nineteenth century " (which created the concept). Only he immediately clarifies it: " The history of salvation is . . . *the* history, the *proper* history, in which all other history is determined " (64). Or as applied to the covenant we may say: " The covenant of grace is *the* theme of history " (64).

But now if creation is God's first work in carrying out the covenant of grace, then it itself belongs to history. It is " not a timeless truth," even as there are no timeless truths in the Bible at all, but only truths as " God's deeds " (64). From this it inevitably follows that creation " occurs *in time* " (72). What does not occur in time is God's eternal " decree of grace and so of creation " (73). The creation itself, however, is temporal, whereby time is understood as " the creature's form of existence " (72). If one wished to speak of a timeless creation, it would have the " illegitimate import " of " denoting an eternal relation of God as Creator to a world eternal like himself," and that would be a " false doctrine " (73). God would not then interest himself in the creature in his, the creature's, form of existence, and that would mean that God is " not gracious to the creature " (74). But God's eternity " is revealed . . . in the act of creation as his readiness for time " (76) ; that is, just for the form, in which the creature exists, and therefore for the creature itself.

Now, to be sure, there is a difference between " time " and " time." The " time of the history of creation " is not to be confused with " *our* time." Our time is just " time without a discernible ground or reason in eternity." In fact, " as the time of lost man " it is necessarily " *lost* time " (78). But on the other hand, neither is the " time of creation " to be equated with the " time of grace," the time of the gracious " now " of fulfillment (79 f.), which, however, in contrast to the time of creation, now has " lost "

time for its " opposing counterpart " (82) . But this time of grace
has found its previous portrayal, as it were, in the time of creation.
The time of grace is simply " the archetype of all time " (82) ;
that is, time in immediate relation to God: the " lifetime of Jesus
Christ " (82) !

Creation is temporal. But it is not " historiographical history "
(84) . For the temporal, which is directly related to God and, as it
were, directly borders on eternity, may not be conceived historiographically. In order to describe this mystery Barth coins the term
" unhistoriographical history " [1] for creation (84) . But only for
creation! For all other history stands at the same time " in an
indirect relation to God as well." To that extent it is " also historiographical "; that is, by way of explanation, it may also be understood in one way or another from a creaturely context. But creation, God's action alone, solely in the creature which first becomes
a creature by this action, is, " in its nature, absolutely unhistoriographical." The meaning is, therefore, that creation is not by any
means to be comprehended in creaturely terms (86) . To be sure,
all history is " unhistoriographical " " in its direct relationship to
God " (87) . But the history of creation " has *only* this element "
(87) . Under these circumstances the history of creation, as literature, can come to us only as " saga "; that is, as an unhistoriographical conception of history, which states " by way of divination " and " poetry " what cannot be expressed at all as historiography; that is to say, it cannot be expressed in creaturely terms.
(They are " historical sagas "; 90.) On the other hand, the view
that the history of creation is a " myth " is to be completely rejected. Barth tells us what he understands by " myth." " The actual theme and content of the myth (in contrast to concrete history) are the essential principles of universal realities and relations
of the natural and spiritual cosmos which are not bound to particular times and places . . ." (91) . But with that we have also
said that " a real myth " has " never yet really had creation as its
theme and subject matter " (that is, as a deed, as a temporal event;
92) . In the last analysis a myth is bound up with " the single reality of man and his cosmos," and hence (in spite of all appearances
to the contrary) it is ultimately " always monistic " (93) . The

---

1 " *Unhistorische Geschichte.*"

Biblical history of creation unquestionably takes myth into account; but in reality it opposes it with its " exact opposite " (95). It speaks of event, deed, time, and history, even if it does not precisely speak of historiography.

In the middle of this whole part there is an exposition of the Biblical history of creation. The preceding considerations ought to have indicated the way in which it is to be understood. As is well known, we have two accounts (Gen. 1:1 to 2:4 a and Gen. 2:4 b ff.). Barth takes them up in succession. According to his interpretation " the creation " appears in the first account " as the external presupposition of the covenant " (103–258); in the second, " the covenant as the internal presupposition of creation " (258–377). In the discussion of both of these Barth makes exhaustive references to contemporary exegesis.

What we have before us in the first account is, as it were, " a work of tremendous preparation, yet carefully planned, completely thought out, and thoroughly comprehensive as well. It is comparable to the erection of a temple, whose design and construction . . . is determined by the liturgy it is to serve . . ." (107). Thus, the entire account is to be understood from the standpoint of its goal. Therefore it must " also be read from back to front in order to understand it properly " (108). This goal, however, is " God's Sabbath freedom, Sabbath rest, and Sabbath joy, in which man is also called to participate " (108). " It is the covenant of God's grace, which in this event, at the culmination and conclusion of the first history of creation, then appears as the starting point for all that follows " (108).

From the wealth of particular observations in regard to this account, attention can be called to only a few.

At the outset one may be reminded of one of the leading thoughts in Barth's doctrine of election, when he now emphatically asserts that the " darkness " (Gen. 1:2) may " in no case be understood as being a positive entity, not even potentially " (117). " As nothing good can come from the *tehom* (Luther: the ' deep '), so neither can anything good come from the darkness " (117). For Barth it is a matter of the greatest consequence that the " deep " or the " darkness " (or evil or unbelief, etc.) do not acquire a sort of independent substantiality over against the Creator. For then we would have a dualism; then God would be " the god of this world " — an imaginary, mythical god (119). No, the much debated verse in Gen. 1:2 does not speak about a raw, primitive state of creation existing as it were before creation, " but about the possibility which God, as he set to work at creation, passed over, and which he passed by in disdain . . ." (119). Barth goes even farther. Unquestionably there is indicated in Gen. 1:2 the possibility of a judgment of God upon what does not originate in his creative Word, and so does not actually " exist." However, in point of fact this judgment is executed only " at a single place in the cosmos he has created, only in a single creature" (121); namely, in the Person of Jesus Christ! " The passage in Gen. 1:2 speaks of the old things which, according to II Cor. 5:17, have radically passed away in the death and resurrection of Jesus Christ " (121)! From the same starting point Barth afterward is able to explain, in regard to Gen. 1:4, that only light really " exists," while darkness " also exists " solely in virtue of being separated from light. " It is not at hand; it is only near at hand " (137). It has, therefore, no essence of its own. And there is a reason for it too: " The Creator of light is also the Lord of darkness " (141).

Of incisive importance is then what Barth says about the creation of man (according to the first account of creation). It will be necessary to dwell somewhat longer on this section.

" Let us make man," it reads in Gen. 1:26. The plural number in " let us " has always been surprising. Barth (rightly) rejects the explanation which apparently lies nearest at hand, namely, that here there is a *pluralis majestaticus*. He does so because the language of the Old Testament has no knowledge of this (215). To think of angels is, according to Barth, equally impossible because man becomes the " image " and " likeness " of him who there speaks in the plural; but man being made in the image of an angel is certainly out of the question (215). So there is, therefore, no other choice possible: God speaks in this peculiar form with himself. It means that there is " already a vis-à-vis in the nature and sphere of the divine " (205). God himself does not exist exactly like a " point, spaceless and timeless "; he is " not dead but alive " (205)! Precisely because this is so, creation is " not a renunciation but a revelation of his divinity " (205)!

Man, whose creation the first account introduces in such an incomparably prominent way, is now created " in our archetype," and that means " as a creature which has its ground and its possibility in the fact that in ' us,' that is, in God's own sphere and nature a divine . . . archetype exists . . ." (205). In this " archetype " man's nature has its " legal basis " (205). But what then is to be said about man " having been made in (this) image of God "? First of all, it may be safely said that it is " not a quality of man " (not a quality distinct from his nature; 206). It exists rather " because man himself and as such exists as God's creature " (207). " He would not be man, if he were not God's image " (207). Materially this has a twofold meaning. First, man is God's " counterpart." That is to say, " the self-encounter and finding oneself, which takes place in God himself " (namely, between the Father and the Son in the Trinity), is " portrayed and copied in God's relation to man." Secondly, however, man is " the counterpart of another of the same sort as himself." " The togetherness and co-operation occurring in God himself " is therefore " repeated in the relation of man to man " (207) ! The " analogy," which is the point in question here, is " existence " " in the vis-à-vis of I and Thou "; *that* is what is " constitutive " for God and for man (207).

" Analogy! " We know how sharply Barth has attacked the concept of " *analogia entis* " time and again. It expresses the idea that between the Creator and the creature, between " grace " and " nature," there is a static, continuous, and logically perceptible relationship, at least just to the extent that Creator and creature both have one " being," and share in the same " being " which embraces them both, only in a different way: one might almost say in a different density. Barth's whole struggle against the Thomistic doctrine, against Protestant modernism, even against Emil Brunner, could be understood as having this concept as its theme. And the objection was also constantly being made against him that the one — Biblical — concept of man having been made in God's image, the *imago Dei*, proves just that, nevertheless, there must be an analogy. It had been said that with the absolute denial of such an analogy the " world " would lapse into sheer senselessness. The Church would make itself the ally of nihilism or of skepticism, and would be indifferent whether the world went on or went to pieces. In short, in disputing the *analogia entis* it appeared as if now "all cats" actually had to be "gray," to quote Barth's own expression. If after all an unbridgeable chasm yawns between the Creator and the creature, yes, between God and the world — as one then had to say — a chasm which could be closed only in an eschatological event, then the Christian can be absolutely indifferent how, for example, the state is governed, whether marriage, for example, is kept holy or broken, etc. Indeed then, seen from God, everything secular is of no consequence; everything is immersed in that twilight, "in which all cats are gray." As is known, these considerations have been constantly urged against Barth. Admittedly at best this could be done with apparent justice only up till 1938, up to the publication of Barth's decisively important pamphlet *Justification and Justice!* [2] And after the section of the *Dogmatics* now to be discussed is presented, surely no one will any longer venture to do so.

Barth actually speaks about an "analogy"! But not of an *analogia entis*. Rather, he speaks of an *analogia relationis*, and in doing so he borrows a term from Dietrich Bonhoeffer (220, 226). What is meant by it? An observation in regard to the text of Gen. 1:27 previously made by Wilhelm Vischer and Dietrich Bonhoeffer constituted the starting point. The verse must be read in a single breath, so to speak: "in the image of God created he him; male and female created he them." So, expressed crudely, the phrase "in the image of God" is expounded by the addition: male and female. "The characteristic feature of God's nature" is "that he includes an I and a Thou in himself"; and the characteristic feature of man's nature is "that he is man and woman" (220)! So Barth concludes: "As the invoking I in God's nature is related to the divine Thou invoked by him, so God is related to the man he has created, so in human existence itself is the I related to the Thou, the man to the woman" (220). So in this relatedness and relation of man and woman, established by God's creative grace, lies the correspondence between the creature and the Creator. Hence, an "*analogia relationis,*" an analogy in the sense of a relation (a corresponding relation)! But the analogy lies *only* in this

[2] Translated into English under the title *Church and State*, by G. Ronald House. Student Christian Movement Press, London, 1939.

relation between man and woman, not perchance in other relations. According to Barth " the sexual differentiation " is the " only one," in which man is created (208) ; in the creation account there is no mention of any others.

May we now say with the Reformers that man has lost the " image of God " through sin? Barth admits that the Reformers had to make such a pronouncement because they understood by the image of God man's original created state, his being in the *status integritatis* (" state of original purity "). However, there is no basis for this conception in the Biblical account. But of the image of God as Barth now presents it, consisting solely in an *analogia relationis,* one cannot say that it has been lost. On the contrary, one must say " that God acknowledges his purpose for him (man) by addressing him as Thou and making him responsible as an I, and that also men among themselves have to work out their destiny together as I and Thou, as male and female " (225). God holds firmly to his purpose! God is not dethroned by the Fall! If an *analogia entis* had been established in the image of God, then one might think that a " remnant " of it still exists, though only through a complete perversion of Biblical truth. If, however, the image of God consists in this *analogia relationis,* then as such it can never cease " to be God's work and gift " (226).

But how is that? Just from what we see Barth advocating we may immediately take the following — that man's being in the image of God always remains " God's work and gift," and simply never " can become a human possession " (226). It is and remains an *analogia relationis,* and not through any sort of back door does it become the *analogia entis* after all! The fact that man copies God's nature, as it were, is never a peculiarity present in or upon him, but always points man forward and away from himself. (For this reason Barth believes that although the phrase " to (be) his image " is " grammatically false," it is really correct; 228.) But where is God's image? Where has that " relation," that original and archetypal relation, really been fulfilled? Barth answers with Paul: in Jesus Christ! " According to I Cor. 11:7 there is indeed one man who is actually the *eikon kai doxa theou* (the image and glory of God), and, seen from him, the same is to be said of every man. And beside this one man there is also a woman who is His

doxa (glory) , as He . . . is the *doxa* of God. Moreover, seen from
her, or rather from the standpoint of her husband, the same is to
be said of every woman "! Let us note that the unity of Christ with
his congregation is hence unfolded for us as the mystery which is
illustrated in the togetherness of husband and wife in marriage.
" *Jesus Christ together with the congregation is God's image.*" And
this " Christological equation " is at the same time an " ecclesio-
logical " equation, " and in connection with it," it is " even an
anthropological equation " (230) !

Thus Barth achieves, as it were, in retrograde, from the side of
Jesus Christ, and therewith from a proper basis, an understanding
of the image of God in creation. And the real nature of this image
of God becomes the promise! Thus one is able to speak even of
fallen man and his world as confidently as the first creation account does — in the light of the goal to which it is directed.

According to Barth the second account of creation is " so to
speak a history of creation from within " (263) . If we said with
Barth that for the first account the covenant is the goal to which
all single statements are directed, and only to that extent is the inner origin, then of course on the basis of the second account the
reverse may be asserted: here creation already prefigures the covenant; indeed, to that extent it already anticipates it (262) . The
new name for God (Yahweh-Elohim) immediately attests this
fact. The God, who acts in this place, is " Yahweh-Elohim, the God
who has revealed his name to Israel, who under this name has
elected and called Israel, and who has dealt with it as its Lord "
(265) . To this corresponds the fact that here (Gen. 2:4 b) the sequence runs: " Earth and heaven." Attention is directed first to
the earth, and for its sake to man, whose existence is now " very
simply that of one commissioned for a service and a work " (269) .

The " humanity " of this man rests " upon God's utterly free
and wholly special electing and turning toward him " (268) . In
this electing and turning toward him by God, man is assured of
being " a living creature." He " does not *have* but *is* that which he
is formed from the earth " (277 f.) . " By the hand and breath of
the same God " he is " altogether both: earthly and living, body
and soul, visible and invisible, inward and outward." For this rea-

son the body certainly cannot be for him " a disgrace, nor a prison, nor an endangerment to the soul at all " (276). But he is what he is exclusively from the Creator. " He is a creature absolutely dependent upon God not ceasing to encounter him anew in this way. . . . He would no longer be man if God were to stop doing it and thus being his Creator " (280)! Ezekiel, ch. 37, is therefore " the strongest commentary on Gen. 2:7 in the Old Testament " (281).

Now this man is transferred to a particular place. To the temporal sanctuary of the Sabbath in the first account corresponds the local sanctuary of " paradise " here in the second (288). However, this sanctuary has for its part a center, a " holy of holies," namely, the two trees (291). Initially, that is, " prior " to Gen. 3:22, there is no intimation that man is denied the tree of life. But it is remarkable that he does not lay hold of it, in fact, not even after the Fall. " Great as was his fall, he was nevertheless supported and upheld even in his fall; he nevertheless remained a possible subject for a future salvation in the fact that the matter actually rested with that previous, voluntary desisting from (the tree of life). He had to die. . . . But he did not do what his condemnation to an eternal, irretrievable dying would have had to mean — a dying which from the first ruled out all resurrection " (292). And so even the Fall cannot have rendered " untrue " the fact that this tree of life (" the center of paradise ") was " the sign of the homeland " (292). The promise of life is held out even for the man thrust into death.

But what about the other tree? It is not (like the tree of life) a sign of a " God-given reality " but a sign of a " possibility God held up and showed to man " (293). " With it God himself shows man " a " possibility of an unheard-of elevation of the creature " (293). For " to know about good and evil, to be able to distinguish and so to be a judge between what ought and ought not to be, between Yes and No, salvation and destruction, life and death, means to be like God, means even to be the Creator and Lord of the creature " (293)! But just this possibility would be death. And the prohibition to eat of this tree is therefore " an act of God's Fatherly and providential care " (294). Death is therefore not a threat added to strengthen the prohibition. On the contrary, " God

forbids because he wants to safeguard man against the threat involved in doing what is forbidden " (294) . " He wants to preserve
what he has created " (295) . But admittedly the threat is then " so
unavoidably necessary that God himself cannot stay its execution "
(295) . God's will has disdainfully passed by this other tree, death,
that is, man's arbitrary knowledge of good and evil; and this means
that it is God's creative will that man should put into effect the
proper and legitimate knowledge of good and evil the Creator has
willed. He should accept God's own knowledge of good and evil,
and glorify God in it (296) . Man is to let him alone be the judge.
If he himself becomes the judge, then he is " a helpless, lost bearer
of divine responsibility " (298) .

But why does the Creator point out to man this other, this impossible, futile, and deadly, possibility? It is true that with it a
freedom is attributed to man. " In this order man is indeed required to acknowledge God's office to judge in his sovereign freedom and therewith consciously to live in obedience to God. But it
is not made a physical necessity " (300) . And " moreover he is
here forbidden " to eat of the tree of knowledge, " though it is not
made physically impossible " (300) . And yet the freedom ascribed
to man is " not a freedom of choice between obedience and disobedience." It is not a " playground on the edge of an abyss," not
a " place midway between obedience and disobedience " (300) .
No, the meaning of the prohibition is " that God has created man
. . . with the ability to verify and confirm his obedience, and for
a decision of his own " (301) . Obedience is " to take place as his
own decision " (301) . So man does not stand " in the middle between good and evil." He stands before God in such a way that he
" is not only subject to the divine decision but can respect it in the
form of a decision of his own " (302) . This " freedom to be obedient " is " the characteristic feature of the fellowship between God
and man already established in his creation " (302) .
    But with this attention is directed, in advance, to all that Scrip-
ture says about the relation between God and man. On the one
hand we see Israel's idolatry as the " final consequence . . . of
man's usurped (unlawfully assumed) knowledge of good and
evil " (309) , and on the other hand, the gift of the divine com-

mandment, with which God graciously recalls Israel from that way
of death and assures it that it lives from its election (308 f.). What
the story of paradise "announces" takes "its shape" in Israel's
history. "However, it is only its provisional form" (314). It receives its final form in the Person "of the Jewish Messiah Jesus of
Nazareth " (315).

The climax of the second account of creation is "the completion
of man's creation, by woman being associated with man" (329).
" In order to be God's partner in this covenant man himself needs
a partner " (331). Indeed, Barth can say that "in virtue of his nature he must be formally prepared for grace " (331). The episode
with the animals (Gen. 2:19 f.) by no means signifies an "unfortunate divine experiment." Rather it serves to bring out that man
" was to recognize, choose, and affirm the assistance appointed and
created for him as such " (334). The man who decides in favor of
being a man does not have the disposal of himself in such a decision, but "decides in favor of a decision that has befallen him "
(335). The deep sleep into which he falls ought then to signify that
man " does not actively share in the creation of woman and so in
the completion of his own creation" (336). However, God does
not create woman merely as a part of man, as something which he
nevertheless had to recognize as "a creature with an independent
character and structure of its own " (338 f.). Rather, he also leads
her to him. "He creates not only I and Thou, man and woman,
but also their relation to one another as such " (340 f.).

But what is meant by that? Barth expresses his misgivings in regard to the familiar idea of an "original state." A "state" would
somehow mean a "standing" by man on his own, and certainly
this account is not concerned with anything like that. "They first
began to 'stand' after they had 'fallen'! " (351). "Man's own
state, his accomplishments and the demonstration of his virtue,
was actually, in distinction to God's primitive state, immediately
his guilty state " (352). This "original state," if we should speak
of such a thing, is in reality nothing but "the clear, necessary reflex of the covenant of grace " (364). The second creation account
points to it from the standpoint of its beginning; the Song of Solomon points to it from the standpoint of its goal (360); and the

prophets point to it insofar as they describe Yahweh's relation to Israel as a covenant of marriage. Ephesians 5:25 f., as a "commentary on Gen. 2:18 f. and on the Song of Solomon as well," points to it in its completion in the New Testament (367). But just because this relation has found its fulfillment not in Israel but solely in the " King who was granted to Israel, rejected by it, but exalted by God," in Jesus Christ, therefore texts like Gen., ch. 2, or the Song of Solomon could "form only the rim " of the Old Testament witness "and not its center." Only " the witness to the Son, the One awaited," could stand in the " center " (370). Thus the second account of creation, instead of being a testimony to a " lost paradise " which makes doleful reading, becomes a joyous announcement of him who has loved and sanctified the congregation for himself in a divine offering up of himself (Eph. 5:25 f.).

It should have become clear in what way and in what sense Barth could provide the most exhaustive section of Vol. III, 1, with the title: " Creation and Covenant " (§ 41). In his teaching, covenant and creation are strictly related to each other. Creation is " the external presupposition of the covenant " (first account), and the covenant is " the internal presupposition of creation " (second account). Consequently the doctrine of creation loses the character of something that properly belongs to the past — an idea that so easily clings to it. In fact, to the superficial observer it may seem as if we are faced with an unavoidable dilemma. *Either* we understand creation as the secret origin of what exists and hence God as the " meaning " of the world, and grace as the transcendence of nature, in which case " creation " is indeed something that is apparently present, but certainly it is not what the Bible understands by the word; *or* we understand creation as a unique act in the past before the Fall. Then God is really a former Creator. Then sin has removed God from the world. Then we cannot confess: " I believe in God the Creator. . . ." It can scarcely be denied that the familiar presentations move along one of these two lines with innumerable variations. Barth follows neither the one line nor the other. No one any longer needs to be told today that Barth does not understand creation as the secret ground of all things. And this report should have made it clear that neither does he understand it as an event belonging to the past and withdrawn from us — however much attenuated or converted. And thence we will now understand why Barth, who understands creation from the side of God's covenant with man fulfilled in Jesus Christ, is able to speak of the " Yea of God the Creator " in the final section of this volume (§ 42, pp. 377–476) .

Barth's presupposed thesis is as follows: " The work of God the Creator consists chiefly in the blessing [3] that what he has created may, within the limits of its creatureliness, exist as actualized by him and may be good as justified by him " (377) .

God's work is a Yea! To be sure it is also a Nay — the Nay of rejection, of preterition, of nonelection. But that which is rejected does not possess true reality. (We recall how often we have already come upon this fundamental truth. For Barth there is absolutely no dualism, no splitting up of reality into two conflicting, balanced " principles.") " Only God's creature is truly real outside of God. And only what is real outside of God is truly God's creature." And so it follows that " what God has not made, what is therefore unreal, must be an object of the divine wrath and judgment " (379) .

Admittedly, however, the knowledge that God's creation is a blessing is impossible as an expression of some kind of optimism. It depends solely upon the fact that God's creation and God's covenant are connected, and it is destroyed with any loosening of this connection (380) . " That the divine creating has the character of a blessing follows, . . . in whatever light it may be viewed, from the fact that it has its purpose and meaning in the covenant between God and man. God's revelation in Jesus Christ, as the fulfillment of the covenant, therefore . . . makes this knowledge imperative " (380) . When creation and covenant are separated, our thinking then falls into what is " diametrically opposed " (382) to the statement that creation is a blessing. Barth illustrates this on the one hand in Marcion, who wanted to know only about the covenant, and nothing about creation, and consequently arrived at a picture of God " without the world " (387) . Likewise, on the other hand, he illustrates this in Schopenhauer, whose picture of the world is without God, and of which it must therefore be true:

---

[3] " Wohltat." Rendered " blessing " in the sense of a beneficent gift, a boon.

" A creation from which God has been excluded can be for honest eyes only an evil creation " (389) .

Meanwhile the Christian doctrine of creation is to be distinguished entirely from every so-called " Weltanschauung." " It not only has a different source, but its subject matter is different. Consequently it takes a different course " (390) . For the divine creating, which is its subject matter, can " never become the subject matter of a Weltanschauung " (390) . But this sentence does not mean, as Barth stresses in an important qualification, that the " pure becoming," which first of all establishes all knowing and being, might not also come within the field of vision of a Weltanschauung. It is true that this does not apply to all Weltanschauungen that have hitherto appeared. But in all of them the problem as such has been posed and " a Christian doctrine of creation would do away with itself, if it were to reckon with the possibility of a Weltanschauung which could be objectively relieved of this disturbing problem " (391) . So in no case can theology simply cast in its lot with skepticism (391) . But even if a Weltanschauung, on its own presuppositions and with its own methods, were once to hit upon the problem of " pure becoming," and to that extent were to arrive at a sort of parallel to the Christian doctrine of creation (which in itself is not out of the question) , even then there would remain a fundamental difference. The Christian doctrine, that is, the doctrine that God in Christ is the Creator, must " confess and recognize " that creation, just as " God's work in Jesus Christ," is a " blessing," whereas a Weltanschauung by nature is not able to do this (393) . So Barth then defines the relation of the doctrine of God the Creator to Weltanschauungen in a few propositions which have to be rendered briefly: 1. The Christian doctrine of creation " cannot itself become a Weltanschauung." 2. " It cannot support itself on a Weltanschauung." 3. It cannot " guarantee any Weltanschauung " (393) . 4. It " cannot enter into a ' debate ' with the Weltanschauungen "; that is, oppose them while in part agreeing with them and in part rejecting them. 5. It " carries on a discussion with the Weltanschauungen in such a way that it places beside and against them . . . its own knowledge of its own subject matter with the arguments and logical consequences peculiar to it, yet not professing to know everything better, but to know in another way." 6. It "meanwhile attends to its own task as part of Christian dogmatics. . . . If the *Weltanschauungen* are not able to help it with its task, so neither will it let itself be troubled by them in pursuing it . . ." (394).

According to Barth the "Yea" of the Creator signifies in the first place that He has "actualized" what has been made, and secondly, that he has "justified" it. Barth pursues these two ideas in detail in the conclusion of this volume (395–476). Any reader of this report will also discover that he needs a fuller explanation of them.

What is meant by "actualization"? It means "that the creature may exist by his Creator and so does exist" (395). "The creature may exist because God exists" (395). We note that here a conclusion is drawn from the reversal of the *analogia entis* Barth developed. Why is the world of men and things actually not an illusion? Why is it not "a form of the Nothing" (395)[4]? From the side of our "self-consciousness and consciousness of the world" this question does not permit of an answer. To be sure, it may be that it actually implies some existence. But whence do we know it? Whence do we even know that we ourselves "exist"? Do we then somehow push out beyond the consciousness of our own existence? No, we would have to have been already assured of the "existence" of ourselves and of our world, as it were, from the outside, from beyond the consciousness of our own existence! "A higher judge . . . would already have to intervene between the consciousness of our own existence and our supposedly inner and outer existence" (396). We would already have "to be told by our Creator that we, and what is outside us, are his creatures" (397). By our Creator — not by our God-consciousness! For even our God-consciousness still belongs to our consciousness (398 f.)! No, the "knowledge of creaturely existence rests entirely and exclusively upon God's self-disclosure and revelation. It is entirely and exclusively an echo and an answer of the creature to what his Creator has said to him" (400). And consequently "it has no interest in the dialectic of a knowledge based upon our consciousness of self, the world, and God" (400). "Normal" is here "only the full, boundless, and unreserved certainty . . . the grateful jubilation

4 "*Eine Gestalt des Nichts.*" See footnotes in Chapter XIII, p. 220.

of the creature over the existence of his Creator . . ." (401).
" The creature exists. We say that because God exists, and because
even God has told us that he and also the creature exist. God is
real. His creation is actualization. So his creature is also real"
(401).

Anyone familiar with traditional thought will find such sentences exceedingly audacious. Is not that which should first be
proved, namely, the reality of the Creator, here made the presupposition of the proof? Is not in this instance the customary sequence reversed, according to which human self-consciousness is
the basis from which everything else, including the reality of the
" idea of God," is first to be proved? Barth enters upon the subject
of discussion in an analysis of Descartes (401 ff.), just because he
most clearly reveals the questionableness of the characteristic
method, in that he at once makes the idea of God, " extracted "
from self-consciousness, to be the presupposition and proof for the
validity of our knowledge of ourselves and the world. In a certain
sense Barth admits this: " Because and as we believe in God, we
believe . . . that we exist, and not that we do not exist; and that
also the world around us exists, and not that it does not exist "
(414). But Descartes's initial mistake lies in not proceeding from
God's own self-witness, but from the " testimony of our own intel-
lect " (414). And for that very reason Descartes's idea of God does
not help us to obtain a certainty that we are not kept in nothingness. This certainty can befall us, as it were, only from a place entirely outside us, whence even our consciousness itself is involved in
a radical questioning. When the Creator himself tells us that we exist, then the vanity of all our positions, even of our consciousness
of self and the world, is unmasked. When the true answer is given
to us, then it first becomes evident how radically we are called in
question. But Descartes got no farther than consciousness. That is
to say, his question was not a radical one — because he did not
start from the revelation of God the Creator but from an innately
given idea of God (415).

But what is meant by the " existence " which the Creator guarantees his creature? By somewhat overstraining Barth's mode of
expression at this point, we can put it best by saying that this " existence " is a full existence. Barth expresses it this way: " God does

not live a barren existence as Creator. Rather, he exists in the
overflowing fullness of his life as Father, Son, and Holy Spirit "
(415). God's Creator-will is truly his covenant-will! And consequently neither does " the creature live a barren existence, but
just as the sphere and object of the covenant, as that existence for
which God intended his pleasure, namely, to share in the overflowing of his fullness " (416). It is the grace of the Creator, which
the Word imparts to us. And the Church " recognizes the existence of the Creator and the existence of his creature in that the
Creator is gracious to his creature " (417). That, therefore, is the
reality which the Creator establishes: not an empty existence " in
itself," as it were, but this existence from and in the Creator's
grace.

With that we have already come to the second thought: " creation as justification " (418 ff.). The meaning is, as we already
heard, that the creature may " be good " (377). " Its existence is
not a neutral one; it is not a bad existence but a proper one "
(418). " It was very good! "
Now it is similar with the goodness of the creature as with its
existence. That is, the Christian doctrine of creation is not affili-
ated with other interpretations, according to which the self or the
world " exist " or " are good." In speaking of the goodness of
the creature it is therefore not a matter here of " introducing the
thought of God in order to rescue an ' optimistic ' theory " (422).
Ordinary optimism is not necessarily an illusion. " Creaturely
existence has indeed something like a bright side to it " (424).
And theology will have to acknowledge that " there is a basis and
justification for even a positive opinion concerning what exists "
(424). But " God's self-disclosure is not bound to this fact of the
creaturely world becoming and being luminous " (425). For the
creaturely world only shines " in the reflection of its light " (425).
Even a " negative opinion about what exists " has " a justification and reason " (427). But " God's self-disclosure is as little
bound to the limiting darkness of existence as it is to its light "
(427). Indeed, (for very obvious reasons) Barth regards it as a
matter of course to call attention to this especially. The fact is that
one has indeed often acted " as if the real perfection of the crea-

turely world were first to begin where its immediate, immanent goodness has been given the lie, as it were, and where it has been unmasked as illusion, and its vanity disclosed " (426). We have seen how Barth ever again guards against letting the Christian witness become lost in an alliance with nihilism, cynicism, or skepticism. So neither does he want to make it an ally of pessimism. God's self-disclosure " takes place in the highest: even in the highest above the misery of existence, fundamentally beyond even the greatest convulsions . . ." (428). Thus, just as there is no way leading from our high places to God's so also there is no way from our depths upward to him. There is not even a negative " natural theology "! (We need to hear that especially in Germany. . . .)

But in view of this manifest discordance in the creaturely world, how is one still to speak about " creation as justification "?

How are we to understand — in the first place — that God's self-disclosure " confirms," and " at any rate also includes," both " aspects " of reality, the bright as well as the dark? (430). How are we to understand that it plainly requires us " to laugh and to weep, to rejoice and to lament " (430)? We can understand it only when we remember the strict relatedness of creation and covenant. On the strength of this covenant the creature is actually subject to a " double determination." " In God's sight the creature possesses an importance and value " in virtue of being God's partner in the covenant. But it is equally clear that in God's sight he stands in need and peril as a creature utterly dependent upon God and His covenant. And the one aspect is just as peculiar to him as the other. The creature is " not Nothing, but Something; but Something on the brink of the Nothing "! (430).

But now — in the second place — it must also be said and understood that God surpasses both of these " aspects " on his own. God's self-disclosure does not allow the creature to hang uncertainly and precariously between brightness and darkness, but it says " unconditionally ' Yes ' and unconditionally ' No ' " (431), and carries the brightness as well as the darkness to its profoundest depths. The reason for this is that God " makes " both aspects of the creature " his own affair." The " humiliation and exaltation " of Jesus Christ " is the self-disclosure of God the Creator " (432). In him the Creator has given the creature a dignity otherwise unthinkable, and has revealed in him a neediness the mind could not suspect; in him he has made " himself the subject of both aspects of existence "! (432) .

Because — thirdly — and only because God has done this has it become manifest that existence is " good in its totality." The Creator himself has borne the " contradiction of creaturely existence." He has " interested himself in the creature before it existed," namely, in his Son (436) . It is true that he has not therewith relieved the creature, standing in this contradiction, of a struggle (435) , but he has made it " to be a free and joyous struggle, delivered from all willfulness and vexation " (435) . " The ' nevertheless ' has already been uttered. . . . This divine ' nevertheless ' is the justification of existence. It is not only permitted but necessary to Christian faith because it has been commanded. It is the freedom in which man may not only be calm before God the Creator but may also become contented with Him, and therefore with His creature's world as well . . ." (436) . Or we may put it in another way: " Because God has suffered to be what we are and as we are, he bears us " (438) ! But God the Creator has also thereby given us the certainty that the discordant aspects are not the last word. God's covenant is aimed at combating and overcoming the " imperfection " of the creature (441) . So Christian faith knows " better than all forms of optimism that the last word about the creaturely world is a positive and not a negative word " (443) . And its " Nay to the creaturely world " (442) , which appears to approach that of pessimism, is directed " never against creatureliness as such, but against the Nothing . . . against sin and death . . ." (442) .

And finally — in the fourth place — we can now see how it is that God's self-disclosure, as it confirms and surpasses both these aspects of existence, and as it reveals to us the perfection of existence in its co-ordination, mediates to us a sure, definitive, and conclusive knowledge of everything (443) . In other words, because we do not have to do with an idea, but with the Creator who discloses himself in Jesus Christ, so a position in this creaturely world is thereby given to us. It is not the position of optimism or pessimism, or a neutral position between the two (444) . It is rather the position of one who, in this existence, may believe in the love of the Creator, and may therefore have trust and confidence in the midst of the tension and discordance of this creaturely world.

Barth clarifies the nature of this Christian confidence by comparing it, in a magnificent vista, with the optimism of the period of the Enlightenment, as Leibniz first developed it. After what has gone before, one will expect, and then also find it confirmed, that Barth is not likely to make a frontal attack, as it were, upon this enlightened optimism because it was " optimistic." What he urges against it is this: that although it was " not exactly lacking " in the knowledge of Jesus Christ (475 f.), it then let it go at that, and when it spoke about the Creator and his goodness, it was not thinking simply of the Father of Jesus Christ, but of a God it already thought it was sure of from some other source — and in this it was following the tradition of the Middle Ages. For that reason it had to give a false interpretation to the dark " aspect " (466). Nor for that reason could it let even the bright side be really bright, but furnished it with superlatives, and vigorously defended it (468). Therefore, for all its sincere appeals to God, in the last analysis he was nevertheless not indispensable to it (470 ff.). And consequently, thoroughly uncertain of its subject, it remained at bottom in the attitude of an observer and a spectator (473 f.). So over against the optimism of the Enlightenment the resultant view is more than ever what Barth now quite explicitly calls a " Christian optimism " (474). — And it may be remarked that this " optimism " lasts, even after its secular opponent no longer finds a following anywhere!

XI

MAN

[Volume III, 2, pp. 1–780]

THE SINGLE chapter (the tenth in the entire work), which forms the content of Vol. III, 2, of the *Church Dogmatics,* bears the title: " The Creature " — a chapter of almost eight hundred pages. Now Barth starts with the fact that " a theological doctrine of the creature " . . . is " in fact anthropology . . . a doctrine of man " (2). By this he certainly does not mean that God, the " Creator of heaven and earth," made only man. It cannot be gainsaid that man lives in the cosmos God has made. However, a theological doctrine of the creature has to take into consideration that God's Word treats " of God and of man " (5), and that consequently we are doubtless given an ontology of man, but not an " ontology of heaven and of earth " (5). In other words, faith " believes in God in his relation to man who exists under heaven on earth; it does not believe in this or that constitution of heaven and earth " (7).

There is therefore no Biblical world view, no Biblical cosmology, no Biblical " *Weltanschauung.*" It is true that from time to time the Biblical witness can be associated with different types of cosmologies (6). But it is not really necessary (7), and never in such a way that a quite definite and invariable cosmology might set itself up as " the " Biblical or Christian cosmology. If faith, on the contrary, were to be linked absolutely to one cosmology, there would be a " partial apostasy " from faith (9). For " cosmology always arises there — in a vacuum — where God's Word, with its peculiar communication, has not yet found a hearing and an obedience with man, or has lost it again " (10). In fact, Barth emphasizes that even " exact science," as long as it remains conscious of its limitations, cannot arrive at an " ontology of the universe " (12 f.). " There is no world view in exact science " (12).

" The bright spot in the world in regard to its relation to God, and from which it is illumined in regard to its relation to God," is

man (19). And therefore a theological doctrine of the creature
has to begin at this point.

Yes, but does not the whole Bible speak of the relation between
God and man? What then is to be the purpose of a special anthropology? Barth replies that anthropology inquires " only about the
human creatureliness presupposed in this relation, and made
known . . . to us by this relation " (20). " It asks: What sort of
being is related to God and with which God stands in that relation? " (20). However, with this question (need it still be said?)
theology does not reach out beyond the sphere of revelation, or
back behind it, but receives from God's Word the basis and truth
of its statements about man (21).

Christian anthropology has to reckon with the fact that there
are also " all sorts of quite different anthropologies " (22). There
is " speculative " anthropology, arising always from a particular
Weltanschauung (23 ff.). In every form it is the " enemy," " which
cannot be met otherwise than by opposing the Christian confession to it " (24). There is an " exact science of man," such as human physiology, biology, psychology, or sociology (25), which " as
such " . . . can " not be an enemy of the Christian confession of
faith " (26). But that science has something else in mind than
Christian doctrine does. It thinks of man as a phenomenon, but
not of man himself, man in his " reality " (27).

But what about this " reality " of man? Where is the point at
which theology must begin if it is to lay hold of it? God's revelation
shows us man — and that is where the problem is to be tackled —
not at all in his creatureliness, but in its " perversion and corruption " (29) ! Man is a " sinner against his creaturely nature " (29).
Now of course it must be said at this juncture " that even as a sinner man is and remains who he is — God's creature " (30). " It
therefore ought not to be said that he no longer exists as the one
God has made " (30). But now how are we to be able to distinguish between man's corruption and man's creatureliness? It could
be done only by our " minimizing " his corruption (31 f.) — and
we are absolutely prevented from doing that. On the other hand,
" the question about the human nature God has made " still remains . . . " meaningful and necessary " (33). The sinner is a
creature! And we also know it. However, " we do not owe this

'nevertheless' of our knowledge to the power . . . of our observation and judgment, but solely to the light of God's Word, just as
we do not already owe the 'nevertheless' of the fact, here to be
known, to our ability . . . but solely to the grace of the same
Word of God . . ." (34). We can know neither our sin nor our
creatureliness, our "nature," by our own ability. Both insights
can be "achieved only in the overlapping knowledge of God's
Word; that is, however, in the knowledge of man as the partner in
the covenant God has concluded with him . . . as the object of
the eternal grace of his Creator and Lord" (34 f.). "If man is the
object of God's grace, then his self-contradiction, as radical and
complete as it is, is actually not the last word which has been said
about him" (35).

Inasmuch as God's covenant and grace is truth, the subject has
to be pursued even still farther. Sinful man "as such," not seen in
the light of God's grace, is not "the real man" at all (36). "The
real man is the sinner who participates in God's grace" (36).
(Again we note how Barth wants to warn against taking sin more
seriously than grace.) Even if we think of the fact that man as a
sinner stands under judgment (36 f.), we must at the same time
consider that "even God's reaction to man's sin . . . is the form
of his grace" (37). "God does not let go of man. So neither can
man be released from his creatureliness, and so from his humanity" (38). Therefore we are unable to regard man's "sin" and
"denature" as an "autonomous principle" (41). To be sure, we
are not able to "relativize" it; that is, somehow to classify it or
distinguish it from our creaturely "nature." But God has "rela-
tivized" it "at the outset" in his grace, and therefore we on our
part may "not absolutize" it (42). God's freedom, that is, the
freedom of his grace, triumphs over our sin (which we can know
in its reality only as those who have been pardoned; 41).

What we certainly can never at any time know about ourselves,
God "knows" about man. And just that which God alone
"knows" about man is "his creaturely nature" (43 f.). However, Barth is also able to say the same thing in another way.
"God's way of acting against sinful man, as revealed in his Word,"
occurs "under the presupposition and within the sphere of the
particular conditions of human existence, which are all indeed de-

termined by sin, but are not changed in their structure by it"
(46). And " by man's creaturely nature " is to be understood " the
total conception of these conditions " (46).

The last-mentioned sentences could be misunderstood to mean
that Barth nevertheless now wanted to discover on or in man —
even if it is merely knowable quite indirectly — something untouched by sin. But how little this is his meaning is shown by the
main thesis of the first section of our chapter, which now immediately follows (" Man as a Problem in Dogmatics "; § 43 in the entire work) : " Since the man Jesus is the revealing Word of God,
he is the source of our knowledge of the human nature God has
made " (47). The first explanatory sentence immediately shows
the connection with the preceding: " God's conduct, in which the
faithfulness of the Creator is manifest and knowable, and therefore the constant conditions of human existence created by him as
well, are quite simply his conduct toward the man Jesus " (47).
Let us note: here we have before us the main point upon which
this whole thought turns. " Ecce homo! " " Behold the man! "
(John 19:5).

With this choice of a starting point Barth has done nothing less,
as he himself stresses, than " ground anthropology upon Christology " (50). The development of the doctrine of man is therefore
to take place — in a departure from tradition — in such a way
that " point for point " attention is first of all directed to the nature of man " as it meets us in the Person of the man Jesus," and
thence first to man's nature " as the nature of every man, of all
other men " (54).

Naturally Barth has no thought of " deriving " anthropology directly from Christology (54). " For he (Jesus) indeed becomes
what we are, but he does not do what we do, and so he is certainly
not now what we are " (55). " He alone is primarily and really
elected . . . the receiver and bestower of grace at the same time.
We can always be only those who have received grace " (57). He
is sinless (59). Of course, his sinlessness " does not consist in a
special constitution of his creaturely nature, by which he would
be so to speak physically removed from sin " (59). It is rather " because he, as the Bearer of human nature, was . . . its Lord " (60),
and thereby held his ground against temptation. And finally the

difference between him and us is that only in him is the real existence of the creature revealed (60 f.), whereas in us it remains un-
recognizable. But in all that, Jesus' nature has, " it is true, another
state " than ours, " but not a different constitution." If we wanted
to look at it otherwise, our Christology would become docetic (63).

Upon this foundation Barth now develops the next section:
" Man as God's Creature " (§ 44, pp. 64–241).

Consequently he begins with a Christological point of view:
" Jesus, the Man for God." The Bible answers the question, Who
is the man Jesus? by testifying to his peculiar historical work. " Jesus is by all means the Bearer of an office " (66). He has no human
existence apart from this office; it is given with the office. " There
is no neutral humanity of Jesus " (66). The Biblical witness is
not at all interested in an ex officio life of Jesus, as it were. In
fact, one must say that " Jesus not only has a history but is himself
this his history " (69) ; that he " not only does, but is his work."
And this work is the work of a Saviour (69). But that means that
this work of his is God's work. " He acts in God's cause, and just
thereby and so in his own " (72). " This man's work consists in
refraining from all other works to do God's work. And to be one
with God in the performance of this work is . . . this man's existence " (73 f.). Hence we can go farther. Barth asks what then
would result as man's reality, if the Person of the Man Jesus were
the only source of our information about it. (He puts the question
in this way as a possible hypothesis; for, as already mentioned, he
knows very well what a difference otherwise yawns between the
man Jesus and men.) Within this particular parenthesis the following may now be stated about the reality of man (or about his
creatureliness) : 1. Man is, " among all creatures, the one in whose
identity with himself we must also immediately establish the identity of God with himself. If God's presence in all other creatures is
for us at least problematical, it is here incontrovertible . . ." (79).
2. God is the One who acts in this man. (Let us remember: in *this*
man, in this *one* man!) " His presence in him consists in the history of his salvation coming to pass " (79). 3. God " does not
thereby lose himself in man." . . . " His willing and doing is and
remains wholly his own " (80). In his action (that is, in his sav-

ing) he demonstrates his sovereignty, his honor. 4. This man, in whom it takes place, exists " within God's dominion "; indeed, he " is the coming Kingdom of God " (80). 5. This man exists wholly in His office and work. He is himself the history he effects. 6. To sum up: this man is " the creature who exists for God " (82).

Let it be stated once again that we cannot read what man is from these statements about the man Jesus. And yet Barth takes from them, as the presupposition for the question about man's nature, first of all the stipulation that the nature of man must be understood " at any rate as one standing naturally in some kind of relation to God " (83). Never at any time will we be able to admit " that a truly godless man is the real man " (84). However, from the above six Christological propositions it is possible to recognize further at least six boundary points, within which the nature of man can be theologically defined. 1. Man's nature must " be seen as coming from God, and above all it must be seen as leading to God " (85). 2. Man's nature occurs in history, and what is more, in a history connected with the history of the man Jesus. 3. Man has his destiny in the honor of God. 4. He stands under God's sovereignty. 5. His freedom " consists in his freedom to decide for God . . ." (86). 6. His existence is spent in " rendering service to God " (86). But these six points are no more than boundary points. With them we have not yet reached a " theological concept of man." It is to be found only " as we contrast man as such . . . with the man Jesus " (86).

At the same time those six points offer the criteria by which other conceptions of man may be judged. These conceptions could indeed still point to particular " phenomena of the human," to which even theology has cause to pay heed.

Barth first mentions the naturalistic conception of man and, in connection with it, the theological apologetic, which was so very anxious to defend man's special place in the biological world over against the Darwinian theory. Barth's answer is that if we want to do this we first need to know about this special thing in man from some other source. By the means used in apologetics we only arrive at a limited, relative knowledge of this special element. What is actually observable are just " phenomena " of the human, but not man's reality.

The second conception of man to which Barth turns is that of idealism. (He takes Fichte's *The Vocation of Man* as an example of it.) It is the phenomenon of human conduct, of " ethics," and of " practical reason " which here becomes the central thing (at which in this connection Barth takes into thorough account concepts like " person " and " personality "). In Barth's opinion " it is a good thing that our view of man is able to move out of the narrow confines of naturalism into the broad field of ethics. But once again it is not so good that we could be persuaded to have thereby advanced to the real man, to man's peculiarity in creation " (111). Even the significant fact that the man who is understood ethically and idealistically finds that he is identical with himself " in two realms " (110) cannot deceive us about the fact that man's peculiarity would first have to be known to us from another source, in order for it to be apparent to us here. Even here we do not push beyond the phenomenon.

The same is true, finally, of existentialism (which Barth describes, drawing freely upon Jaspers). In this instance, to be sure, there is an advance to a " crisis situation." And " the advantage " which the anthropology of existential philosophy has over the other two is " that it would like man's existence to be seen as his movement and in his fundamental openness; as his action in relation to another than himself and in his encounter with this other, instead of being grounded, reposing and moved in himself " (134). But what it lacks is " any concrete certainty in regard to man's counterpart . . . which establishes this movement " (134). And who proves to us that this " counterpart " has met us just in these crises? Does not contemporary man — after all! — prove that it need not be so? " Mankind has a tough hide . . ." (135). " The Lord was not in the storm, nor in the earthquake, nor in the fire (I Kings 19:11 f.). No, not at all " (135). In fact, " it is simply not so that certain situations, specially weighted in the negative, have, as such, a way of being the bearers of the mystery of transcendence and so of the mystery of human existence " (135). Besides, do not the majority of men react just to crises with notorious indifference (138 f.)? And when a man is admonished to become conscious of the transcendent through unconditional surrender, is it not actually presupposed that he already secretly carries it along with him

(140) ? Has not the break-through into transcendence thereby become an illusion (141) ?

Barth concludes these reflections thus: " We have not caught sight of the real man along this entire way " (140) . Phenomena of the human, to be sure; and hence none of these three conceptions could be flatly contradicted (144) . However, they are only phenomena. Everything that is to be known along those ways is " parenthetical." " The decisive instruction about man " can " not ensue within this parenthesis. On the contrary, it can, at all events, be expected only from a place and a factor outside this parenthesis " (145) . The relation of man to God, which all these experiments for their part more or less rule out, proves to be, noetically (that is, in knowing) and ontically (that is, in being) , the constituent fact for the reality of man: " Man is never without God " (146) . If, however, it is man's nature that he is constituted by God's Word — as Barth admits in a discussion which follows now of Emil Brunner's " Man in Contradiction " [1] — then his nature has therewith been decided upon; then he does not find himself in the situation of having a " merely neutral capacity " (as Barth ascertains to be Brunner's position) , but in his reality (156) .

Thus the way is open for Barth's " constructive " statements. The last part of the section may be entitled " The Real Man." We are able to speak about him if — with Barth — it has been clear that " the ontological determination of man is grounded in the fact that in the midst of all other men there is the one man Jesus " (158) . It may be expressed in another way: every man is " as such Jesus' fellow man " (159) . In the Person of Jesus man is " placed before his divine counterpart " (160) . " Man is together with God because he is together with Jesus " (163) . And " consequently " godlessness is " an impossibility " (as surely as it is also, according to Barth, a fact). Rather, it is " the ontological impossibility of human existence." " If he denies God, then he denies himself " (162) .

Now, of course, " every creature " has " the same concrete divine counterpart in common with man " (164) . But " what secretly

[1] Translated into English under the title *Man in Revolt* by Olive Wyon. The Westminster Press, Philadelphia, 1947.

constitutes the existence of all creatures is revealed as human existence because Jesus is man " (165) .

But how is this human existence materially defined? Barth gives
a twofold answer. In the first place it is, " as a togetherness with
Jesus, an existence which rests upon God's election " (170–176) .
Secondly it is, " again as a togetherness with Jesus, an existence
which consists in hearing God's Word " (176–188) . Barth then
summarizes both thus: " The existence of man is a history " (188–
196) .

Existence which rests upon *election!* " Man as such, insofar as he
exists together with Jesus and so with God, is himself a creature
elected in God's election by grace. We must put it more exactly:
he is conjointly or additionally elected " (174) . However, Barth
immediately adds that naturally it is not true of man *in abstracto.*
(Looking at man in and for himself, from his side, " The Fall "
would be rather " a straightforward ontological necessity "; 175.)
But man is seen as such a one " whose existence is a togetherness
with God " (175) . Man, then, can never simply appeal to his
" helplessness," to the " superior power of the Nihil," [2] to which
he had been delivered up. (We recall what has been said repeatedly.) If he decides against God, then " he thereby actually
does that for which there is no excuse, and for which only a restoration of a legal state, to be expected from God alone, and that means
only divine forgiveness, can intervene for his justification " (176) .
At any rate man as a creature is intended " to be victorious and
not to be overcome " (176) .

Existence which consists in hearing God's *Word!* " To be man
is to exist in that sphere of the creaturely world in which God's
Word is uttered and becomes known " (179) ! To that extent man
is " ' in the Word of God ' from the very first " (179) . Human
existence has absolutely nothing else " ahead of it "; it has its character as existence exclusively in the Word of the Creator. In itself
it has not even a potentiality for existence. Looked at by itself, it
actually exists *ex nihilo,* out of nothing. (Barth now enters into a
careful study of this concept; 182 ff.) The *creatio ex nihilo* (creation out of nothing) is " not a speculative construction, but the
most natural expression for man's understanding of himself based

2 " *Übermacht des Nichtigen.*" See footnotes in Chapter XIII, p. 187.

upon God's revelation in the man Jesus " (187).

Existence as *history!* " The history of a creature begins, continues, and ends because something other than itself, something
transcending its nature, encounters it, is added to it, and determines its existence in its own nature . . ." (189). The opposite
term for " history " is " state." Now actually, apart from the revelation in Jesus Christ, everything historical could also be interpreted
as a " state actuated in itself " (190). Only in virtue of the history
of Jesus Christ (that is, in virtue of the fulfilled election of grace
and the revealed Word!) can and must we speak of history in that
primary, original sense. " Existence is here the identity of the
Creator with the creature " (190) and, indeed, as an event. The
man Jesus *is* this event, this history. Other men are certainly not
this event. Rather, " their existence is history in or with the history which occurs in the existence of the man Jesus " (193). Perhaps we could also say: as man acquires an " existence in the
history founded by Jesus," he has real, human existence (193).
Or in still another way: " To be man means to be preserved by
God's mercy for Jesus' sake, and to adhere to God's righteousness
for Jesus' sake " (194).

To interrupt this report for a moment, some reader or other
may possibly think that Barth is always talking here about man,
while describing what is promised to the *Christian*. This is just
what should prove to be true. And this is just what is actually
necessary. For if passages like Eph. 4:24 or Col. 3:10 retain their
importance, then indeed the very thing that is promised and given
to the Christian as his own *in Christ* is just that he is a — creature,
a creature in God's image! So here, and in everything we further
read in Barth, we shall have to notice that what we have before
us is Christology and hence eschatology. And it is not the least of
Karl Barth's services that he has closed the circle of creatureliness
and salvation so securely.

Barth now concludes the discussions about the " real man " by
defining even more precisely that existence which is realized in
election, in hearing the Word, and in history. And he does so
again from two sides. Human existence, coming from God, is to
be understood as an existence under grace (196 ff.), which is cor-

respondingly realized in gratitude. It is an " existence in thanks-giving." And from man's side, human existence is defined as " responsibility " " toward God " (207 ff.). The " real man," man in his creatureliness, man in the reality of the man Jesus, man as Jesus' fellow man — this man is truly a " subject in pure spontaneity " (207). We no longer need to stress that he is not this of himself. An existence proceeding from himself would be nothing but the perversion of his existence. Therefore, it would not be spontaneity, not responsibility, and not freedom. The subject existence of the " real man " is an " act and . . . an occurrence of a response to God's Word " (208). But it is thereby, " in its place and in its way, itself a word." Yet certainly as a human word it is a " word of gratitude," and not " the Word of grace . . ." (209). It is a word in response.

As an existence in responsibility to God, human existence possesses the character " of knowledge of God " (209), " of obedience to God " (213), of invocation to God (222), and of " freedom God has given it " (229).

After Barth has spoken about the " real man," he can now return to those " phenomena of the human " already discussed. As we also remember, he had neither rejected them nor made them the basis of theological propositions. They never refer to the real man, but to a " shadow of man " (87, 236). Now, however, in retrospect, Barth can say that at the same time they indicate symptoms of the real man. Natural science seeks man in the cosmos — and the real man actually belongs within the cosmos. Idealistic ethics sees man " in the act of distinguishing himself in the midst of the cosmos " (239). It is demonstrated that the real man has the ability " to be an . . . active subject himself in his history " (239)! Existential philosophy sees man " in his openness toward that which is outside," outside " in a genuine transcendence " (239). And the real man is capable of being related to such an " extraneous entity " (and we heard Who it is). So even a non-theological, " yet proper," science of man is theologically " possible, justified in principle and necessary in principle " (241).

But " it certainly is not able to lead and guide us to the knowledge
of the real man." It can come only from there (241) !

In regard to its positive content Barth's anthropology is divided
into four sections, of which we have so far taken up the first (§ 44:
" Man as God's Creature "). Each further section, like the one already discussed, also begins with statements about the man Jesus,
in keeping with the Christological basis of this anthropology.
When (in § 45) the subject for discussion is man " in his appoint-
ment to be God's covenant partner," Barth begins with a subsection: " Jesus the Man for Other Men." When (in § 46) he speaks
about man " as soul and body," he begins with a part on " Jesus,
the Whole Man." And when finally, in the most exhaustive section, he presents us with explications of man " in his time " (§ 47),
he begins with " Jesus, the Lord of Time." Thus anthropology is
always developed (though not in a direct line) from the doctrine
of Jesus Christ.

Hitherto we have been speaking about man's " existence." And
Barth's reflections have pushed forward to the " real man "
through all the profusion of other (nontheological) anthropologies. But for what purpose has this man been created? That is the
question now to follow. Well, it could already be answered from
what has been said above: he is made for God. But we cannot
catch sight of the reality of Jesus of Nazareth without immediately
adding that " he is the man for other men " (248). Jesus does not
also exist for other men; that is, as if his existence for other men
were additional to his own nature. We are concerned here " with
a matter having an ontological character " (251). Jesus' humanity
is radically, " originally, and intrinsically cohumanity " (252).
Therefore he can only be thought of as " coming from and going
toward his fellow man " (257). That such is the case, however,
rests upon the fact that he " obeys God perfectly " (258); his
existence for man is first of all God's existence for man (259). But
with that we are referred back to the mystery of God himself, yes,
in God himself. God does not *also* exist for man. It is not something added to him. He does not *also* exist in relation to man.
Rather, " there is a relation . . . in his own inner divine being "

(260). And this relation, which " is repeated and portrayed " in
" God's eternal covenant with man," becomes " manifest and
effectual " in the fulfillment of this covenant " in the humanity of
Jesus in time " (261). So we have to say that over against his existence for God, Jesus' " existence " for his fellow man represents a
" correspondence and likeness integral to God." " His humanity
. . . is the image of God, the *imago Dei* " (261) ! It is understandable that at this point Barth again has recourse to the already developed concept of *analogia relationis* (262).

We are now able to go on from here in thinking further about
anthropology. Once again we cannot pursue our thought directly;
for " Christology is not anthropology " (264). What is " exclusively peculiar " to the humanity of the man Jesus — namely, the
direct relation of correspondence between God's relation in himself and his, Jesus', relation to other men — cannot possibly be
transferred to another man, who on the contrary is truly a sinner
and for that reason is neither an authentic " I " nor can have a
proper relation to a " Thou " (265). And yet by indirection we
can carry the thought farther. For with all the dissimilarity between Jesus and another man there is still agreement " in some
basic form." There is a " basic form of humanity," in which the
" presupposition " for it has been given in " that the man Jesus
can exist for him " (266). There is a " covenant capacity " of the
creature for his God (267). Naturally it is not a virtue, merit, or
right of man, but grace (267). What is this basic form of humanity?

From the preceding it follows of itself that there can by no
means be a humanity without the fellow man. Indeed, it would be
the very opposite of the humanity of Jesus. In impressive fashion
Barth shows with what uncanny consistency Nietzsche carried
both of these to their logical conclusion in " *Ecce homo*": a
humanity without the fellow man and a humanity against the Crucified (276 ff.). The one does not exist without the other — Nietzsche saw that with a clarity which one could have wished for theology.

To put the matter positively: when I say " *I*," I do not thereby
mean something empty, not an " abyss " (294), " but a full reality.

As I exist, there is also another like myself" (294). And that signifies: "humanity is the determination of our existence as an
existence in an encounter with another man" (296). "He who
says man, says history" (295). "I am, because thou art" (299).

Now this "existence in an encounter" is first of all "an existence in which one looks the other squarely in the eye." It means
above all that there is no vis-à-vis of one number of people and another. "Where one man imagines he sees and recognizes a group,
or a group an individual, or one group another group, there is already something at least approaching ambiguity" (301). In the
second place, existence in an encounter consists in "speaking to
another and listening to one another" (302). Thirdly, it consists
in mutual aid (312). "Both would be inhuman: an action in
which we refuse to help another person, and an action in which we
wanted to renounce his help" (314). And fourthly, it consists in
all this give-and-take "occurring gladly" (318); that is, not "neu-
trally" (320), nor with a capacity to do otherwise, but actually
out of the profound mystery of existence. Precisely with what we
have just said we stand before the "mystery" of humanity (319,
etc.). And we could forthwith characterize this peculiar freedom
(no longer the freedom to choose but to put into execution) as
man's "nature" (329).

Now Barth is very anxious to emphasize that humanity, so cir-
cumscribed, is not the same as Christian love (329 ff.). The latter
is "not a determination of human nature" (321), and conversely
it is not a matter of asserting that humanity might not also be
sought and found, at all events in the proper direction, outside of
the Christian sphere (333). If we remember especially that humanity does not mean solitude but companionship, it is also not at
all necessary to conceive the relation of Eros and Agape, of "natural" and Christian love, to be as sharply opposed, as is so often
done (340 ff.). We again note the importance Barth attaches to
this fact, though, of course, not in the — then mistaken — interest
of grace to "debase human nature as much as possible" (330).
And we also observe how wide is the arc within which he sees the
freedom of grace to be efficacious.

Humanity, however, " is not an ideal and not a virtue but an un-

assailable continuum of human existence " (349) . Here we again
note that Barth is not — as perhaps the last remarks could be misunderstood — speaking in praise of man. He is not speaking of an
accomplishment and worthiness man has somehow acquired, but
of a determination of his existence. And this is cohumanity. More
precisely it is the vis-à-vis of man and woman (at which we recall
Barth's exegesis of the second creation account in particular, to
which he again refers) . He frankly calls the passage about the creation of woman for man (Gen. 2:18–25) " the Old Testament
Magna Charta of humanity " (351) . The togetherness of man and
woman is " the original and true form of cohumanity " (353) .
Just in this form we see what Barth means when he speaks of " humanity being parable and hope." The unique position of marriage
is not founded upon the fact that naturally and sociologically it
represents a value above other values but upon the fact that " behind the relation of man and woman " stands " a governing archetype ": " the relation of the God Yahweh-Elohim to his people
Israel " (358) . And in the new covenant this relation is " revealed " as the relation of Jesus Christ to his congregation. The
New Testament does not speak gratuitously when it speaks about
Christ and the congregation and thereby " about the goal of all
heavenly and earthly things," about a marriage covenant (as Barth
then expounds it in a detailed explanation of II Cor. 11:2; Rom.
7:3 f.; I Cor. 6:16 f.; 11:11 f.; and especially of Eph. 5:22 ff.) . As
we know, Eph. 5:32 specifically speaks of a " mystery." Barth is
now able to assert more confidently than at the beginning of this
section that " man's humanity " is actually . . . " a mystery of
faith " (382) . He has now given us an insight into this mystery of
faith.

But is man — man in his cohumanity — really " God's covenant
partner "? Barth ends by insisting: no, he is not. He is certainly
" not by nature " (385) . He is created for the purpose of being so;
but this is not the way he is constituted. Thus the correspondence,
about which we have spoken so often, is always a correspondence
in dissimilarity, a correspondence by reason of hope. Only on the
strength of this hope may it be said that human existence is an
" existence corresponding to God himself," and that man is God's
image (390) .

But now how is human existence, so defined, constituted? What about its " *Dasein* and *Sosein* "? [3] The next section (§ 46) answers this question: " Man as Soul and Body." Once again let us immediately quote the presupposed thesis: " By God's Spirit man is the subject, the form, and the life of a material organism. He is the soul of a body — both completely and simultaneously: in an irrevocable diversity, in inseparable unity, in indestructible order (391).

As mentioned, Barth also begins here logically with Christological propositions (391–414). And in doing so he first explains that the pair of concepts " soul and body " do not so properly apply to Jesus. For the first impression the New Testament gives us of Jesus is that of a " united and whole " man (394). The fellowship we have with him is correspondingly not just a spiritual one, but affords us " a corporal contact and fellowship " (395). (This is said by a Reformed Churchman.) But just as surely it can also be " nothing else than a question of a secret — we would say ' inner ' or ' spiritual ' — tasting and sampling of the heavenly bread, of the powers of the world to come " (395). However, what immediately strikes the eye in the Biblical witness is that " the unity, the wholeness of this human life, is formed, constructed, and designed out of itself and hence it comes from within and is therefore necessarily and always sensuous " (399). " He is not only his soul, he is also his body " (400). " The New Testament has not even given the slightest intimation either of an emancipation of the corporal life of Jesus over against the psychical,[4] or even of an ascetic conflict of Jesus' soul against his body. The Spirit resting upon him manifestly makes the one to be impossible and the other superfluous " (407). And yet something further may be recognized. The oneness of this man Jesus is truly grounded in the oneness of his existence with the existence of God (410). And according to Barth one can say that in him " soul and body are so related to one another, as his nature as the Son and Word of God the Creator is related to his creaturely constitution as the soul and body of this man " (410). Between Jesus' soul and body there is therefore the same corresponding relation as there is between his

[3] " Thereness and thusness," or, " being there and being thus."
[4] " *Seelisch.*"

divinity and his humanity. A " corresponding relation " — nothing more. For " Jesus' soul is not his divinity " (410) ; " there are only the same proportions in which in the higher sphere divinity and humanity, in the lower soul and body, confront each other " (410). In fact, Barth poses the question " whether Jesus' soul and body might not also be so related to one another as heaven and earth in creation as a whole; or as justification and sanctification in Christ's work of reconciliation; or as the gospel and the law in God's Word; or as faith and works in man's responsibility to God; or as sermon and sacrament in the congregation's service of God; or as the confessional word and an attitude and action in keeping with a confession in her Confession of Faith; or as Church and State in the inner structure of Christ's Kingdom " (412). What perspectives!

" Wholeness in a rational ordering of human existence " — that is the picture of the man Jesus (413). This quality does not belong to our human existence. But Barth again infers, as we have already seen repeatedly: " The picture of the man Jesus requires an understanding of man which is governed by this point of view " (413).

Wherein lies the one thing by which wholeness is intended for man's life? Barth replies: In the fact that man exists from God (" we are his offspring "; Acts 17:28. It is " baptized wisdom, so to speak, and therefore no longer pagan wisdom "; 417). " Man lives and dies contingent upon God's being the living God " (419). But this applies to man as " soul of his body " (420). And it actually pertains to the " covenant partnership," for which man is destined, " that man exhibits the whole reality of creation and therefore also participates fully and seriously in the visible, material side, and so is not only soul but soul of a body " (423).

That opening sentence, however, that man " is soul of his body . . . by and from God, and moreover by and from Israel's God, and indeed by his ever-new act of grace," can and must be comprehended as follows: " Man exists because he possesses the Spirit " (425) — or " because the Spirit possesses him " (426). In this connection by " Spirit " is to be understood — as the existence and operation of the Holy Spirit *ad extra,* externally — " an action and attitude of the Creator with respect to his creature " (428).

The Spirit therefore operates not only in the " new " man, but the
Spirit is — in the sense of a presupposition and hope — to be
frankly designated as the " principle " of man's " creatureliness "
(432) . As he, in anticipation of the order of the covenant of grace
to be established in him, effects all creaturely life, so more than
ever does he effect the wholeness and unity of man's existence. " He
is the principle which makes man to be a subject " (437) . He is
the " ground of the soul and of the body," as Barth states in the
heading of the whole section we have here (very summarily) sur-
veyed.

Proceeding from this basic insight, Barth turns now to the question of the " inner structure " of our creatureliness (440) . He first
inquires about its inner unity; secondly about its differentiation,
that is, about the particularity of soul and body; and thirdly about
the order in their correlation.[5]
As to the unity of soul and body, Barth starts from the insight
(already previously underscored) that man indeed has Spirit but
he is not spirit. He is a creature through and through. So he cannot want to be a copy of the difference between Creator and creature perhaps in the difference between body and soul. That would
be " not only an insolent but a dreadful thought " (443) . Just for
this reason man can " only be relatively different" in himself
(445) . His soul is " not something like an extension and continuation " of God's creative " action," but it is a creature (447) . It
does not exist for itself but is the " animation of a body " (452) .
And moreover the body, as an animated body, ceases to be a " mere
carcass "; it becomes a " body " precisely in virtue of this relatedness to an active subject (453) . Thus man is " at once and altogether soul and body " (455) . A " Greek " (but also an Early
Church!) dualism is thereby forbidden, but likewise an abstract
monism (458 ff.) as well as a monistic spiritualism (468 ff.) . " If
materialism with its denial of the soul makes man ' subjectless,'
then spiritualism with its denial of the body makes him ' object-
less ' " (470) . Both solutions, however, result from " abstracting
the Spirit and so the act of the living God the Creator." When
that is done, one must also " make an abstraction between soul

5 " Zusammengehörigkeit," lit., " belonging together."

and body" (472). In the light of the Biblical witness we must speak, on the contrary, of a concrete monism (471) as of a concrete dualism (472) in opposition to every abstract solution.

In order to show " soul and body in their particularity," Barth first avails himself of the concept of " apprehending." [6] One who apprehends (like one who decides) is a man who apprehends " not without his body, nor as body, but as soul " (cf. 477). Now " the man who apprehends " is " always . . . a man apprehending God " (482). However, as a rule God does not encounter him directly, but indirectly, and so in the sphere of the creaturely world (which we do not perceive without the body). The act of apprehension is therefore twofold: " an act of perceiving and of thinking " (483). That is also true in the Bible, to which, by the way, the idea of a " special religious apprehension " is alien (492). However, within this twofold and complete happening we must then still speak of a " primacy of the soul " (486), and indeed because the soul is " man himself." Something quite similar may be recognized, when we have the other aspect of man's behavior in view, namely, " that he is able to be active . . . corresponding to that which he apprehends of God " (487). Even here there is a double feature: desiring and willing. Desiring is more peculiar to the body, willing to the soul (489 f.) ; but the soul, as the subject, first allows the desiring to be " my " desiring. In summarizing, Barth can say: " Man is the apprehending and active soul of his body, which puts his apprehension and activity into operation " (500).

When finally, as the conclusion to this section, Barth speaks about " the order of soul and body," he has already cleared the way by having asserted the " primacy of the soul " (in apprehending and in being active). He now condenses this knowledge by teaching that man is to be recognized as a " rational being " (502), and what is more, according to body and soul (503), but yet so that " the soul rules . . . the body serves " (505). Man, however, is a rational being (not of himself but) because " God has addressed him as such and because therein . . . it is presupposed that God has made him such " (507). If man understands himself as a rational being in this way, then he cannot possibly understand

6 " *Vernehmen.*"

himself as merely a soul (509 f.), merely as a body (510 f.), or as
a creature split up into a body and a soul as it were (511 f.). Only
then can he think of himself as a unity. Barth's intention is to show
this more clearly in a debate with the philosophical theory of psy-
chophysical parallelism, to which he opposes what is peculiarly
central to the Biblical understanding of body and soul and which
is absolutely unintelligible except theologically. There man is an
ordered unity in soul and body just because he does not carry in
himself that which makes him to be man and thereby a whole, but
receives it in God's Word. All this is shown most emphatically by
the Biblical concept of the " heart," with which Barth here concludes (523 f.).

The last section in this volume is the most exhaustive: " Man in
His Time " (§ 47, pp. 524–780!). Consequently it is at this point
that the reader of this concise report has to put up with the worst
abbreviations, and even drastic abbreviations at that.

The point at which Barth begins this investigation of his — he
embodies it in the title: " Jesus the Lord of Time " — lies in the
fact that " the man Jesus in this time was manifestly among them
(the witnesses of the resurrection) in the mode of God " (537).
What the New Testament would understand by the " time " of the
man Jesus is covered not only by the years 1 to 30, but is decisively
determined by the fact of Easter. (The debate in this connection
with Rudolph Bultmann's conception of Jesus' resurrection must
be omitted here. It has been reprinted as an extract in the sym-
posium *Demythologizing,* Confessional Church series, No. 4, Stutt-
gart, 1949, pp. 94–103.) " The time of Easter is . . . the time of
the revelation of the mystery of the time of the life and death of
the man Jesus previous to it " (546). We thereupon come to the
concept of " fulfilled time " in the sense of Gal. 4:4. The point
especially important to Barth is this: The fulfillment of time is
" itself a time-fulfilling event, an event that begins, continues, and
ends " (555). God's time is time " in the midst of other times "
(555). That means that " in its beginning, its duration, and its end
it happened then and there but once. It was present from the
standpoint of the times of certain other men. It was future from
the standpoint of yet other times. And it was past as seen from

still other times, as for example from our own " (555). If one
wanted to deny this, he would have to advocate a docetic Christology.

Jesus Christ — that mean's God's time in our time. But it does
not mean God's time within the limits of our time. Jesus' time
begins once and once was still future. " But that does not mean
that at that time it was not yet " (556). Jesus' time has a duration
and was once present. However, " that . . . does not signify that
it was present . . . only in this its duration." Jesus' life ends once;
his time became the past. " But that does not mean that it was once
no longer " (557). No, to all that we shall have to say: Jesus' time,
" as the time of a man," is " at once God's time " (557), " eternal
time." He is the Lord of time! His present, his past, his future, is
truly " his," " the man Jesus' own time " (574). " I am . . .
which is, and which was, and which is to come " (Rev. 1:8). Barth
now interprets this verse of the Bible by bringing to light in a
masterly way a mass of Biblical statements. (This is perhaps the
most grandiose single portion of the entire work so far; pp. 560–
616.) No single element of that hymn, that dogmatic statement
from the Apocalypse, can be taken in isolation by the congregation; she always has to do with the whole Christ in his time, in his
time which, as man's time, is God's time and as God's time is the
time of a man.

Thus the time of other men is certainly not like the time of
Jesus (616 ff.). We exist " in time," and how we exist is described
very aptly by Hölderlin in " Hyperion's Song of Fate ": ". . . no
place at which to rest . . . tossed like water from one reef to another, year in and year out downward into uncertainty " (621).
And yet that is an actual description of " sinful man in time "
(623). " In the existence of the man Jesus," however, it has been
" decided and also revealed that God has in no way made man in
that state of being tossed ' from one reef to another ' " (624).
Jesus' existence in time is God's " protest," which reveals our existence in time as standing in judgment. And this protest of God
" makes it objectively impossible for man to be really satisfied with
his existence in time " (624). At the same time, however, God's
existence in the man Jesus means that the Creator himself " takes

time and has time for us "; that he " is temporal in our midst just as we are " (625). And with it a " true and proper existence in time " is opened to us (627) — an existence, we can say, in the time God has willed, affirmed, and assumed.

This signifies (and it is basic for what follows) that time " has been given to man by God and is therefore real " (628). It is for us " a condition superior " to us (633). We receive it, and now we also actually " have it "; it has been effectively given to us.

The meaning is first of all that I may and ought to take my present, the urgent and peremptory " Now," as the Now God has prepared for me. " We do not first exist now, but first God exists now " (638); " to exist in time, to exist now, means for us: to exist under and with God " (639). It means further that I may and ought to take my past really as *my* past. I am myself the one who has " been "; I can and may not run away from remembrance. And again it is true: " First God was; he was already then our Creator, Saviour, and Preserver " (647). And for that reason our remembrance may and ought to be one of gratitude. For that reason we are also permitted — in God's name — to forget (without in the meantime being forced to forget in order to be able to live at all). And finally we can and may reckon with the fact " that as God's will and action is the meaning and ground of our existence in time in general, so it is also that of our existence in the future " (659). Or: " In relation to that which God will be, want, and do, we also will be . . ." (660). " We will be in the Lord's hands, who from eternity has been our ally and friend " (665). In each and every circumstance: " My time is in Thy hands! "

Of what man is all that true? We have seen that it is true only from the standpoint of Jesus. (" In Jesus God is eternal . . . eternal for us . . ."; 669.) But for whom? Barth again answers that it is not for Christians alone. " The man whom Jesus has saved, preserved, and placed in an eternal fellowship with God, the man who once will be revealed beyond all time, is . . . , to be sure, much more than the natural man " (670). But nevertheless what has been said applies to the " natural " man insofar as Christ has " suffered, fought, and conquered " for him. And just for that reason he " is to be seen and understood in the light of his resurrec-

tion " (670). " Just as no ontological godlessness, so also no ontological inhumanity is to be ascribed " to this man, " not even with
respect to the temporality of his existence! " (670).

This time, in which man (this man!) " exists," is a " set span "
of time (671 ff.). No doubt a limitation is thereby predicated.
Nevertheless it is not only so; for it is not only appropriate but
salutary for man — who is manifestly not God, not " eternal " —
to be allowed to live in a set period of time (683). For just in this
fixed span it is possible for us " to be those whom God confronts,
speaking to them and dealing with them " (687). God's free grace,
which has truly appeared to us in the midst of a set span of time —
in the incarnation of the Word — encounters us in just this set
span of time (694).

A fixed span of time — that means a time that begins and ends.
Man only exists as one who comes from a beginning and goes toward an end. But whence does he come? To be sure, " his nonexistence " is " somewhere " prior to the existence of the individual and of mankind (698). But the boundary which surrounds
our time and first makes it to be a set span of time, a time that begins and comes to an end, is — in the light of the revelation in
Jesus Christ — " not an abyss." On the contrary, we come " hither
from this God." Hence it is true that we come from our nonexistence, " but not therefore out of nothingness " (701)! Whence do
I know this? Not from myself, not even (like the Old Testament
man) from a history of salvation prepared perhaps for my people
and in it also for me, but from where the beginning plainly has
become manifest and with it the origin of my own life as well: I
know it — *post Christum!* — from my baptism (713)! (At which
Barth does not neglect to reproach the prevailing Church practice
of baptism for concealing just this truth!) There I am thrown
back, as it were, upon my origin; there I am told that I — in my
temporality — " come from Jesus Christ, from his birth, from his
baptism at Jordan, from his crucifixion and resurrection " (713)!

Time that *ends!* " Thither goes time, hither comes death "!
If time as a set span is God's institution and therefore also a divine
boon (as we saw), so this is also true of its drawing to an end — of

course, only under an important presupposition. This drawing to
an end of our time would then be " a negative thing, an evil," if
" our end were to consist in our having to enter not only into our
nonexistence but into our nothingness " (724).

But does death belong at all " to man's nature created by God
and therefore to his good nature " (726) ? Barth's answer is in the
negative; that certainly cannot be said of death as it actually meets
us (726). It is " the sign of God's judgment upon us " (725). And
only in the light of the death Jesus suffered in our stead — and
that is only from the New Testament on — are we told how very
true that is (736). No preacher of the law (and not even Heidegger and Sartre; 736) can truly express the No according to which
our life deserves death. (With all preachers of a law it is only a
human No which cannot do justice to death or to life.) But because it is God's judgment, whose sign death is, and because Jesus
Christ suffered this judgment for us, we have to go farther and say
that something much worse than death befalls us in death (740).
In death we are " confronted by God " (739) ! Truly the power of
death simply consists in " convicting the creature who fights
against God, sinful and guilty man, of his vanity in comparison
with God " (740).

However, the God who " awaits us in death, and as the Lord of
death, is the gracious God — the God who is for man " (741). And
therefore we really cannot fear death; we can only " fear him "
(742). " Our death is our boundary. But our God is also the
boundary of our death " (743) ! In the light of the New Testament
we may hear God's answer concerning our — irrevocable, and
irrevocable precisely in the light of the New Testament — end.
And hence we " by no means " say " too much, when we simply
say of God's existence that it is just our abundant comfort, confidence and hope in our death." But also we " by no means " say
" too little when we say that our comfort, our confidence and hope
in death, is restricted to God's existence . . ." (749). Barth sets
forth in an exhaustive exegesis of familiar Biblical passages what
this signifies in detail.

But once again: Does death as such belong to our created nature? Barth has shown that our actual dying is a " death sentence."
But does this character of judgment necessarily belong to the na-

ture of death? Barth answers this question in the negative. The "identity of our end with our death sentence" is only a "relative" reality (769). "It also belongs to man's nature . . . that man's existence is finite, that man is mortal" (770). And because it is so, there is also a dying which does not bear the character of judgment, namely, that which the New Testament calls "falling asleep" (778). Its opposite is dying in the "second death" (in the language of the book of Revelation), a dying in judgment.

It may be said that the volume we have reviewed — as briefly as possible — is a theological symphony as it were, overpowering in the profusion of ideas, in the clarity of its themes and motifs. It would be pedantic [7] at this point to elucidate certain details critically. The purpose of this report could only be to open up a view of the whole in its ordered variety. Unfortunately, however, in doing so it has not been accomplished without drastic abridgment, even curtailment. It can only be hoped that too great distortions have not occurred.

[7] " *Beckmesserei.*"

XII

GOD'S PROVIDENCE

[Volume III, 3, pp. 1–326]

A s WILL be recalled, Barth had dealt with the doctrine of God's gracious election before the doctrine of creation (II, 2). In that case he understands creation as the " external presupposition " of the covenant established in God's election, and the covenant in turn as the "inner presupposition " of creation (III, 1). It is no wonder that he now also sees the doctrine of God's providence placed in the light of predestination. This is the way he had already announced it in II, 1, 47 ff., and this is the way it is now developed. " Predestination is . . . the presupposition, and its accomplishment in history is the constitutive center of the divine government of the world, the ground and the goal of its execution " (III, 3, 2). If the doctrine of election belonged to the doctrine of God, then the doctrine of providence belongs to the doctrine of creation (3 f.). Providence pertains to the " realization " of the " decree " of predestination (3). It is, as Barth defines it, " the sovereign action of the Creator with his creature, the wisdom, omnipotence, and goodness in which he preserves and rules in time, according to the standard of his own will, this reality which as such is distinguished from himself " (1). If we remember how emphatically Barth understood predestination as proceeding from and leading to Jesus Christ, then we can immediately expect the same in the doctrine of providence.

Creation and providence belong together. God is no " demiurge " (9), not a mere artificer of the world who leaves the world to itself. For creation itself is in fact already an act of his faithfulness; it is the execution of his covenant will, his election. Consequently earlier theology was right in directing its attack against Epicureanism, against Aristotle, and later against deism (10 ff.). However, creation and providence, it so happens, are also not the same thing. " In creation it is a matter of the founding, of the

incomparable beginning of the relationship between the Creator
and the creature; in providence it is a question of its duration and
history which takes place in a series of continually different periods
which, however, in themselves may nevertheless be compared "
(7). If we were to equate creation and providence, we should have
to assume that a continual creation of the world takes place
(*creatio continua*). Barth now (unlike previously; cf. I, 2, 772)
sharply rejects these ideas (4, 78–80). As a result of such preliminary reflections Barth formulates the doctrine thus: " The simple
meaning of the doctrine of providence may therefore be summed
up in the sentence that in the act of creation God, in his capacity
as Creator, has joined himself to his creature as such, as the Lord
of its history, and remains faithful to it as such. God the Creator
coexists with his creature, and so his creature exists under the presupposition, and under the conditions, given with it, of the coexistence of its Creator " (12). He " coexists " with him, but " as
one who acts, and, what is more, in an uninterrupted . . . action " (13).

Now it so happens that " Christian faith in providence," to
which Barth next turns his attention (14 ff.), has all along been
confused with a " view of the world," with a " hypothesis about
God," a " postulate " (17) — quite contrary to Questions 26–28
of the Heidelberg Catechism from which Barth takes his start. It
has been regarded as a sort of " vestibule " to Christian faith (30),
and has thereby been detached from the true substance of Christian faith. For this reason it is a good thing that Barth makes clear-
cut demarcations as he did in the doctrine of creation. Christian
faith in providence, as he first states (15), is " faith in the strictest
sense of the word, and that means that it is first of all a hearing,
receiving, and accepting of God's Word." It is, secondly, " purely
and simply faith in God himself " (20), and therefore not in some
ever so powerfully convincing view of the world, of history, or of
life. (Such a " view " is " out of the question as a conception of
God," 22.) It is, therefore, least of all to be confused with some
philosophy of history (23 ff.). Its structure is determined rather by
a " prophetic relation to history " (27). To be sure, it takes note
of " dispensations and the ways of providence, warnings and signs,
boundaries that have been set and possibilities that have been

opened up, threats and judgments, merciful preservations and de-
liverances " (22) ; it is not blind to history. Yet neither is it determined by history, but by God alone. The " seeing," which is
undoubtedly inherent to it, is " not a theoretical but a practical,
not programmatic but a spontaneous seeing; it is not infallible, but
subject to correction " (29). Thirdly, " Christian faith in providence is substantially *Christian* faith, faith in Christ " (29). Here
it is not a matter of " any kind of Lordship," but " the Fatherly
Lordship of God," who is " the eternal Father of our Lord Jesus
Christ " (32; cf. Ques. 26 of the Heidelberg Catechism). Consequently here, as in predestination, it is true: " Christian faith in
providence does not gaze into empty space or into darkness " (32).
And as in matters pertaining to predestination, so here too Barth
has to reproach the old Protestant doctrine for having " neglected
almost along the whole line . . . even so much as to ask about the
Christian meaning and character of the doctrine of providence "
(34). That is true even of the Reformers, and it is most certainly
true of orthodoxy, which was thoroughly " liberal " in this respect (37).

Following all these preliminary reflections and delineations
Barth is now able to go on to outline the distinctive features of his
development of the doctrine of providence (38 ff.). He does it by
asking about the relation of the " history of the covenant " or " history of salvation " to the " history of creation." The " history of
the covenant " is carried out, in fact, " in the midst of the totality "
of " creaturely events " (42). " The special event in Israel, in
Jesus Christ, in his congregation," is " not only embedded in these
general events, but is interwoven until it is indistinguishable "
(43). How, then, are these two things related to each other? Barth
answers with the bold statement that in both it is simply a question
of two " points of view," and moreover, of such " that . . . the
viewpoint relative to the history of creation receives its light from
that of the history of salvation " (46). Or even more precisely: " It
is God's faithfulness that under his Lordship he co-ordinates and
subordinates creaturely events and lets them serve the event of the
covenant, of grace, and of salvation . . ." (47). Or to express it
in a similar way: " The history of the covenant " (not simply its
beginning in creation) " also has its external presupposition con-

tinually in the existence, in the history of the creature. And in the
government of divine providence it is a matter just of providing
and preserving this external presupposition of the history of the
covenant " (53). The creature, together with its history, plays the
part of a " service " (53) or of an " instrument " (54). " Created
existence " has its " co-ordination and annexation to the history of
the covenant " in that it provides " time, space, and an opportunity
for the divine will and action in the covenant of grace " (54). In
fact, the " primary divine activity," the " history of the covenant
of grace " (57), is related to " creaturely events " as an " archetype " to a " mirror " (57): the " history of the creature " is
" along the whole line similar . . . to the history of salvation . . ." (58). Of course, all this may not be said " in the sense
of an ontological definition "; The creature " is " God's servant
and instrument and exists in this " similarity " only " in the event
of a co-ordination and ' annexation ' which has been accomplished
by God, in the event of a ' co-operation ' with the good, to which
he has called, authorized, and qualified it " (60). There can therefore be no talk of an " independent co-operation of the creature "
(62); creaturely events can only " receive " the importance which
is due them as the " external presupposition " of the history of
the covenant (62). The Biblical texts, to which Barth referred
especially in the foregoing (Rom. 8:28; Matt. 6:33), afforded no
information about a capacity inherent in creaturely events " in
themselves," but testify to God's choice and decision.

Let it be noticed here immediately that the idea just given of a
" similarity " or correspondence between the history of the covenant and creaturely history, founded upon God's choice and decision, belongs to the leading ideas of the whole book. Barth contradicts the idea of *analogia entis* as flatly now as he ever did. But
just as emphatically does he espouse that " analogy " which God —
ever acting, choosing, and deciding — establishes, and which he
erects as the Lord in his free grace.

After Barth (in the section now briefly outlined: § 48) has
spoken about the " presupposition " and " structure " of the doctrine of providence, he proceeds to a detailed development of the
content of the doctrine. He does it under the characteristic title:

" God the Father as Lord of His Creature " (§ 49, pp. 67 ff.) . The
Fatherhood of God is his Lordship and vice versa. God is, as the
Lord, for his creature — " in his Son " (68) .

In the division of this section Barth follows the older dogmatics:
he speaks of God's " preservation " (conservatio) , " concurrence "
(concursus) , and " government " (gubernatio) .

What does it mean: God preserves his creature? It means " that
he affirms it as such in its existence in this present time " (70) and,
moreover, " within the limitations corresponding to its creaturely
nature " (70) . This delimitation is of great consequence: There
is history only " among and for limited creatures " (71) . But then
how can one speak of " preservation," not to mention a " perfect
preservation "? One can and must do so because this preservation
is connected with the " inner and real " preservation of the creature " through its participation in Christ's Kingdom " (71) ; therefore it stands completely in the light of the promise which is held
out for the creature.

The preservation of the creature, however, occurs indirectly,
not — like creation — in the direct act of God (73) . Even this is
a reflection of what has been established in God's covenant of
grace: The creature has a commission to fulfill to the " fellow creature " (74) .[1] Thus also the fact that every creature is directed to
every other creature — in the widest sense — is not by any means
to be based upon a law inherent to the creature as such, but on
the contrary upon God's " freely decreeing " " action " (77, 75) .
Actually everything that is to be said here rests upon this. Indeed, Barth again stresses at this point how dangerous it is to
speak of a continuous creation (creatio continua) (78–80) . But all
the more clearly it must be seen that the preservation of the creature is due to God's faithfulness — revealed solely in the election
by grace — who does not " regret " " having entered into this in-

[1] TRANSLATOR'S NOTE: The meaning is that as God commissions some men to be
witnesses and messengers to their fellow men, so in God's work of preservation the
creature is commissioned to be the means for the preservation of the creature, always provided, of course, that the Creator wants to use the creature as such. And
this is the indirect way in which God acts in the preservation of his creation.

corporation [2] with his creature " (81), and " who actually stands
by his choice of his creature " (82). If the manner and way in
which God preserves his creature has been said to be " incomprehensible " (77) — this is the incomprehensible fact!

But Barth goes even farther in his deliberations. The preservation of the creature presupposes that the creature is constantly " in
need " of this benevolence of the Creator (83), and indeed, because it always stands under the threat of the " Nothing " or of the
" Nihil " [3] (86); it is not only endangered by " nonexistence," but
it exists in this danger (which is first made to be a serious peril)
precisely by the " Nihil," by the " Chaos " (86). Here for the first
time in this volume appears that reality which Barth deals with
fully in a later section (§ 50: " God and the Nihil "). But he is
most anxious to state right now that as surely as the " Nothing "
is " a factor which, in relation to the creature, is absolutely supreme " (87), just as surely does its power depend entirely upon
God's No (his " wrath, rejection, and judgment "; 87), yet upon
a negation which God does not want to turn against the otherwise
helpless creature itself, but which he himself has taken upon himself. " He allowed himself to be negated in order thereby to abolish the negation, in order just thereby and in this way to carry out
the work of his wrath but also the work of his grace " (90). In
other words, the preservation, the *conservatio* of the creature,
stands " in the light of this accomplished *servatio*," of the de-
liverance of the creature from the power of the divine No which
alone gives power to the Nihil (90). The creature is utterly dependent upon God's preserving it; yet precisely in this its neediness " proclaims " that it " is to partake of the *servatio* " (91).
Thus " even existence in this neediness " is " a creaturely existence
which corresponds to our participation in God's covenant of
grace " (92). But even so " the situation of the creature was, in
Jesus Christ, also that of its Creator, and that means: it is a sanctified, a blessed situation, one that is full of promise " (93).

The creature may exist for the purpose God made it! And it
may — " within its limits " — " exist and abide eternally " before

---

2 " *Zugehörigkeit.*"

3 See the following chapter of this book and the footnotes on p. 187 for the
meaning of the " Nothing " and the " Nihil."

God (99). This eternal preservation of the creature does not mean that it could have a continuation over and beyond its end, its limits. What would be the purpose of this continuation " after the creature . . . will have reached its goal in the revelation of Jesus Christ " (100)? We do not mean a continuation when we speak of the eternal preservation of the creature. However, we certainly do mean that its " destruction " is " precluded ": God has " too deeply, too unconditionally associated " himself with his creature " for him to be able subsequently to regret it again, and for him not to be able subsequently to want to be the only one again, and so to be without his creature " (101). Why should the creature not " exist," seeing that, " even after its end," it nevertheless " will exist before him, present with him, as that which it then only will have been " (102)? The mercy of God, which then " endureth forever " (Ps. 136), is the mystery of the eternal preservation of the creature!

When we speak of the divine " concurrence," we mean thereby " God's Lordship in its relation to the creature's own free agency " (102); for the creature, " as the object of the creative and preserving *operatio* of God," is now " for its part engaged in an *operatio* " (an activity) (102 f.). The creature is active in its " coexistence with God," and God is the One who " affirms, approves, acknowledges, and respects " this independent activity of the creature. He " does not act as a tyrant upon him " (104). His Lordship is absolute, absolutely boundless. Yet as the Lordship of the Father it is nevertheless not the removal but the creation of genuine freedom for the creature.

According to Barth, the doctrine of the divine " concurrence," of " *concursus*," was in itself adequately developed by the older dogmatics. It by no means constituted, as he shows, a " specialty of Lutheran dogmatics " (108). However, the Lutherans have had a greater interest in the " relative independence of creaturely activity "; the Reformed Churchmen a greater interest in the " absolute superordination of the divine over creaturely activity " (109), and in this the Lutherans again stood in some proximity to the contemporary Jesuits, the Reformed Churchmen to the Thomists (110). It is Barth's opinion that neither may one forthwith reproach orthodoxy for having created confusion by the applica-

tion of the concept of causality (111 ff.). Under certain conditions
— carefully worked out by Barth — it is rather quite serviceable.
" Between *causare,* God's activity and that of the creature," there
is undoubtedly a "similarity, and so a correspondence, compar-
ableness, analogy," yet just as surely no " equality " (115). Therefore, the concept of causality may not be understood, as it were,
as a common denominator to which God's activity and that of the
creature are in like manner subordinated. Activity here and activity there correspond; but God as a " subject " and the creature
as a " subject " are absolutely incomparable (116). An analogy
again exists (which Barth here characterizes as an " *analogia op-
erationis* "; 116) ; but there is simply no *analogia entis* of whatever
kind, no " *analogia causae* " (117).

Though with these considerations Barth " formally " acknowledges the truth of orthodoxy (113), he opposes it in regard to its
content. In the doctrine of *concursus* it also lacks " the Christian
element " (113). God is thought of altogether too much as an " ultimate being." It lacks the connection between creation and the
covenant of grace, between " world history and the history of salvation " (113). It lacks the insight that " the entire doctrine of
God's providence " must " be developed in a distinct relation between the first and second articles of the Creed " (118, 120). In
opposition to it Barth, returning to the thought of God's " coexistence " with his creature, decisively shows that God coexists with
the creature " in the supremacy of his activity " (123). Of course,
God uses his " freedom " precisely and solely " to offer himself as
a companion " to the creature (124), and " in his supremacy —
the supremacy of his love — on his part to co-operate in all creaturely activity " (124). However, the order of precedence between
the Creator and the creature is irreversible (125). " It is a question of God ' concurring ' with his creature but not of the creature
with God " (127). Where that is not seen, a *Weltanschauung*
could all too easily be made out of the doctrine of *concursus* and,
what is more, become then only a " magical " *Weltanschauung*
(125 f.). Or on the other hand the idea of a " sovereign despotism "
of God could be constructed out of it, and from it would follow, instead of the obedience of faith, resignation or protest, or then finally, as a reaction, the attempt to reverse the idea of *concursus*

and to see God's activity in some sense determined or limited by
that of the creature (126 ff.) . In what has been briefly reported in
the last sentence Barth sees "the tragedy of the specifically Reformed doctrine of providence " (130), which could then lead in
the end to Schleiermacher's " monism " (132) . The mistake of Reformed teaching is that it did not abide by what is back of Questions 26–28 in the Heidelberg Catechism, and for that reason
lacked the proper foundation " which would have distinguished it
from a questionable philosophical theory " (131) . It proceeded
from " empty " concepts rather than from those which were
" filled with a Christian content " (cf. 132) . If the doctrine of
providence is to be Christian, God must also be truly recognized
as the triune God. His will must be understood as " his Fatherly
good will, his gracious decree in Jesus Christ . . ." and even
therein and for that reason as his " royal," his " sovereign will."
His activity must appear as " his action in the history of the covenant which has been established upon his gracious decree " and
" then, as such, also " as " the operation of his power in the whole
realm of his creatures " (132 f.) . When that happens, then even
the notion " that his omnipotence abolishes the creature's own
free activity " (133) disappears, and with it also the possibility of
resignation, of protest, or even of that attempt " to make out of the
' God who is all in all ' a mere ' God who is many things in many '
. . . and thus to regard the divine *concursus* as reversible " (134) .

Barth arranges the separate expositions in three parts: first,
God's activity " precedes the activity of his creature " (*praecur-
rit*) ; secondly, it " accompanies " that activity (*concurrit*) ; and
thirdly, it " follows " it (*succurrit*) .

In regard to the first point Barth notes first of all that in it it is
not a question of God's merely knowing in advance (135 ff.) , but
of God's *praedeterminatio,* of his " predetermination," which, as
such, is to be distinguished from every other determination to
which the creature could be subject, and which " is to be ranked
before and above it " (137) . In this connection Barth comes to
speak, among other things, about the " laws of nature " (140 ff.) .
He first explains that all such " laws " are predetermining " only
with respect to the form and order of creaturely activity " (142),
but that they cannot " predetermine " this creaturely happening

" itself and as such " (143) . They are " attempts, within the framework of our experience of creaturely events and within the framework of our rational possibilities and the necessities of logic to establish and to justify that there are such ontic laws, that there is a predetermined form and order of all creaturely events " (144) . In fact, Barth is able to say in plain terms that, as a subject of human verification, in creaturely events " there prevails " " not accident but constancy, not caprice but faithfulness " (144) . But there can be " no talk " of " being able to interpret God's predestination from the standpoint of our ideas of law " (145) . The " laws of nature " cannot constitute " an independently ruling subject " between God and the creature, so that we would be directly concerned with them, but only indirectly with God. On the contrary, " what we know as law can only remind us of *the* law and therefore of him " (146) . God's activity occurs in freedom. His miracles bear witness to this freedom, and in them " the rule of the divine activity, namely, the free, good will of God himself, is revealed " (147) . So it is to be said that God's activity does not, it is true, abolish the other determinants to which the creature is subject, and in particular the so-called laws of nature, but " relativizes " them (147) . God " does not have his greatness in the suppression of his creature " (147) : he is a merciful God. Nor does he need anything to represent him, for he " is always and everywhere immediately present to his creature through his Holy Spirit " (148) . He who is the " Father of Jesus Christ " does not let his creature out of his hands (148) .

As to the second point, God accompanies the activity of the creature. He " effects creaturely activity " (149) . God is with the creature. " Certainly in an understanding of the universal governing of God's providence one cannot take too seriously this ' Immanuel,' the meaning and force of which is only revealed, of course, in the history of the covenant of grace . . ." (149) . How is this coactivity of God to be conceived? Barth's answer is that God acts " in that he utters his Word to all creatures that have the power, the wisdom, and the goodness of his Holy Spirit. Or expressed the other way round: He acts when his Holy Spirit, who is the Spirit of his Word, is the power, wisdom, and goodness actuating all creatures. His activity is thus a Fatherly activity " (161) . Thus knowledge again takes the central place in the theological propositions and again we see an analogy. Even there where God does not " directly encounter " us, " as he does in the history of the covenant of grace or in Jesus Christ," there he also acts ás the One who encounters us in Jesus Christ. And he acts " everywhere and always . . . in the way in which he is there manifest to us " (162) . " That the Lord of the world is our Father depends upon his activity even in the world, being that of his Word and Spirit " (162) . However, if that is how matters stand, then, in fact, there is reason and sense to the statement that in his sovereignty God does not menace and suppress the " freedom of creaturely activity in its peculiarity and variety," but, on the contrary, establishes it (165) . It is truly the Father of Jesus Christ, it is our Father, who acts: not a principle, not a mysterious power, not a coercive law.

But once that is recognized, there is then no need for us now on the contrary to want to safeguard our creaturely freedom by taking anything away from God's activity. Then the " fear complex " must subside, " as if God were a stranger to his creature " (166) . " What good does all our thinking and talking about Christ and his resurrection really do us after all . . . , if, in the face of the simple demand to acknowledge God as the One who works all in all, we are seized with anxiety, as if thereby perhaps too much could be said about God, and too little about the creature . . . , as if human freedom and responsibility in particular could thereby be infringed! " (166) . Back of such anxiety lies a " fear of God and for the creature " (167) . But this is due to a refusal, right within Christendom, " to speak up freely in favor of loving God more than fearing him," and " after all " just this " is the only relevant and intriguing form of human sin " (167) ! The God revealed in Christ has " taken man, his creature, seriously as his partner " (167) . Who then wants to look for a boundary between the activity of the creature God has accepted and God's activity? The creature may live his life, and " complete the circle of his existence," [4]

---

[4] TRANSLATOR'S NOTE: I am indebted to Professor Weber for pointing out to me that this is a line from a verse of Goethe's poem *Das Göttliche*. (See also p. 176.)

> " *Nach ewigen, ehrnen,*
> *Grossen Gesetzen*
> *Müssen wir alle*
> *Unseres Daseins*
> *Kreise vollenden.*"

just in the light of the sovereignty of the Creator (168). The Creator's activity does not simply absorb the creature's activity into itself or blot it out (169). The Lord, who in his grace is free, does not merely acquiesce in — the creaturely — freedom of the creature, but first truly grants it to him (170). Even the " imprisonment, which arises through the work of the Word and Spirit," is " real freedom " (170). And " what kind of conception of freedom would it be which could induce us to want to protect the creature in the face of the imprisonment threatening here? " (170).

The third point — God's activity " follows " the activity of the creatures — really belongs much rather to the next section: " The Divine Government " (171). What Barth chiefly wishes to show is that the effect of whatever the creature does is now no longer in the creature's hands, but acquires a " history " of its own (173). This history, however, in its independence of the creature and of all other creatures, " is the freedom of God and of his government " (173). But because such is the case, because God does not cease to act where the creature's activity ends, the action of the creature may therefore take place in " trust, confidence, and hope " (174). For the God who in his freedom makes creaturely action to be an object of his plan and execution, this God is " not an unknown God, but in Jesus Christ is our Father — the eternal Father of all his creatures " (175).

Barth's exposition of " the divine government " occupies the most space in this section. The purpose of our report will be best served if it heads as directly as possible toward the point at which the theological decision becomes apparent.

God rules. In the first place that can only mean: " He alone rules " (177). It means further that he himself is "alone the goal . . . which he has set for his creature " (179). His government is truly that of the Lord, and for that reason it takes place in " plain sovereignty " (180). God is " not one of the necessities

E. A. Bowring, in *The Poems of Goethe*, New York, 1882, has rendered this verse as follows:

> " After laws mighty,
> Brazen, eternal,
> Must all we mortals
> Finish the circuit
> Of our existence."

which make themselves felt in the course of the world . . . neither is he their embodiment and sum total " (181) . Nor is his governing identical with the " sequence " in which natural events occur according to the so-called laws of nature (181) , or with which we " see ourselves obligated " by a moral law (182) , or with some other experiential sequence of, say, historical and economic events (182) . His government is certainly not only to be found " in the extraordinary " (although one will surely " have to grant, regardless of what one's view of the world may be, that it also performs genuine and true miracles "; 182) . Rather, " to the manifestation of his wisdom belong also ever again the triumphs of common sense . . . also the wonderful revelation, especially precious to the Holy Spirit, that two times two is four and not five . . ." (183) . But his dominion is not to be confused or equated with any necessity, his constancy with any statics, his power with any dynamics. He governs — as stated in a somewhat different connection — the creature's activity " just as much when it is free as when it is necessary " (187) .

God's governing is a regulating (186 ff.) . Barth takes up again something he had already mentioned in reference to the fact that God's regulating is not the elimination but just the divine, and therefore Fatherly, control of creaturely activity (187) . Precisely because he regulates all things " thither to himself " (190) and preserves his own glory, it is nevertheless a matter of the " justification, salvation, and blessedness " — and ultimately also of the " glory even of his creature " (191) . The lowliness of the creature " in relation to God " is in truth just its " glory " (193) . " For though it is relative to him, it shares in his absoluteness with its activity and in its effects " (193) . And moreover, as Barth stresses, not merely indirectly, because it is part of a whole (perhaps of the " universe " which Schleiermacher had in mind) but in such a way that within this whole, while " serving the common goal," it also " may advance toward its own special goal and be assured of it " (196) .

But what is the standpoint from which all this is said? From what standpoint can it be said that all creaturely events, as a whole and each individually, stand in an order, serve a plan, and at the same time make sense? Here Barth's leading proposition is introduced.

When we speak of " God's governing," of the " kingship " which
all things serve, then we mean that " Israel's King is King of the
world " (200). Whether or not we believe in God's government
of the world is decided by the attitude we take to this knowledge,
or rather, by a proper or improper relation to this reality (201).
This King has uttered his " I am " (200, etc.) " in the midst of
world history." With this " I am " — which in the Old Testament
" preponderantly " occurs as an "overpoweringly issued dictum,"
and in the New Testament " preponderantly " as an " overpowering deed " (205) — he has established the covenant in which he
took the creature's part when he revealed himself as its Lord.

This " I am," this " covenant of free grace " (207), and with it
the " center " of the divine government, is now the reality from
which and to which world events are to be seen as ruled by God.
The " history of salvation " is permanently connected with " world
events." But conversely even " world events " cannot " be seen and
understood in themselves." " They are related to the history of
salvation " (211). Only from this standpoint is Barth now able to
take up again those first propositions with a proper grounding,
namely, the sentences that God alone rules, that God makes himself to be the purpose for all creaturely events, and that God's government is sovereignly above all mundane contradictions such as
freedom and necessity, etc. (211 ff.). It is the freedom of God's
grace, the omnipotence of his mercy, which, revealed in the history
of salvation, now also beams upon world events. And because it is
so, we do not here stare " into the empty framework of an idea of
God but at a form, into a face, into a history " (216). If God had
no face, then talk about his government would be a " luxury
truth," whose practical importance could not be made apparent to
anyone. But this is the way in which " the thought of the divine
government of the world " acquires " practical significance. . . .
It determines human existence . . ." (217). It is now no longer
something about which to speculate. On the contrary, the man
who conceives the thought of God's government of the world now
" finds himself," as he conceives that thought, " for his part already started and on the way to acting in accordance with it "
(220). Even now he knows himself as " a creature who is gov-

erned by a sovereign Creator, and who may recognize and conduct himself as such " (220).

World events under the government of God, of " Israel's King," follow a line, a direction. They have a " whence " and a " whither." They are " not to be compared to an amorphous and diffuse mass set in motion, but to an organism or to a structure " (221). They are subject to an " economy " (221). And " it is the name of Jesus Christ in which this economy is comprehended " (221). Only in the light of the reality of Christ can world events be revealed as ruled by God (223). Nevertheless Barth is able to say that " there are certain constant elements in the midst of general world events as such. They also belong, and indeed altogether, to these world events. They do not represent . . . in themselves a further revelation." But they are now nevertheless " something like permanent enigmas," and " signs and testimonies " of the fact " that even general world events are actually ruled from thence, that is, by him who there, at that unique place, is called ' God ' " (225). Barth enumerates four such " constant elements ": " the history of Holy Scripture " (227 ff.), " the history of the Church " (231 ff.), " the history of the Jews " (238 ff.), and — " the limitation of human life " (256 ff.). Our report can single out only certain few points from Barth's detailed and tremendously impressive exposition. All the while we will be burdened by the question: How can these phenomena, which transpire right within world events, now nevertheless be " signs " and " testimonies " of him who meets us as Lord and Ruler only in the " history of salvation "?

The history of the Church. " Even the Church belongs to this time " — as surely as her time is the " last time " (231). " She is not a continuation or repetition of the Biblical revelation " (232). But what gives her prominence, what grants " priority " to her history over against all the rest of history (234), is her claim. It is further the capacity she has shown " for an outward, and, above all, for an inner resistance " (234).[5] It is, lastly, her capacity for

5 TRANSLATOR'S NOTE: The Church's " claim " is just that her history is the inner meaning of all history; that her time characterizes the time of our world as the " last time " before Christ's Second Coming. By her resistance is meant her resistance to all that is foreign and contradictory to what she believes and proclaims concerning her Lord.

"renewal" (236). Church history is not only "a history of res-
torations, but also a history of reformations" (237). According to
Barth nothing, of course, has been "proven" by these three facts
(226), but something has indeed been attested, advertised, and
demonstrated.

The history of the Jews: it is well known that it has already often been frankly regarded as a "proof" of God's government of
the world. Barth also declares: "It is easier for the uninitiated to
shut his eyes to the history of the Bible and to Church history
than to overlook this history" (238). Since the destruction of Jerusalem there is, "on the one hand, no further continuation of
the history of the covenant as a history between God and this people to the exclusion of the other nations." Nevertheless there is,
"on the other hand, in the midst of world history, a special history of the Jews. It is now no longer a preliminary history. But according to all indications it is a history of the Jews with definitive
character" (239). What are they actually? Not a race in themselves (241), not a people with a language of their own (241),
not a people with a special culture (242). In fact, when they are
not even a "people" at all in the usual sense (243), even the concept, "the Jews," is wholly problematical (242). They are actually
a "phenomenon *sui generis*," incomparable to anything history
knows (244). They can be understood only from the standpoint
of God's election. After all similarities to other people have been
left out, similarities which so often became a snare to Israel, they
can actually "only continue to be God's people and his people
exclusively" (246). They are, however, the "people which has
been unfaithful to its election" (248). And precisely thereby they
"embody and reveal" "what, in the light of divine election and
calling, mankind is, and how man exists as the object of God's free
grace" (248). Hence they must be a riddle. Their history stands
as a huge "question mark" in the midst of world history (245).
"It vexes us . . . that in them, in their nature, we have held up
before us our own nature . . ." (250). For even in them "that
which . . . is concealed in all men is not concealed, what is . . .
hidden in all is not hidden in them" (251). "It vexes us . . .
that, in the existence of the Jews and in their strange character of
not being a people while as such being a people, we are very defi-

nitely placed before the fact of God's electing grace, before the
fact of his mercy, as the one, single, yet powerful ground of human
existence " (253) . They " painfully remind us of the relativity of
our own existence " (253 f.) . They irritatingly refer us to the fact
that in God's free grace just this one people, this people which is
not a people,[6] is elected, and not some other people; that therefore
" God's election " is " the election of another " (255) . This
" other," however, is the *one* Jew, " the *one* Jesus Christ," " who
is now even for us the *one* elect man precisely as the new Head of
all mankind " (255) . We understand when Barth tells us that
even the history of the Jews is itself not sufficient to reveal what
this history actually demonstrates to the nations. " It needs " in
addition " the gospel and faith; it needs their gathering into the
congregation of Jesus Christ . . ." (252) . Howbeit that question
still stands!

But now to what extent does " the limitation of human life "
likewise belong to those " signs " which point to God's government of the world? What makes those two boundary points, birth
and death, about which we have now to speak, to be events which
" characterize all that lies between " (260) ? Barth replies: " Obviously it is the fact that in them . . . are reflected the two great
deeds of God at the beginning and at the end of all things: the creation and the consummation " (260) . And it is the fact that
" among all other creatures man is the one whom God has called
upon to receive the revelation of this mystery . . ." (260 f.) .
Again that idea of a reflection which we have already encountered
several times. But how is man now determined by those symbolic
boundary points of his life? The answer is that he is a creature who
lives but once. He is a self (262) , in whose " tiny creaturely
uniqueness " is reflected " the eternal oneness of God " (262 f.) .
Those two boundary points alone make our life to be a " history "
(263) . But the fact that I have this history of mine only within
those limits, which are in no way at my disposal, can become for
me a sign: " The establishment of who and what I myself may
actually now be . . . is manifestly not my decision but stands in
the judgment of him who, in limiting me in this way, lets me live
before him in such a unique manner " (264 f.) . However, we must

[6] " *Nichtvolk.*"

again call attention to the fact that we have here no more than a
sign. It is " not for nothing " that in this matter we can only then
be a " witness," " when we already know the God whose action is
actually designated and attested by our living that limited human
life " (266 f.) . Then, however, when we have this knowledge, we
" again " recognize in the limitation of our life " the faithfulness
in which he has bound himself to the unfaithful, the predomi-
nance of his grace, the severity and goodness of Israel's King "
(267) . Indeed, Barth is able to go still a step farther. Because our
life history in its two extremities mirrors God's deed in the beginning as at the end, " the whole of world history " occurs " *in nuce,*
yet most truly " in it (266) . He who sets limits to us, and within
these limits our own existence, thereby places us " in solidarity "
with the existence of " heaven and earth " (266) . The " limitation " of our life does not therefore shut it off, but " opens " it
" toward the whole " (266) .

Since in the course of our book so far, there has already been
frequent mention of the practical character of a doctrine of providence inspired by the witness of the Bible, it is understandable
when Barth now ends with a section entitled " The Christian Under the Universal Rule of God the Father " (271 ff.) . The Christian is that " creaturely subject " who " not only is actually
affected " by God's universal rule " but who also knows and acknowledges it, who is grateful for it and therefore also wishes to rely
upon it and act according to it " (271) . In the Christian congregation, and only in it, does the " self-evident revealedness of God's
universal rule " become " possible and real " (272) . " The Christian utters the Yea about which man is interrogated " (272) . As
surely as he has no advantage over other creatures at all, indeed, as
surely as he especially does not want, and cannot have, any advantage over them, he is " quite simply the true creature " just in that
fact (272 f.) .

The meaning is not that a Christian has at his disposal a speculative insight others do not possess (277) . The meaning is rather
that for him God's providence and universal rule are " not only
true " but, because he is " in agreement " with the Creator and
Lord (276) and his universal rule is " reflected " in him " as in

a clear mirror," they are also " actual " for him (277). Such is the
case " when he believes, when he obeys, and when he prays. They
are the three forms of an active and complete Christian conduct "
(278). These three forms belong inseparably together. Any splitting up of them must lead to " a preoccupation with a law in whose
fulfillment Christian conduct would then consist " (278 f.). On
the other hand, " understood in the freedom of the gospel," " each
of those three forms " is " at once the whole " (279).

Faith is " the acceptance of God's Word as such. It is the conscious trust in which the Christian knows and acknowledges that
the Word is uttered by God and to him personally, so that he does
not question it as such " (279). It is not a " magical quality "
(280), but neither is it an action of which man is capable of himself; not a " blind submission," nor even a self-acquired " conviction " (280). It lives beyond all these contradictions, " as it is
awakened by God's Word " (281). Faith is " God's work in man "
(284), but at the same time it is " man's own work " (284). It is
man's complete " imprisonment," yet at the same time his complete " liberation " (285). Hence obedience as well as prayer are
necessarily included in it (285 ff.). In this faith " the Christian
now shares . . . in God's providence and government of the
world " (281). Here we come upon the same thought we have often met before. Faith is, " in the first place, . . . a participation in
Jesus Christ and in his work of grace and salvation." But then, " in
a second movement resulting from the first," faith " begins " and
" reaches away back," as it were, and " comes to trust that this happening in Jesus Christ is . . . foreordained long before all other
happenings . . . and that to Jesus Christ alone is given all power
in heaven and on earth " (281). Faith is " here," that is, in regard
to Christ's work in the first sense, a " light which is kindled from
the light "; and " there," that is, in regard to world events, it is a
" light that shines in darkness " (281). Whatever faith is able " to
do " is done by the Word; but just for that reason it is now also
done by faith itself which is awakened by the Word. In this connection it is not a question of whether faith is " great " or " small,"
" weak " or " strong," but " only whether it is really faith and not
an illusion " (283) ; " whether it is a participation in Jesus Christ "
. . . " whether it really clings to the Word . . ." and is not " in

some sense the Christian's faith in himself" (283). Where there is such faith, freedom prevails. There the "reason" for all world events, which it ascribes to its Lord, becomes "without further ado" the "nevertheless" in the face of them (284), the laughter over all "spurious ideas and hallucinations concerning the world" (283), the defiance in the face of all temporal reality.

Obedience is "doing God's Word. It is the conscious responsibility in which the Christian decides in favor of the Word against himself, against every man, and against the whole world, in which the Christian himself becomes a righteous man. For man's righteousness consists in his having and using the freedom to decide in favor of God's Word" (288). "He becomes a Christian as he believes, and he is a Christian as he obeys" (288). Obedience is not an achievement which claims to be meritorious. But neither is it "optional," or "avoidable" (288). It is subject "to no external law at all." Yet at the same time it is "the exact opposite of all human arbitrariness and caprice" (289). It comes indeed from the Holy Spirit. Here Barth now follows the same train of thought he adopted in the case of faith. Obedience is "first of all" "simply the Christian's participation in Jesus Christ: in the kingdom of grace which has appeared and is effective in him" (289). It is to that extent "acquiescence as a member" in the "order" Jesus Christ gives to his congregation. In fact, it is "co-operation in carrying out" God's "imperial ideas" (290). But again, from this first "movement" of obedience results a second, "again going farther back"; for the "Lord of the congregation" is also truly Lord of "general world events" (290). Consequently in obedience the Christian is also "absorbed in secular and temporal affairs," and in "politics, social questions, science, and aesthetics" (291). Thus here also a so to speak "centripetal" movement and a "centrifugal" movement exist together — different and yet united. With them the first is decisive. Everything depends upon "participation in Jesus Christ" and correspondingly upon the "work" of the Spirit (292). But once again it so happens that it is the Christian who performs this obedience — however enlightened or unenlightened, stouthearted or disheartened, it may be. Where there is real obedience, there the Christian is always "appointed and used in a particular place and in a particular way"

(294). For that purpose he certainly does not need a seat " in the council of God " or even so much as to know " the ' grand lines ' of God's imperial ideas " (294 f.). " When and to the extent that he is obedient, he has his function within the framework of the divine strategy . . ." (295)! This obedience is " not something he has earned " but a " voluntary act " (295): the Christian obeys on the ground of the " reward he has already secretly received " (296)! This obedience is subject to " no statute "; for in contrast to the sole authority " of the Holy Spirit in God's Word," no such dignity belongs to any of the " orders and laws " the Christian might encounter in the course of the world, such that true and therefore Christian obedience should be rendered to them (296 f.). The " dignity and respect " which obtains here is always conditional. And the obedience of the Christian consists in a freedom with respect to those orders or laws under " real authority " (297).

Barth characterizes prayer — as an element of obedience — as " the most intimate and powerful form of Christian activity " (300). In its exercise it can be " praise and thanksgiving, confession and repentance, supplication and intercession, and praise and thanksgiving again." But the proper " center " around which prayer revolves (301) is not adoration, not repentance, but supplication. The fact that man comes to God with his petition " makes him to be one who prays " (303). For that which is " truly and primarily astonishing in the Christian situation " is not the greatness or the holiness or the riches of God but that through his Word precisely the great, holy, and rich God draws so nigh to insignificant, unworthy, and poor man (304). " The Christian is permitted to take; for God gives himself to him and all that is his " (305)! The answer to prayer " really precedes " such asking (306); for the " one great divine gift and answer is Jesus Christ " (307). God is " present to his people " in him (308), and moreover, in such a way that each individual, as " a member of this Christian congregation " (309), may apply this presence of God to himself " personally." And so to the Christian as a " connoisseur " of the " prophetic, priestly, and royal office of Jesus Christ," " yes . . . , as a participant in this office," " world events are manifestly and palpably not something left to themselves but

preserved, accompanied, and governed by God . . ." (309). So
the "meaning" of supplication may be formulated first of all as
"that taking and receiving which is in order where this one great
divine gift and answer to prayer is present for man in Jesus
Christ" (310). On the other hand, the supplication of the congregation is at bottom only an "echoing prayer" (314). For "the
man who first and truly prays is . . . none other than Jesus Christ
himself" (311). "In his dealings as a man" he is "simply one
who prays and nothing more" (312). But — since he is never to
be thought of as being alone — his existence as the Son of Man
was, "as a supplication," at the same time an "intercession"
(313). The congregation, which "echoes his prayer," can therefore be nothing else than an intercessory congregation; her "participation in Jesus Christ," as Barth likes to express it, signifies
that she stands "together with her Lord before God for the whole
creation" (316).

"Christian conduct" in these "three forms" is a conduct of
the creature, and it takes place "in the depths under God's universal rule." But "precisely in the form of prayer" it points "upward," "over and beyond all immanence of the creaturely subject," and comes to "share in God's universal rule" (322).
"There is no unlimited dominion and exclusive agency of God
limiting . . . the freedom of the creature. But there is a freedom
of God's friends, which he has not only permitted but willed, yes,
created, in relation to whom God determines, without letting the
reins out of his own hands even for a moment, to let himself in
turn also be determined by them" (323). "In obedience the
Christian is the servant, in faith he is the child, but in prayer he
is, as a child and a servant, just the friend of God" (324)! In fact,
Barth can close with the statement: "Where the Christian believes, obeys, and prays, the finger, hand, and scepter of the God
who rules the world is secretly and yet most truly at work . . . in
the movement of the creature. Even more, there God's heart is
stirred. . . . There we find ourselves right in the seat of government, in the very mystery and meaning of all world events . . ."
(326).

XIII

GOD AND THE NIHIL

[*Volume III, 3, pp. 327–425*]

T HERE has already been a discussion of the " Nihil " [1]: the
" preservation " of the creature is his being kept from the
threat of the " Nihil " (83 ff., 328). This very thing had already
been specially designated as " the Nothing " [2] in III, 1, 119 f., in
the exegesis of Gen. 1:2 (in connection with an expression used
by W. Zimmerli). It is " that which has been destroyed through
God's act of creation." It is a " possibility " which God " has
scornfully passed over " (*loc. cit.*, 119). The Nihil, let it be immediately said, is, in its nature, " evil " (407), or the " Chaos " (as
mentioned frequently, e.g., p. 86). It still needs to be clearly shown
why Barth prefers the term " Nihil." It followed fundamentally

---

[1] TRANSLATOR'S NOTE: The word *Nichtige*, which has been translated as the
" Nihil," has no precise equivalent in English. It is a noun which Barth has formed
from the German adjective *nichtig*. In Barth's use of it, it possesses a variety of
meanings, which prevents its being rendered satisfactorily by any one English word.
Although the *Nichtige* exists, it does not exist as the Creator and the creature do;
it exists as that which has been negated and abrogated by God. It denotes what
is null and void, what has been nullified and annulled, and is therefore invalid
(*ungültig*) and nugatory. But as Barth himself explains in a letter, "' *nichtig* '
contains not only a negative but a distinctly disqualifying note. That which is
' *nichtig* ' is not only ineffectual, insignificant, and trifling but is downright abomi-
nable — yes, accursed. Strictly speaking, the word may only be used in the way I have
done: to denote the Chaos, sin, the devil, and the demons. Used in any other way,
it is too strong, too sharp." Since no single word in English is suitable, I decided
to coin the word " Nihil." It bears the negative aspect of the German word " *nichtig*,"
and suggests — at least in its derivative " nihilism " — what is evil and destructive.
However, our use of the expression " the Nihil " must not be confused with philosophical, ethical, and political nihilism, although for Christian faith these indeed
may be outward signs of the power and activity of the Nihil, the evil one. The full
meaning of the Nihil (*das Nichtige*) can be gleaned only from the context in which
it is used.

[2] TRANSLATOR'S NOTE: " *Das Nichts* " — " the Nothing." The term is borrowed
from contemporary existentialist philosophy in Europe, notably that of Martin
Heidegger. It could be translated literally as "nothingness," though Heidegger's
translator has more correctly rendered it the " Nothing." See *Existence and Being*,
Henry Regnery Co., Chicago, 1949. Barth, however, prefers the term " *das Nichtige*,"
doubtless to distinguish it from the word used in existentialism, and because he
gives it a distinctly theological connotation. This is an additional reason why I
have coined the term " the Nihil."

from the previous expositions in the *Church Dogmatics,* III, 1. If creation is " justification," " actualization," and a " blessing," as set forth in III, 1, then evidently evil is not to be understood otherwise than as the Nihil. It stands to reason that we ought not thereby to say that the " Nihil " perhaps does not exist. The entire subsection we are here discussing carries the heading " The Reality of the Nihil "!

Barth first outlines " the problem of the Nihil." He proceeds from the fact that " in the creaturely sphere under the Creator's dominion there is something at work which is to be explained . . . neither from the side of the Creator nor from that of the creature, but is to be reckoned with in all its peculiarity." Accordingly, neither the Creator himself may be " charged " " with the nihility of the Nihil," [3] nor may the Nihil be derived " solely from the activity of the creature." The Nihil is not to be looked upon as a sort of " antigod," nor on the other hand may it be made into a " principle at one's disposal " (330 f.). The Nihil may not be overrated in its relation to God, or underrated in its " power as opposed to us."

However, before Barth is able to speak positively about the " knowledge of the Nihil," he refers to the " misconception of Nihil," that is, to the widespread confusion of the Nihil with the " shadowy side " of the creaturely world (334 ff.). Already in III, 1 (426 ff.), Barth had brought out that there is this " shadowy side." Here he is at pains to show that " the justification of creaturely existence " is not bound to this shadowy side. He now wants to prove the reverse — that it represents a fatal mistake " to identify " this " shadowy side " with the " Nihil." To be sure, it is a " reminder " that the creature is " threatened " by the Nihil (336); but it is not true that creation as such has already " succumbed " to this threat in virtue of this shadowy side (336). That would be a " calumny of creation " (336). For if the whole creature, in both of its aspects, is " founded upon Jesus Christ," then it must be said that " in both of its aspects, and hence also in its negative aspect," it is God's " good creation " (337).

The confusion, against which Barth contends at this point, which thus equates night, suffering, decay, and death as such with

---

[3] " *Mit der Nichtigkeit des Nichtigen.*"

" the Nihil," is actually the plain " triumph of the Nihil." It is its
" most cunning camouflage," because in what now seems to be the
" Nihil " the true Nihil is no longer recognized at all, and because
in the end one undertakes to " deal " with it on one's own. This is
because it has either been rendered harmless or " demythologized "
(340), or even " classified " by treating the devil, for example, as
" the last candidate for a salvation which, by reason of a universal
apokatastasis is also due him " (340). (It is to be noted that this
passage is very important because it shows how false it is to number Barth among the advocates of " *apokatastasis*.") Thus that confusion proves itself to be really a victory for the Nihil; the enemy
is " sought . . . where he does not exist " (342), and " in the
end " he thereby acquires an " innocuous form " (342), while on
the other hand the whole of God's Yea to the whole of his creation is no longer heard and no longer responded to.

The " knowledge of the Nihil," on the contrary, has to start
with what " is revealed " in Jesus Christ (342). And that is not
simply " the goodness of God's creation in its twofold form " but
actually " also " what is " really the Nihil, the enemy; . . . the
negative which is not merely the complement of a positive standing over against it; the sinistral which is not held in equilibrium
by any dextral; the antithesis which is certainly no longer a merely
inner-worldly, and thus merely dialectical antithesis . . ." (342).
It is an enemy who is not to be classified in any higher category
knowable to us, and who is therefore not amenable to any " synthesis." It is an antithesis above which God indeed stands, but not
the creature, and therefore not even theology. The incarnation of
the Word had " manifestly not been necessary " . . . " if it had
only been for the revelation of the goodness of God's creation "
(344). The Word became flesh, and that means a " lost creature "
(345). Here God appears to carry out his universal dominion
against the enemy who undertook " an attack upon his own cause "
(345). " The Nihil is the ' reality ' for whose sake (that is, in opposition to it) God himself willed to become a creature in the
creaturely world, to which he willed to surrender and subject himself in Jesus Christ, and just in this way to overcome it. . . . What
brought Jesus to the cross and what he conquered on the cross —

that is the real Nihil" (346)! Only from this standpoint do we
come to see what "real evil, real death, the real devil, real hell,"
and also what man's "real sin" is (347).

In this context "real" means "in opposition to the totality of
God's creation" (353). Hence it must also be said: "The Nihil is
not exhausted in sin" (352). And in this connection, in order to
recognize the Nihil, we may not start from our own reason, our
consciousness of sin, nor from our "consciousness of the Nihil"
(347 ff.). In doing so we always encounter only what is mediate.
Only God in the flesh, only Jesus Christ can directly accuse me of
being a sinner, a real sinner. Only in Jesus Christ does it now happen — something no "abstract law of God" can do — that the
real God also becomes knowable to me as the adversary and sub-
duer of the Nihil: the God whose "goodness toward his creature"
is demonstrated precisely in that he "has also vindicated and restored the natural right of his creature with his own right to his
creature" (351). God is himself the One attacked when his creature is attacked, and — as he repels the totality of the attack — he
"forgives not only the sins of men; he also removes the cause of
their suffering" (354).

With such sentences Barth has already given an implicit criticism of the conception of the Nihil, of evil, in Julius Müller, Leibniz, and Schleiermacher, as well as in Martin Heidegger and Jean
Paul Sartre. In what follows he addresses himself to this criticism
in an analysis which goes into the greatest detail (355–402).

Barth's main objection to Julius Müller is that, though perhaps
unintentionally, he at any rate did not consciously and consider-
ately take his bearings "from the heart of the gospel." Consequently he did not understand the law, by which sin is known, concretely as the "law of the covenant," but as an "abstract demand,"
as "the moral law" (358). Corresponding to this stricture there
is then also the circumstance that he looks upon sin too much as
an "isolated phenomenon." "Where the whole Saviour, the perfect Comforter does not stand at the beginning as the source of
knowledge, it is not to be expected that in the end there will result
a knowledge of the whole misery of the creature, of the perfect
negation, which is the source of the misery" (359).

Barth's chief objection to Leibniz is that he accomplished that confusion of the Nihil with the shadowy side of the creaturely world, and then in turn arranged it in his over-all picture, so that the " adversary " is " domesticated " (362 f.) ; in fact, in the end the Nihil becomes simply " nothingness," the " absence of something " (364) , something " in the good," indeed a " special form " of the good (363) . The result is that after Leibniz has converted the Nihil into something positive he no longer even catches sight of what is " really positive " (365) .

Barth energetically defends Schleiermacher against some frequent misinterpretations. He cannot be reproached on the ground that for him sin has no reality (370 f.) ; or that he simply equates it with " sensuality " (371 f.) ; or that in his teaching it is, especially in its form as original sin, merely a " state " (372) ; and that he wants to evade the idea of a " punishment for sin " (373) . Rather, attention must be definitely called to the fact that according to Schleiermacher (in which Barth agrees with him) the nature of Nihil is " that which God has negated in his omnipotent grace," and therefore " only exists in this relation to it " (373) . God is the " author " of sin " in that he negates it " (374) ! But — and this is now Barth's serious objection — in Schleiermacher it is then actually still a question of a subjective occurrence: " In virtue of his holiness God permits the discord in our existence to become sin for us through conscience. He himself has here no antagonist and enemy " (377) ! But then what is to prevent man perhaps on his part from giving a new interpretation to or denying what meets him in conscience, or making evil to be merely the reverse side of the good? (" Evil compensates the good," Barth explains; 382) . Must not the opposite be said, if man's need of redemption is to be treated seriously, namely, that " God himself is chiefly engaged in that powerful negation of the Nihil "; that it is a matter " of his very special concern " (378) ? The reason Schleiermacher does not see this is because he somehow wants to know the Nihil from the absolutely established reality of Christian consciousness, apart from the " relation " in which it (the Nihil) alone is " real," that is, apart from the " reality which God has opposed in Jesus Christ " (380) . For that reason he never did catch sight of real sin (383) .

In Barth's view Heidegger and Sartre are also not to be equated. They stand " together only back to back as it were " (383) . Sartre has " behind him " what Heidegger " has before him " (389) . " In Heidegger we have to do with the premise of Sartre's view, in Sartre with the consequence of Heidegger's view " (389) . With both it is a matter of " the Nothing [4] having become a principle, a dimension, and commandment "; " but with Heidegger it is almost solely in order to show its powerfulness over against existence [5]; with Sartre, in order to show the existence of which that principle has taken possession " (389) . In Heidegger the Nothing [4] is revealed in " dread," and precisely the Nothing,[4] which is so revealed, therewith renders possible the " revealedness of what exists as being such for human existence " [5] (387) . Heidegger has never been a " nihilist " [6] (390) . Even Sartre's existentialism does not bear the usual features of nihilism. On the other hand, Sartre regards himself as an atheist; Heidegger does not. But that does not matter much — it could also be the reverse. Actually in both the Nothing is plainly a " pseudonym " for divinity (395) , only that in Heidegger the Nothing itself becomes a substitute for God, whereas in Sartre it is " man " who " finds, chooses, wills himself and lives responsibly under the Nothing " (393; 395) . However, Barth's objection to both is that while they think " in and from a real encounter with the Nihil " (397) , they certainly have not yet thereby " advanced into the dimension " " in which the Nihil, according to Christian knowledge, is to be seen and to be broached as the real Nihil " (398) . They are both fundamentally still with Cartesius. So long as man is still able " to put ' the Nihil ' behind him," just so long is the true enemy still unknown (399) . The " dragon," which is here " visualized," is " relatively harmless " (399) . That is especially true of Sartre. In opposition to Heidegger it is to be said that his concept of " being," as he has recently understood it, as well as his concept of " the Nothing," as he earlier stated it, are " ambivalent," ambiguous, and in certain instances interchange-

---

[4] " Das Nichts."

[5] " Dasein " — a term to which Heidegger has given prominence. Lit., " thereness."

[6] " Nihilist " is here used in its usual philosophical sense of one who denies any objective ground for truth or moral principles.

able. The concept of the " real Nihil " is, however, " in truth not
an ambivalent concept " (401).

In a concluding summary Barth now speaks about the " reality
of the Nihil " (402 ff.).

The Nihil does not " exist " in the sense that God " exists " and
the creature " exists." " What actually and truly exists can in fact
only be God and his creature " (402). However, the Nihil is also
not simply " nothing," that is, nonexistent. It really exists, but
only in a way peculiar to itself and known only to God, because it
is grounded in his negation. " The creature knows it only because
God knows it in his existence and in his way of acting against the
Nihil " (404). Only in God's action does the Nihil have its " ontic
coherence "; it is " the other," from which God " separates " himself and in opposition to which he " accomplishes " his will (405).
God is truly also " Lord of the sinister." Hence the Nihil is " not
accidental." But it is also " not a second God " (405). It lives
solely from the fact that it " is what God does not will " (406).
When Barth further calls it " evil," he thereby means a " being
alien to grace, contrary to grace, devoid of grace," and adds: " This
negation of grace is the Chaos " (407).

The dispute with the Nihil — Barth stresses this very explicitly
— " is primarily and essentially God's affair " (409). For the Nihil
is aimed against God himself, and, though the creature is certainly
threatened, it cannot be primarily its business to ward it off. " The
creature has always succumbed to the real Nihil " (413). And
Gen., ch. 3, shows that it is lost just because it tries to conduct the
dispute itself, to be " here itself the sufferer, fighter, hero, and
victor," and so to be like God (413). If it is really the " mystery
of God's free grace " to make " his own " the cause of the creature
which has succumbed to the Nihil (411), then it is iniquitous
when the creature, disdaining this grace, undertakes " to help and
to save himself " (414), especially when it thinks that it is itself
the " party which is first and really concerned." In Barth's view it
is one of the most dangerous " heresies " to regard God as " standing over against " the Nihil " more or less untouched and uncon-
cerned," and man on the other hand as having the " task " of set-

tling the dispute with the Nihil "on his own" (415). For "a God which was not gracious" would be, in whatever form, "an evil, a nihilistic [7] God." And a creature, which wanted to help itself, would be necessarily "an evil, a nihilistic [7] creature" (416). "The whole concept of the Nihil depends upon the fact that the original antithesis and the original encounter, in which it has its nature, is its opposition to God himself" (416).

However, in this opposition — fulfilled in the Crucified — it must also now be true of the Nihil that it "possesses no permanence" (416). It has certainly "not been created by God," [8] and (that means) there is "no divine covenant" with it (417). But the goal of God's work in Christ is that the negated and rejected actually be "put to rout" (420), and that there be "no enemy with which God has to do" but "still only his creature" (418). "In looking back upon Jesus Christ's resurrection and forward to his Second Coming," that is, "in the knowledge and confession of the Christian faith," the only thing we can still say about the Nihil is that it is the "monster [9] which in Jesus Christ has passed away" (419). The "Kingdom of the Nihil . . . is destroyed" (424). Now naturally Barth also knows what texts like I Peter 5:8 say. The "general revelation" of the "destruction" of evil has "not yet happened" (424). However, the Christian does not look timidly and fearfully at the Nihil but back to Christ's resurrection and forward to the Second Coming, and in this vision he has "the freedom" "to consider the Nihil as done away with" (421).

[7] "Nichtig."
[8] The text (of the Dogmatik) reveals a typographical error on p. 417; instead of "nicht" it supplies an obviously unintentional "wohl."
[9] "Unwesen."

XIV

THE ANGELS

[Volume III, 3, pp. 426–623]

———

BARTH's doctrine of the angels is the first large-scale project of this kind in a very long time. The reason why Barth deals with the angels, and with " the Kingdom of Heaven " in general, and thus with the " invisible " sphere of creaturely reality, here first in connection with the doctrine of providence, indeed, in its wider context, and therefore not already in his doctrine of the " creature " (III, 2), is because, contrary to the dogmatic tradition, he does not in the first instance ask about the " nature " of angels but about their " service." (See especially pp. 525 ff.)

Correspondingly, in the first part of our section (§ 51: " The Kingdom of Heaven, God's Messengers and Their Adversaries ") Barth calls special attention to the fact that " strictly speaking " the doctrine of angels has " no meaning and content of its own " (428). Even the otherwise so strictly maintained connection of every dogmatic proposition with the Person of Jesus Christ is here more indirect. Angelology is " not, like anthropology, a consequence and an analogy of Christology. For God did not become an angel in Christ." Angelology must rather be understood as an " annex to Christology "; since God is present to man in Christ, this presence of his always includes that of the angels as well (586).

Under these circumstances it is appropriate for Barth to speak first of the " Limits of Angelology " (426–486). In the first place, here especially it can be only a matter of assertions in which Scripture is the " teacher and master " (429 f.; accordingly this section is also particularly rich in exegetical expositions). Further than this, the Scriptural witness is really to be " pondered," to be " understood and explained " (430 ff.). In this connection it is to be considered that angelology, like demonology, takes us in a special way into an area in which " history, which is rationally conceivable according to the common analogies of world events familiar to us, passes over into saga or legends which are not historiographically

verifiable " (432) . Nevertheless they are then " true saga or legends " (432) , and when we — " demythologizing "! — undertake
to " translate " them, that is what they must at all events remain.
It is still better " to relate this history in language which is less intelligible today than to introduce another history in language
which in our day is supposedly or actually more intelligible "
(433) . The transition which the Biblical statements accentuate —
between " history " and " saga and legend " — is only a reflection
of the transition which the angels themselves represent; for with
them it is a matter of a " projection of the unfathomable into the
fathomable " (433) . " Divination," " phantasy," and " poetry "
are absolutely necessary in order to speak about them. But, in view
of the transition character of the subject (the angels) , as well as of
statements about them, we also need order, rationality, and discipline (435) . Thirdly, Barth makes the reservation that in the doctrine of the angels we must also proceed strictly according to the
rule: *credo ut intelligam* — I believe in order to understand. Right
here, where we are plainly in the realm of mystery, it would be especially dangerous, on the basis of certain " preconceptions "
(438) , to want to know in advance what the angels might well be
— and at this spot Barth then protests against the whole tradition
of angelology in the Early Church and in the Middle Ages. To be
sure, he pays Pseudo-Dionysius Areopagita, whose angelology
stamped the thinking of centuries, the compliment of acknowledg-
ing this impressive intellectual achievement (445–452) , and the
same applies to the angelology of Thomas Aquinas (452 ff.) . But
both, from their general presuppositions based upon a conception
of the world, inquire about something that is not answered in the
Bible, and ignore the real nature of the angels, namely, their service (see particularly pp. 455, 460) , however energetically and logically they refer to dimensions in which we are here indeed obliged
to think. On the other hand, in view of that: " I believe in order
to know," the attempt of an " enlightened " Protestant theology is
impossible which looks with one eye at the " angels in the Bible,"
as it were, and with the other at some " real or invented category "
on the assumption that it is identical with them (466 ff.) . Here
one thinks of all those views in which the angels are transferred to
the realm of " ideas " or to the " realm of spirits." Lastly, Barth

averts what he calls an " angelology of shrugging one's shoulders "
(479 f.), that angelology in which the only vital question is just
what are we to "make" of the angels or can make of them — a
question which Barth declares is falsely posed (478). (Unfortunately within the limits of this report we cannot go more fully into
exceedingly important details of the extensive sections in small
print, here but briefly touched upon.)

The foundation of angelology is offered by Barth in the section
" The Kingdom of Heaven " (486–558).

" He who in the Biblical sense . . . says God also says heaven,
and he who in this sense . . . says man also says earth " (487).
Therefore theology cannot be treated abstractly, disregarding
" heaven " and " earth," as solely a doctrine of God and man. But
now — as Barth has often emphasized already — heaven is " God's
creature " (488). If it is so that there is an " eminence " of heaven
or of angels, it is not identical with the pre-eminence of the Creator above his creature. Nevertheless, there is doubtless a " correspondence " here: the whole creaturely reality, heaven and earth,
is a correspondence " of that for which it has been created — of
the encounter, history, and fellowship between God and man "
(490). Because and as God deals with man, therefore and thus
there are the " above " and the " before " of the heavenly creaturely sphere, and the " below " and the " afterward " of the
earthly (491). It is therefore the history of God's dealing with
man, in which the superiority of " heaven " over the " earth " is
revealed, a superiority, for which Barth is willing to allow the
concept of a " hierarchy " to stand, which Pseudo-Dionysius introduced (492). With " heaven " as the upper creaturely sphere, a
" boundary " is set to man together with his " earth." God is
" closer " to heaven " than to earth " (496), and so heaven " in its
relation to earth " is a " parable of God in his relation to man "
(496). That does not depend upon the " nature " of heaven
(497 f.), and hence there is no " independent ontology of heaven "
(515); rather, " heaven " and " earth," that is, the invisible and
visible creaturely world, are " qualified " solely by God's action,
solely by this history (492, 498).

With the doctrine of the " Kingdom of Heaven " we are, accord-

ing to Barth, " at the peak of the entire doctrine of creation "
(498) . In the light of the second article of the Creed we must again
speak of God's " condescension," his " faithfulness," and his
" Kingdom " (498) . The " act " of creation was seen in this light;
and everything that " exceeds " it (thus the whole event of divine
servatio and *conservatio,* of divine operation and co-operation and
divine government) first appears as that which it is: as a " movement proceeding from God, aimed at the creature, and extending
to it " (499) . " That is truly the height and depth of God's free
grace: He has chosen himself and he has chosen the world he has
created to the end that he be altogether living, active, and busy in
it . . ." (501) . Because it is so, the " below " of the earth in no
way signifies a devaluation (502) . To this " below " reaches a
movement whose origin is that " above " — heaven! God's action
as history, as " movement," has a Whence and a Whither. In an
earlier place (II, 1, 527) attention has already been drawn to the
fact that we may not ascribe spacelessness to God. " Spacelessness
means an absence of distance. And an absence of distance means
identity." Barth now returns to this thought. God has " his own
peculiar sphere " within the creaturely world, and that is heaven
(503) . Heaven is really a " place," even if an " inconceivable
place "; it is a " created place," yet " God's place " (509) . For that
reason the term " Kingdom of Heaven," prevalent in Matthew, is,
it is true, a figure of speech, but one that is of " very real import "
(505) . And hence it is also understandable when God's governing
activity is described in other Biblical figures of speech as proceeding from heaven and takes place " by heaven sharing in it " (506) .
At the same time it is not a matter of something " cosmicly higher,"
but of " the Higher " to whom all thought is raised (509) . The
" standard definition of heaven in the Bible " is Col. 3:1. " Where
is heaven? Answer: There where Christ is. But Christ sits at the
right hand of God " (511) . That certainly does not mean that God
is limited in Jesus Christ to one place, though no doubt an " on
high " is thereby " established " — the exalted Christ is truly the
One who is coming and who is present! However, we ought not to
lose sight of the heavenly " Whence " in the earthly human
" Whither " of God's action in Christ. Otherwise our theology
could only become an " unmysterious," and therewith an " unan-

gelic," and then at bottom an " ungodly " business (558) !

What substantially may we say about heaven from this stand-point? In the first place it is certainly the sphere of mystery (515). But it is not an inflexible, sealed-up sphere but one that comes to us in God's action! And thus heaven proves to be, " it is true, an inaccessible and unknown yet real category of existence." It is " definitely not a vacuum " (517). Its " existence " is not self-suffi-cient but an " obedient existence " (518). In heaven " something happens," namely, " the will of God " (518). Barth is referring to Matt. 6:10. But if we bear in mind that what happens there has earth and man as its goal, and that God's action is not " mis-shapen " but takes place in an organized diversity, then we must also say that that heavenly event is for its part " an event which is ordered, organized, unified but also differentiated in itself " (521). Here Barth refers in particular to the Biblical idea of the " Lord of hosts " [1] and to the fact that in the Old Testament " heaven " is in the plural (522 ff.). However, if that statement about the di-versity, order, and differentiation of heaven, and of the event pro-ceeding from it, must be maintained, then we must further say that in the Kingdom of Heaven there are also " elements," " mem-bers," " singularity," " individuals " (525) — a statement which, like all the rest, can only be uttered in a thorough respect for the inconceivability of the " Kingdom of Heaven," and hence it can-not amount to a " definition " of the heavenly creature (525). When we speak of such individual beings, we are to think of the service which they perform in the structural unity of God's action and which, as a service of the " merciful " God, is also a service to the " earthly creature " (527). Here we naturally think of Heb. 1:14 (" ministering spirits ") in connection with which the ex-planation of the term as referring to a " liturgical " service is re-jected as one-sided (529 f.; cf. 440, 443). The designation of an-gels as " celestial beings," " holy ones," or even as " gods " (Ps. 82:1) or " sons of God," also belongs here. What is meant is that they belong especially to God; never that they have a power or im-portance of their own (530). Barth finds it worthy of note that the multiplicity of Biblical statements elude any systematizing — the names which emerge from time to time " melt away " " in one's

---

1 " *Jahwe der Heerscharen.*"

hands, as it were," and this is just what is "impressive" about them (532). No significance of their own! Nor any hierarchy! All we can say is that there is an "order in function" or an "order in service" (536). That is especially true in regard to those "principalities, powers, and dominions appearing in the New Testament . . . ," "which then" (perhaps Rom. 13:1) "find their antitype in the earthly political powers as powers of a relative peace" (535).

We reported that we cannot speak of the angels' having a power or importance of their own. Even their activity can "not consist in their doing something that God alone can do" (537). They would be truly "their own apes," indeed, they would be "demons," if, "under the pretext and appearance of being helpers, saviors, comforters, prophets, priests, and kings themselves . . . they were . . . to turn the earthly creature's attention, veneration, and gratitude to themselves" (537)! Their real service "is the service of witnesses" (538), and what is more, of "primary, . . . authentic, . . . constant, . . . unchangeable, and infallible witnesses" (540). Not because they are celestial creatures but because God has appointed and called them to be witnesses, their existence is to that extent an "exemplary" one: in their testimony all testimony of all creatures has its model and prototype (541). Of course this is not intended to mean that possibly the Church had to imitate the angels directly — especially in their "cultic" function. The ministry of angels serves the God "who did not become an angel but man," and hence the Church's service must be peculiar to her, and different from that of angels (556). This last point was made particularly in a discussion with Erik Peterson, and in the course of a thorough interpretation of Rev., chs. 4 and 5, with which this subsection closes.

The subsection "God's Messengers and Their Adversaries" (558–623) forms the conclusion of the section and with it of the whole volume. It is angelology and demonology in the narrower sense.

"Where God is, there is heaven, and there are the angels also" (558 f., 487). This sentence stands out like a theme. Barth immediately explains that one ought not to speak of an "experience of

angels." Whatever might be meant by that, in Scripture it is always
" experience of God and of Jesus Christ " (559) . For where God
acts, he is also " surrounded and accompanied, ministered and
testified to by a heavenly creature " (559) . Then in a quite definite sense angels are mediators of his grace in that they are simply
" at hand " without prejudice to God's exclusive activity (559,
579) .

With that the first question is: What and how are the angels
related to God (561–577) ? First of all they are *his* angels — very
often with the possessive pronoun so designated in the Bible (561) .
That is the way they exist, and only therein are they angels. They
would, in fact, be false spirits, if they wanted to be anything else
than humble servants, if they wanted to draw the attention and
love of a fellow creature to themselves (562 f.) . Their service in
this utter dependence is then characterized again as that of " pure
witnesses " (566) . At that, however, " all genuine witness to God "
lives " from the witness, and so from the service of angels " (567) .
This witness guarantees that " there can be room for God's mystery on earth," and that God will not be confused " with some sort
of static or dynamic, spiritual or material datum of the created
cosmos " (567) . " The dimension and category of the divine " is
brought to light in the angels (568, 572) as a boundary and as —
an opened boundary. They stand " on God's side opposite us ";
but precisely as such they have " to do with us " (568 f.) . What the
Old Testament says about the " *maleak Yahweh*," about the messenger of Yahweh, can — under certain circumstances in the same
context, e.g., Judg. 13:2 ff. — also be said of Yahweh himself in
his relation to man. But Yahweh's messenger proves quite definitely that in his appearance Yahweh draws near to man in a way
that cannot be gainsaid, and through its accompanying witness the
angel immediately brings the event into relief from among all that
is ordinary, as well as from all that may be meant by religion and
piety (571 ff.) . However, angelic apparitions, as in Gen., ch. 18, for
example, ought not to have been connected with the *Logos,* with
the second Person of the Trinity; the angel is " God's angel for
Israel " (570) , " a functionary of Yahweh's special relationship
of grace " (571; a quotation from G. v. Rad) . For Christ is " more
than a pure witness of God. He is, like the Old Testament cov-

enant God (and as the reality of Him who is hidden in the Old
Testament, though already proclaimed in the form of mere promise), the Godhead itself, speaking and acting upon earth." No
angel is " identical with him "; neither is he " prefigured " by
any (570) !

The second question concerns the " nature and meaning " of
the " service " of angels (577–599). On this point Barth attaches
the greatest importance to the fact that the ministry of angels
always bears the character of indirectness (578). It certainly can
never take the place of God's action. As mentioned, only in a very
restricted sense can we even speak of a " mediation." " God is
present upon earth even without the angels. . . . But where his
presence becomes an event, an experience, and a decision for the
earthly creature, then there is the activity of angels in which this
becomes true as coming from him." It is " God himself who speaks
with man." But when he does so, then " it is just his angels by
whom he distinguishes his voice from all others." " God himself,
and God alone," is " the Lord in the covenant of grace." But if,
" in carrying out his covenant . . . , he continually proves to be
powerful, strong, and mighty, then this proof is made . . . in his
angels' being on hand " (580 f.). The angels, we heard, are " pure
witnesses." To that extent they are " the archetypes of the prophets
and apostles " (581), without their service being able perhaps to
replace " that of the prophets and apostles, or the congregation's
position as a witness " (583). What " is to occur finally on earth "
is not the witness of angels but that of man (584), in the event of
which " already the last times, already the consummation,"
" dawns " (583). Barth then shows the peculiar indirectness of the
witness of angels in a thorough discussion of the relation of the
" activity of angels " to the work of Jesus Christ (585 ff.). It is remarkable enough that both in the Gospel narrative and in the account of the " forty days " (593) the witness of the angels is indeed
heard at the beginning and at the end, but not in the middle. It nowhere appears beside Jesus' own acting and speaking (587). And
with good reason; for it is just here that the angels' " holy want of
independence " comes to light (587). " The ' He must increase,
but I must decrease ' of John 3:30, also applies to them " (588).
They announce, they point — but they retreat where Jesus ap-

pears! That does not mean, to be sure, that they are not at hand; but it does mean that they remain hidden with respect to him whom, indeed, they simply announce, simply attest.

Thirdly, Barth asks about the name or concept which would best do justice to the position and ministry of angels (599–608). In all the variety of Biblical usage he finds that "angel" is still the most suitable; the concept clearly refers to a "function and activity." He "characterizes" this activity as a "delivery of a message," the "making of an announcement," the "execution of evidence" (599). For, as we already reported, the angels must be understood entirely from the standpoint of their service. "We only know them in what they do" (600), and their service is that of messengers (601, 567). We immediately get off on the wrong track if we understand them otherwise than as coming from the God to whom Scripture bears witness. (Then they become intermediaries, "hypostases" on their own, etc.) As surely as their service is an action upon men, just as surely is it strictly God's action. If, for example, we are going to speak about "national angels," then it is not thereby a matter of representing national interests, as it were, but "God's interest in order and power" (607). And if we are going to speak about "guardian angels" at all (which, according to Barth, can only mean that the Christian may know that all God's heavenly host is summoned to his aid), then it is definitely not a matter of the "granting of certain favors." On the contrary, the assistance of the angels consists in "advertising God's assistance" for man (606). It would be an insult to the angels to fancy their being elsewhere than there where they actually are: in the service of God who intercedes in favor of man.

The demons, which are now discussed in closing, are designated as the "adversaries" of "God's messengers" in the heading of the section. According to Barth they are absolutely nothing else. In no respect do they belong together with the angels in the same sphere. "There is no common denominator to which they both could be reduced" (609). To be sure, God is also their Lord, but only in their negation and subjugation, and ultimately in their annihilation (611). For that reason one cannot also believe in the devil and in demons, "in the way that one believes in God, and may also believe in angels " (611). They are "the myth of all mythologies." Hence, a faith in God, with respect to them, can only be a " demythologizing," " disbelief " (611). However, it is just this fact which precludes wanting to " demythologize " them together " with the angels, with the miracles connected with the act of atonement and Christ's resurrection, and in the end with God " (611)! But " in this way it suits . . . them perfectly! "

In what he goes on to explain, Barth naturally follows his teaching about the " Nihil "; for it is the " origin and nature " of demons (613). Consequently they indeed " exist," but " only improperly " [2] (613). They belong to the " kingdom " of the Nihil (614) which, it is true, bears a " resemblance " to that of angels, just as a lie bears a " resemblance " to the truth. But in no respect are they homogeneous (615 f.). Under these circumstances two basic mistakes are to be avoided. If we " ignore " the demons, they " deceive us in that they conceal their power from us." If we " absolutize " them, and if we fear them " as veritable powers," then one is deceived in that they conceal their character as lies (616 ff.). They exist; but they are nothing but lies. And therefore " only the truth is a match " for them (620). God's truth " puts an end to them." Where it does not prevail, they are certainly able to do their lying work. But where God's truth is present, they are " revealed, unmasked, and exposed as pseudo powers " (620). Connected with this is the fact that their appearance in the New Testament is much more palpable than in the Old. In the light of " God's Kingdom coming from heaven to earth " the opposition and contradiction naturally " become much more concretely manifest." However, this opposition and contradiction become manifest precisely as the Nihil (621). Thus a " Biblical demonology " can, " in fact, only be the negative reflex of Biblical Christology and soteriology " (621) — a doctrine of the enemy which has been overcome and of a " world which has lost its demonic spell " (622).

[2] " *Nur uneigentlich.*"

XV

COMMANDMENT AND FREEDOM

[*Volume III, 4, pp. 1–126*]

—————

A s BARTH finished his doctrine of God (II, 2, 564 ff.) with a chapter on " God's Commandment " and thereby defined " ethics as a task of the doctrine of God," so now his " doctrine of creation " also opens up into ethics which — as the twelfth chapter of the entire work — bears the title: " The Commandment of God the Creator." [1] With this we are not offered a complete ethics. In the foreword it is stated that " in particular the whole complex of the state, society, and justice could here only be touched upon in passing." Barth would contradict himself and annul the trinitarian approach of his work, if he wanted to countenance the opinion that " beside this commandment (that of God the Creator) there is another commandment of God the Reconciler separated from it, and then yet again a third separate commandment of God the Redeemer " (35). However, as the doctrine of the Trinity allows to the Father, Son, and Holy Spirit each a special work of its own (the doctrine of *appropriationes*) so there is now indeed a " differentiation of spheres " in which the one commandment of the triune God takes place. Therefore (in the imposed " inadequacy " of human knowledge), theology may and should nevertheless consider separately that which in itself is certainly a unity (36). This means, for the development of the work as planned, that each of the awaited fourth and fifth volumes will also close with an ethics attached to it. Thus the state, which Barth designates as a " genuine and special ordinance of the covenant " (343), properly belongs at the end of Vol. IV. Naturally, however, even already in the present chapter the state and society, yes, also the nation and the fatherland, cannot fail to loom in sight, although certainly not as " orders of creation " in the ordinary sense. In distinction from the " general ethics " [2] presented in II, 2, we now

[1] Zollikon, 1951. 810 pages.

[2] TRANSLATOR'S NOTE: Naturally the term " general ethics " does not here refer to abstract, philosophical ethics but to the nature of God's commandment in general.

have a " special " ethics in which attention is directed to the man who is placed under God's commandment, and what is more, to his concrete action. " Here, in the realm of the concrete, the particular and the special in regard to human possibility and reality, it needs to be seen and shown that, and to what extent, there is a good human action under the dominion and efficacy of the divine commandment " (5). Concreteness, however, does not produce casuistry (5 ff.). " Casuistry is an infringement of the divine mystery in the ethical event " (11). It is the attempted removal of and threat to human freedom in action. It is man's attempt to place himself upon God's throne and — in advance — to know of himself what is good and evil. What is more, it always fallaciously presupposes that God's commandment is a general rule (11 f.). It is therefore as much an encroachment upon the mystery of God as it is upon human freedom established by God's commandment.

Then the question is whether, in obedience to God's commandment, man is not dependent, from moment to moment as it were, upon ever new individual revelations. How often may this question have been put to Barth in the course of the years! Is not his whole theology — so it was asked — a constant reference to that " perpendicular from above," to that " vertical " which, incalculable and underivable, ever in and from God's freedom, can meet and dissect our reality, time, and history? And must not ethics, as it might seem, in order to escape from the fanaticism which lies at the door (it has recently been called " the logic of the hour " [3]), inevitably take refuge in speaking (like Brunner) about the commandment and the orders, or in the end even simply about " orders of creation " ? Now there really could be no doubt about Barth's not being a defender of a theology concerned with what is exclusively " vertical," for even the first pages of III, 1, would conclusively show that. But it is clear that in our context Barth must once again return to the same point from another angle. The way in which he answers here fundamentally determines his whole ethics. " When one stands before the ethical question, one has not simply a vertical to pay attention to; not simply that occurrence, those many occurrences, of the encounter between God's commandment and human action in their . . . once-and-for-all-

[3] " kairologisch."

ness and uniqueness. For just these events take place . . . each
in a particular context. . . . Only because the vertical intersects
a horizontal can it itself be vertical " (17 f.) . But now, however,
there is a " constant factor in the divine commanding " (18) , just
as in the light of this commanding there is a " constancy and con-
tinuity of human action as well " (17) . However, this horizontal
is not to be recognized anywhere else than once again in God's
Word. In no sense does it constitute an independent, and so perhaps " natural," magnitude over against the Word, which we could
know by ourselves. (This sentence is directed against Emil Brunner; 20 ff.) Nor is it to be understood (as Bonhoeffer tried) by
the idea of a divine " mandate." For in regard to the horizontal it
is " purely and simply a matter of showing certain constant conditions as such " (23) , and these do not possess the character of an
" imperative." And yet — there is this horizontal: " the ethical
event, as an encounter of the concrete God with a concrete man,"
takes place in a " particular place." For this reason there is actually
a special ethics (28) . The " particular spheres and conditions,"
which become " visible " in the encounter between God and man,
could also be called " orders " (31) . Yet then it would appear as
if they, as such, were already " laws, precepts, imperatives," whereas
in truth they are " spheres," " but not laws " (31) . Consequently
it also follows then that " reality," in terms of our experience which
has been determined for us in one way or another, cannot serve
as that horizontal (39) .[4]

What we just now found to be characterized as the " horizontal "
becomes clearer when in the following Barth speaks about the
" sphere " in which man, " without prejudice to his oneness and
wholeness," is " specifically God's creature " (49) . God's commandment, as inculcated time and again, does not meet man in a
vacuum, as it were, but already in his " creaturely existence." But
this means that it does not meet him in a sort of neutral or even
independent " reality " (39) , or in an " order of creation " understood in this sense, but rather as the creature for which Jesus Christ

4 TRANSLATOR'S NOTE: Another reference to Emil Brunner's conception of " reality " set forth in his book *Das Gebot und die Ordnungen* (1932), translated by
Olive Wyon under the title *The Divine Imperative*, The Westminster Press, Philadelphia, 1947.

is the ground of knowledge and therefore the " real ground " of
its creation (43) . The man, whom God's commandment befalls,
is " the creature . . . to which God in Jesus Christ is gracious "
(44) . In fact, " he is the creature whom God has created, willed,
and called into existence in a quite definite peculiarity, and who
then, as such, is a transgressor who, in spite of his guilt, has been
preserved and delivered from his lost condition, and who, as such,
is also in the end honored as a child of the Father " (46) . Accordingly we should be permitted to say, though no doubt abbreviated,
that even that horizontal, even that which could be called " natural," is not " nature " but grace, but it is really grace in the proper
sense of the word — grace which God manifests in Jesus Christ
and nowhere else. Hence Barth's description of man's genuine
" reality " is grounded solely upon " God's existence as man in
Jesus Christ " (47 f.) . Thus God's commandment, as the commandment of the Creator, does not meet man in a vacuum and
not in a neutral or independent sphere but just in the human
existence which God himself has established in Jesus Christ and
has chosen for himself! If this is true, then it also follows that the
commandment — as the thesis for the first section of our chapter
(52) reads — is " the sanctification even of man's creaturely actions." In this sense Barth too can now speak of an " order of creation." He understands by it " the order," " that is," the special
" sphere of divine commanding and human action, in which the
God who is gracious to man in Jesus Christ here also commands
as the Creator, and where the man to whom God is gracious in
Jesus Christ also stands before him as his creature, and is to be
sanctified and liberated by his commandment " (49) .

Liberated! It is, in fact, a basic contention of Barth's that in the
commandment, and in the sanctification of " man's creaturely actions " which takes place through the commandment, man is
placed in freedom. " Where God commands . . . it is ultimately
and decisively a matter of man's . . . exaltation, precisely in his
inevitable subordination, adaptation, humbling, and humiliation
in the midst of his limitations. There he is placed by the law — it
is, of course, the ' law of the Spirit of life ' and not the law of sin
and death (Rom. 8:2) which he now comes to hear and to which
he now becomes obedient — not under a law but is called into

freedom " (745) . This basic idea is developed thematically; in
each of the sections of our chapter (and of the volume) , in which
the meaning is unfolded, God's commandment is discussed in such
a way that " freedom before God " (§ 53) , " freedom in community " (§ 54) , " freedom to live " (§ 55) , and " freedom within
limitations " (§ 56) is granted to man by the commandment. And
this fourfold aspect of human reality in turn is taken, once again,
not from general experience but from God's existence as man in
Jesus Christ. As such it is 1. existence " in a history," the existence
of a creature who is called to be responsible to God; 2. " existence
in encounter "; 3. existence as " the subject of a material organism "; and finally 4. a " temporally limited span of . . . existence " (48) . Along these " four lines " man's " particular structure " as God's creature is recognizable — and right here, at the
place so designated, the commandment is man's liberation (50) .

We now have before us the essential basic ideas Barth develops
in this chapter. They are to a large extent the basic ideas which we
already learned from his doctrine of man as a creature. Only now
it is a matter of the sanctification, and that means at the same time,
of the freedom of man as a creature. This combination of sanctification and freedom is rooted in Barth's doctrine of the law as the
" form of the gospel " (II, 2, 564) , a doctrine which he put forward long ago (and which since then has been much disputed) . It
finds its clearest expression in the fact that Barth begins his " special ethics " with the day of rest. " In the commandment for a day
of rest it is a matter . . . of human action which, precisely as rest
from one's own work, consists — to put it comprehensively — in
a readiness for the gospel. The import of Holy Scripture, even
where it commands, is the gospel " (55) . Thus the day of rest is
" the sign of the freedom which (according to Gen. 2:3) God the
Creator has reserved for himself," and at the same time of the
" freedom which he has given to his creature and which he has
thereby required of him " (57) . An ethics which begins in this
way will consequently see the commandment and freedom together in all their aspects. Such is the case, for example, in the
section on " Man and Woman " (127 ff.) . There a natural law
does not rule, not even a natural law raised to the dignity of meta-

physics. On the contrary, there a man and a woman are called into
marriage by the commandment (205). At the same time an ab-
stention from marriage, depending likewise upon a divine calling,
and hence celibacy, is kept in view (205, 159 ff.). Thus the decision to live together is also understood as a voluntary arrangement. The case is similar in regard to what Barth has to say about
calling and vocation (686 ff.). Strongly opposed to a widespread
tradition, he contends against equating the two. Calling [5] is an
ever-new event resulting from God's freedom. However, it always
finds man already at his " place " of responsibility. (Barth here
adopts Bonhoeffer's expression.) To be sure, it is once more the
place which God himself, as the Creator, had assigned to him
(687). Barth is constantly concerned about two things. In the first
place he is anxious that that concrete " place," the concrete " field "
of human action, be not neutralized over against God and be not
regarded as something self-sufficient, as it were, which as such
would be shut off from God's ever-new, free call, or in relation to
which this call for its part would be like a self-enclosed glass bulb
(692). His second concern is lest the immensity of this " place " or
" field " should, just for this reason, also become a tyranny within
which there is no more freedom. God himself is the one who acts
in his commanding on either side. For this very reason his commandment is man's preservation from the totalitarian power of
" orders " which have been rendered independent, as well as from
being directed into an empty space in which there could no longer
be any concrete action or obedience at all.

We have already mentioned that Barth begins with the day of
rest. We might add that this whole ethics, though it actually does
not hesitate to touch upon everyday problems, acquires something
intrinsically joyous and festive about it because of its axiomatic
and thematic starting point. " The commandment for a day of
rest interprets all other commandments or all other forms of the
one commandment! " (58). As the course of all history (" natural
history and world history ") is secretly determined by the " special history of the covenant and of salvation " hidden in it (60),
so all of man's actions are determined by this one day that has been

5 " Berufung."

singled out. This one day, as the goal of the history of creation, is at the same time the manifestation of the final day of all history from which all other days, hastening toward it, receive their meaning (61). The rule governing the day of rest is also the rule for the workday (69)! And that definitely means that the day of rest is based upon God's commandment to man to acquiesce in God himself having " taken " his cause " into his own hands " and " so out of the hands of men " (63). God therefore demands " faith " of man, that is, a " renunciation " of all arbitrary willing and doing (64, etc.). He therefore forbids him to have " a faith in his (own) planning and willing " (58). The day of rest is to be understood from the standpoint of that faith in God the Creator and that creaturely renunciation. Then, but only then, do the humanitarian and also religious aspects follow as a matter of course. But if such is the case, the commandment for a day of rest can in no sense be reduced to a sort of generalization. Then it actually requires that one particular day be singled out (just as the history of salvation is a particular history) — a day which " belongs to God and not to man " (72). For that reason it is a " day which is to be free of every necessity," a day which has its meaning in joy, in the " celebrating of a festival " (73), and thus not in an " artificially enforced unemployment " (74), and which is not given to a man in his " isolation " but " together with his fellow man " (75). This last specifically means that the day of rest serves the " assembling of the congregation " " which God has charged with hearing and proclaiming the witness to himself " (77). That this one day is not then an isolated day in the succession of days, shut off by itself, is shown by the fact that it is not the last but the first day of the week. " Just in its particularity " it is " a sign of that which is the meaning of every day " (78).

Perhaps many a reader of this ethics will now be a bit astonished that Barth, who otherwise shows no fear of " secularism," should begin in such a peculiarly " ecclesiastical " fashion. Well, this is also the way he continues, right to the last page. And he does so, moreover, not for the sake of a " sacred " realm sealed off by itself, but simply because in none of the creaturely aspects of his life can man be really free unless God is known and worshiped as the Creator. Accordingly Barth — still in the section (53) which

deals with " freedom before God " — links confession (79 ff.) and
prayer (95 ff.) with the day of rest, and both, indeed, as the required confirmation of that freedom before God. Here he is also
concerned to show that, since the day of rest is a particular day, it
is not merely a matter of a perpetual " attitude " of confession
and prayer, so to speak, but in both instances of concrete acts. Confession is, " in fact, also and truly a confession of the lips " (82),
and prayer, though " perpetual," " may and must " " also be ever
again a single act, and have the character of a particular concrete
action " (97). In every respect they belong together. " One can
only be God's witness as one becomes a witness ever again. And
that is just what is involved in prayer " (96)! It is true of both that
they are only meaningful as an activity within the congregation
(90 ff., 112 ff.), though charged, as such, to the individual. As surely
as they have been commanded, both are just for that reason a voluntary activity. Confession is " undesigning," since it is done
" solely to the honor of God " (84). It is " positive " even when
it is " faith's protest "; it first says Yes, and not No (89). As a free,
responsible action it is " not confined to any calendar or to any
hour " (93). This is also the reason why it cannot be thought of
as a " permanent state " (86); the man who confesses " sets foot
upon a mountain peak above which there is only heaven " (93)!
And prayer, moreover, depends neither upon our needs and
wishes, nor upon an ever so reasonable desire in man, but solely
upon a " freedom before God " granted to man, and to that extent,
upon God's " bidding and commandment " (104). Not to want to
pray because of a supposed humility is an illicit " luxury " (105).
However, just because prayer rests upon the freedom granted to
us before God, it may be therefore " definitely supplication "
(106 ff.) into which even gratitude, even repentance, and even
adoration merge (108 ff.). Of special importance is also what
Barth says about the hearing of prayer. He describes it as " human
supplication taken up and into the plan and will of God " (117).
The idea that, since God is " unchangeable," he is not able to answer prayer, Barth calls (as he did similarly in II, 1) a " miserable
anthropomorphism " (119). For God's unchangeableness simply
means that he is unchangeable " in his being the living God, in the
mercy in which he interests himself in his creature " (120)!

Man before God — that is the subject with which Barth has commenced his ethics. And in so doing he has separated himself from many teachers of ethics, who, possibly like Emil Brunner or no doubt Albrecht Ritschl, wanted to exclude man's relationship to God as such from the sphere of " morality " (52) . He has tried to show, on the contrary, that since ethics begins with God, even it begins with freedom. And that ought to be of considerable importance not only for theology but for the pastoral ministry as well.

XVI

FREEDOM IN COMMUNITY

[Volume III, 4, pp. 127–366]

IN THE doctrine of creation (III, 1) Barth had laid great stress upon the fact that God did not intend himself to be a lonely God, and that correspondingly man's creation in the image of God, as the creature called to be God's covenant partner, consists in his "cohumanity," and what is more, primarily and originally in the relationship of man to woman and woman to man. In this connection he had taken over from Bonhoeffer the concept of an *analogia relationis* (of the correspondence between God and man existing just in this mutual relationship). Consequently, we could expect Barth's doctrine of the "commandment of God the Creator" to give a prominent place to the relation of man and woman. Indeed, here the lines which had been prepared in III, 1, are extended.

"Cohumanity" is "natural" to man; it is assigned to him "naturally" (127). And the commandment of God the Creator addresses him on the basis of that fact (128). In addition, the "distinction and relation" between man and woman is "the original, and at the same time exemplary, sphere of cohumanity." (128). It is, in particular, as Barth reiterates at this point, the only one which rests upon a "structural and functional difference" (129; cf. III, 1, 208). God's commandment signifies, when it has reference to the encounter between man and woman, first, that here "what is truly transcendent appears on the scene" (132). Thus even in this area man is neither "without a lord" nor "abandoned by his Creator" (132). It signifies, secondly, the "radical relativizing" of the encounter between man and woman, the complete exclusion of any myth which so easily emerges at this point, as well as of the confusion which just as easily arises here (133). Lastly, the commandment signifies that in this area also, and precisely in this area, man is ushered "into freedom" (133 f.). Hence, the attempt to elevate the relation of man and woman into the metaphysical (like Schleiermacher) or to raise it to a sacra-

ment (like the Roman Church) is forbidden. Every effort to
undertake an " apotheosis," and thereby to lift man out of his creaturely situation as man in relation to woman (138 ff.), is cate-
gorically forbidden. Here especially man is really only a creature,
and not somehow " creative." And therefore while it is true that
man is a creature in " analogy " to the Creator, he is, just for that
reason, by no means in an " identity " with him (138). Thus God's
commandment undeniably effects a " limitation " here as in every
other sphere (142).

But, on the other hand, the " soberness," which the commandment produces, lies in the fact that it is addressed to the whole
man. In the light of the commandment the relation of man to
woman cannot possibly be regarded merely as a " sexual problem "
(143). The sexual relationship can therefore never lead a " life of
its own " (145). Sexuality for its own sake would be rather a
" demonic affair " (146), or, as Barth repeats: " Coitus without coexistence is a demonic affair " (148). If, according to Gen. 2:24
and I Cor. 6:16, man and woman become " one flesh," or, according to Eph. 5:31 (cf. v. 28), one " body," then we have to consider
that in the Bible " flesh " and " body " do not simply denote the
physical body (148).

At any rate, as Barth now argues in defining the subject more
narrowly, the ethical question, in its bearing upon the relation of
man and woman, can by no means be restricted to marriage
(154 ff.). Unquestionably marriage is the " goal " and the " center " of the sphere now under discussion (155). And " undoubtedly everything " that happens within this area is " to be measured " by the standards which apply to marriage. " Whatever is
. . . in keeping with marriage is good in this whole sphere; whatever in this sphere is contrary to marriage is evil " (155). However, this does not mean that marriage in some way absorbs the
existence of man and woman into itself, as it were; there is also a
" periphery " of marriage, " within which the male is also a male,
the woman is also a woman, man is also man, and within which
the ethical question is also an actual one " (156). Above all it must
be considered that — " in the congregation of New Testament
times " (159) — marriage is actually not an " obligatorium." In
the Old Testament, as long as the One Son is awaited, " no provi-

sion is made, so to speak," for celibacy (157). In the New Testament, on the other hand, now that "necessity for the procreation of children in the history of the covenant" has lapsed (158), the renunciation of marriage may also be "understood and appreciated as one course, and as a matter of a special gift and calling" (159); in which, indeed, I Cor., ch. 7, instructs us.

Barth now continues in such a way that, without directly entering upon marriage (though it always lies within his "field of vision"), he first of all endeavors to achieve "certain viewpoints" concerning what might be good or evil in the relation of man and woman (165 ff.), in order to turn next to marriage itself (202 ff.).

In the initial chain of ideas Barth first advances the thesis that God's commandment for man and woman alike is that they should be "truly and wholly" man or woman. Each is God's creature in the way in which it is what it is, "and each is as such God's image" (168). Admittedly it is not quite possible for us to describe more precisely in terms of ethics, over and beyond this theological insight, the specific differentiation of both; ultimately it will always be a "mystery" (167). What is discoverable here by way of typology is by no means ever a commandment (169). But most certainly God's commandment puts "the man always in his place and woman always in hers" (171). For that reason they are both prevented from exchanging with one another what is peculiar to each, or from allowing it to be merged in a supposedly higher unity, thus becoming a "nondescript" creature (173). Of course, they are both human beings; but their unity is to be sought only "in the unity of God" (175). It is never to be acquired by their leaping over the boundaries which have been established for them in their individuality, and thus in the end not wanting to be either man or woman. Where the ever-special sexual determination becomes a matter of indifference, indeed, a "burden," supposedly "in favor of a superior human existence," there "begins a flight from God which, as such, is then without fail a flight into inhumanity as well" (177).

Secondly, God's commandment mutually destines man and woman to be co-ordinated, to belong together and to turn to each

other. Here Barth refers especially to I Cor. 11:11. Their " adjust-
ment " to each other determines the " nature of both of them "
(181 f.) . " In the Lord " — as Gal. 3:28 shows — the Jew can only
exist in his turning to the Greek, and the man can only exist in his
turning to the woman (183) . " They are one in the Lord. That is
what keeps them together " (183) . Barth understands this mutual
co-ordination of man and woman (wherever they meet each other,
and not merely in love or in marriage) as the basic form of cohumanity. Consequently we are here concerned with the " very
heart and core " of everything that is to be said about " freedom in
community " (183) . Accordingly, everything then that looks like
a hermitage for men or women, as well as all male or female
" orders," is " sheer disobedience " (184) , and the sickness of
homosexuality can all too easily ensue where man no longer
acknowledges the commandment which directs him as a man to
woman and vice versa. It is a consequence of " failing to recognize
God," which then also results in a " failure to recognize man " and
becomes a " humanity without one's fellow man " (184) . As opposed to this, the commandment intends that man and woman
" mutually see each other "; that they " know themselves as ques-
tioned " by each other, and " give account to each other " (185 ff.) .
The " other " is " always and everywhere present " " as a standard
and criterion " (187) .

Thirdly, the dissimilarity and mutuality of both sexes in relation to each other is subject to a " definite order " (187 ff.) . Here
there is actually a priority and a posteriority, a superordination
and a subordination (189) ! Just in that fact woman possesses a
dignity which belongs especially to her. And man does not thereby
acquire some sort of " personal glorification " (189) , since he too
is " subjected to an order " (191) . Because this order, about which
we are here speaking, " is realized first in Christ himself " (193) ,
woman is " subordinated by the same Lord by whom man is ex-
celled " (193) . In her subordination woman is an " image of the
congregation which is obedient to Jesus Christ." Precisely in that
fact there is, in a certain sense, a " primacy " which has been given
to her. Here Barth refers as he had previously done in III, 1, and
even more in III, 2, to familiar passages, especially in Eph. 5:22 ff.

and I Cor. 11:3 ff. To state the matter comprehensively: " In an
imitation of the conduct of Jesus Christ " man " may and should
take precedence " over woman, " as she may and should take precedence over him in an imitation of the conduct of the congregation
and therefore in discipleship " (195 f.). Both have, each in his
place, a pre-eminence — but each one in his place! That means,
however, that the man who — in obedience — adheres to the
order given to both parties is the " strong " man, that is, the man
who knows and exercises his " special responsibility " for just this
order (197). The woman, who corresponds to this man, is a " mature " woman who, likewise, takes " her proper place within that
order " (197). The opposite type is that of the " tyrannical " man
and the " slavish " woman (198). These " mutually give rise to
each other " (199) ; and on the other hand, a " rebellious " woman
and a " weak " man likewise give rise to each other (199 f.).
When things are done properly, the " strong " man proves to be
" gracious," and the " mature " woman to be " unassuming "; and
these again mutually give rise to each other (201 f.).

An introductory report, especially at this point, could sketch
only in barest outline the thoughts of a book which, even humanly
speaking, are extremely impressive and always exceedingly sober;
otherwise whole pages would have to be reprinted here.

Barth now turns to the subject of marriage (202 ff.). If the relation of man and woman is the exemplary form of cohumanity
in general, then marriage in turn appears as the " exemplary form
of the meeting of the sexes " (203). It appears as the " once-and-
for-all," " unrepeatable," and " incomparable " relation of man
and woman. It is therefore a " life companionship," and as such,
it is " complete," " exclusive," and " lasting " (203). It does " not
simply exist "; rather, its realization has its origin in a " decision
and act " of both partners, in " love's choice," in a *diligere,* in a
loving selection (204). What, then, is God's commandment at this
point (which Barth expressly distinguishes from what follows
from the institutional character of marriage; 251 ff.) ?

In keeping with the fact that the commandment and freedom
belong together, Barth begins his separate expositions by declaring
that the pathway to marriage certainly does not spring at all from

a " necessity of nature," and not even from a universally valid commandment of God which required marriage of everyone. On the contrary, it " is a matter of a highly special, divine calling " (205). For precisely in the light of God's commandment there is also a pathway leading to celibacy. Thus marriage is again seen to be " a matter of freedom, not of an old humdrum way " (205). Under these circumstances one can understand why Barth devotes special attention to the establishment and realization of marriage (208, 239 ff.). It is not something that can be taken for granted, and, in the light of Matt. 19:1–12, it certainly can never appear so (207). If here God's calling is effective, then it is thereby said at the same time that marriage in its entirety becomes " subject to God's commandment " (206). It is thus — as a " life companionship " — " more than love." Its nature is such that in it love is, " of necessity," " repeated," and that also certainly means in suffering, in growing old, and in sickness (209).

A " life companionship," however, is a " task "; it " does not fall into anyone's lap "; indeed, it is a " work of art," requiring constant " labor " (210). Such a special task is not to be subordinated to any other purpose, neither to that of sexual satisfaction, nor to that of providing a maintenance, nor even to that of begetting children. It includes, it is true, " the inherent readiness to have children "; but it does not " depend upon the coexistence of a child " (211). The family is not placed above marriage but is " coordinated " with it (211).

Marriage, as we already heard, is a " complete " life companionship. That does not, of course, imply an " equalization "; such would, indeed, presuppose that that " order " of a reciprocal relationship had already been destroyed (213). However, it does mean that both march together " in step." When both persevere in it, they carry out the idea of " marital fidelity " according to its " positive and primary meaning " (214). The " order," which is required in the relation of husband and wife, does not destroy the inequality (216 f.), but primarily lays upon the husband the responsibility for the fellowship being one that occurs in freedom. " In the last analysis all complaints that are raised in marriage " fall " upon him " (216).

Marriage is an " exclusive " life companionship; it is, " in its

nature, monogamous " (218). Here it now becomes completely
clear that Barth's doctrine of marriage is theological ethics. For
the history of the " institution " of marriage, as we know, also reveals polygamy (218). The commandment of God — " of the God
who in his grace is free and yet is the freely electing God " (221) —
requires monogamy unconditionally, or more correctly: monogamy is " really not a demand and a law at all, but a gift, a gospel "
(221). And here a difference between the Old and the New Testament plainly appears. (Barth has sharply called attention to it
elsewhere in this volume, and thus apart from this particular context; 229 ff., 243 f., 277 f., 299, 456.) " The question whether marriage should be monogamous or polygamous could still appear to
be an open one within the Old Testament sphere of the promise
and the announcement of the Kingdom " (223). For the covenant, which had indeed been established, was, in its exclusiveness, only announced (224). Only the " fulfillment of the covenant " (224) finally opened the way for monogamy, and moreover,
now as an imperative; so that the Church must also " demand
monogamy in institutional marriage." However, she must not confuse its existence with the commandment (227). — Incidentally,
according to Barth the exclusiveness of marriage renders the entrance into a second marriage after the loss of one's husband or
wife " even less a matter of course " than the entrance into marriage at all (226); and for this he refers to I Tim. 3:2; Titus 1:6.

Marriage is a " lasting " life companionship. " The person who
enters upon marriage thereby gives up the possibility of with-
drawing from it again " (228). Also in this respect the Old and
the New Testaments part company. In the light of the " fulfilled
covenant," of the " appearance of the Son of Man," the law does not
in some way experience an " intensification," but is " surpassed "
(230). What the Old Testament reader read out of Gen. 2:18–25
had to be something else than what may now — Mark 10:5 f. — be
read out of it. The covenant, which was undoubtedly the " internal
presupposition of creation " even for the Old Covenant (III, 1),
has been revealed in the New Covenant. That also signifies something new for marriage, since it receives its permanence from the
fact that it is " directly confronted with the manifest will of God "
(230). Thus the lifelong marriage has not been " devised " by any

authority but has been "discovered in this truth besides which
there is no other," and to which an institutional lifelong marriage
can never give anything but inadequate expression (231). In the
light of God's commandment which has now been revealed, there
cannot be, in principle, any divorce, and even less perhaps a "marriage on time" (231). "What God hath joined together, let not
man put asunder!" Meanwhile, what has God joined together?
As Barth raises this question, there again appears, as in the question of the establishment and existence of marriage, the divine calling, which alone makes marriage to be marriage and whose presence in every marriage can by no means be taken for granted
(233). For Barth this means positively above all that without faith
and the Word of God no marriage can be entered into, preserved,
and kept (234 ff.). But it also means, negatively, that a "borderline case" can arise in which a marriage becomes separable because
it has not actually been joined together by God but is "based
upon human arbitrariness and human error," and therefore "in
God's judgment . . . has never been contracted and has never
come into existence at all" (236). "Even this negative decision,
the submission to a judgment upon a marriage, recognized as final, can become possible and necessary in freedom, and thus is in
the obedience of faith" (237). At all events it would be a false
Biblicism to rule out the Old Testament allowance for divorce as
"law," but to regard the opposite New Testament position as
"canon law" when, in truth, it is the "gospel," an "offer of freedom" (237). But then it stands to reason that civil divorce is not
an essential part of . . . God's commandment but pertains to
marriage as an institution. However, such a course is not absolutely closed to a believer, provided he accepts it simply "as
(God's) judicial sentence" (238). In view of the "hardness of
men's hearts" divorce can never be, it is true, a good way; yet it
can be the "better" way. It can be a return to a point from which
two people "can be restored to new obedience" (239). Hence
Barth is also opposed to refusing, on principle, a wedding service
in the case of a second marriage then about to be entered upon
(239).

If marriage is such a serious business, as Barth teaches us to regard it, then it should be especially important to ask what God's

commandment means for the way in which marriage comes about.
In Barth's opinion Christian thought in general says too little in
this respect (208). And moreover, the " misfortune of most (not
all?) ' unhappy ' marriages " goes back " to a misfortune precisely
in the inner way in which they came into existence " (240). It is
there and then that where possible an arbitrariness prevails which
does not inquire about " God's calling and gift " (241). We have
already seen more than once what emphasis Barth places upon
this point. To be sure, the two people who enter into a marriage
may and should " choose." In their choosing they may " at least
imitate, portray, and exhibit " the " incomparable history " of
God's covenant (242), and it corresponds to the already repeatedly
discussed relation of the New to the Old Testament, that this
choosing, in which God's election by grace is mirrored, as it were
(242), has now emerged from the " shadow " which lies " upon
the whole sphere of marriage " under the Old Covenant (243).
The " choosing " which man may and should do is that of love.
But in Barth's mind love is " the free decision of a man and
woman, in which they may know each other, give themselves to
each other, and desire each other (the last in this order; 244), as
those who have been joined by God in a conjugal life companionship, and thus are called and endowed for one another." When
love is this, then the human " intentions, purposes, and ventures "
in it are directed toward that which in the divine calling is " not
at the disposal of men," but just for that reason it is to occur " in
the free decision of a man and a woman " (245). When man conducts himself in this attitude, then his reciprocal " understanding," " surrendering," and " desiring," that is, the eros, is " sanctified by God's commandment " (246). Under these circumstances
Barth is able to speak very soberly about eros. " True love is . . .
a sensible love " (247). He is able to make a careful and yet " sensible " distinction between love and affection, and can issue a drastic warning against the intermediate area between love and affection (against love affairs as being the more dangerous, because
they are thoroughly irresponsible; and against the flirt, as being
less dangerous, because it is the type that moves more along aesthetic lines; 248). But he can do so only from the side of that theological point of departure, and simply in view of the fact that in

reality a "sanctified *eros*" exists only where a man and a woman "also have Christian love and therefore faith; where they are united not only in *eros* but also, and first of all, in *agape*" (250). From this standpoint he can ask whether, in truth, the "whole dilemma of love" is not "also and primarily a dilemma of faith" (250).

It is also in keeping with the requisite soberness that the "institutional side of marriage," thus in particular the "wedding," is for Barth — as we mentioned — nowhere identical with marriage which is subject to God's commandment (253, etc.), though it is to be seen in connection with it. Marriage is "also an outwardly" responsible act "in relation to human society" (251). It "cannot and does not want to be carried out simply as a private undertaking" (252). In this connection Barth takes into account the circumstance that a wedding has a "domestic" side to it. A marriage without the willingness to come to an understanding with the parents is "in most cases" an "unsuccessful" enterprise even though parents cannot make a marriage, and though we have to consider that the partners are "adults" and hence "on their own," and even though they, in turn, should be "respectful" and "ready to learn." In addition, the wedding has a "legal aspect," and finally, it doubtless has an "ecclesiastical" side as well — even though a church "wedding service" is neither Biblically, nor essentially, an "unconditional requirement" (255).

But who keeps the commandment of God which determines man and woman in their dissimilarity and in what they have in common? Barth's answer is given in a kind of theological paraenesis. And he argues that surely the only one who keeps the commandment is he who "acknowledges and accepts" it in its unity and entirety (259). That, however, is the man who at the same time allows himself to be told that in respect to the commandment he is "in error"; that he is therefore an "adulterer" (260). Precisely because man lets this be told to him, and admits God's judgment upon him, he cannot possibly "rest satisfied with being a transgressor" (265). For God's judgment distinguishes between the man who must recognize himself as "God's good creature" and the "man who has incurred his judgment in the state of his transgression" (265). Thus, the "Go, and sin no more" (John

8:11) amounts to " God's call to war " (266) which puts man in a
" state of alarm," in the light of which, however, there is now no
longer the possibility of seeing this whole sphere as all black.
" When man does not keep the commandment, then the commandment itself keeps man " (269) ! And as everyone is here placed under judgment, so there is also no one who would not somehow " be
reached by God's goodness and in his way be preserved and comforted " (268) .

In Barth's view the relation of man and woman under God's
commandment is " exemplary " for " freedom in community." It
is therefore not the only form in which that freedom is valid. And
if it is to be said that that exemplary form — however indirect it
may be — reflects God's covenant, it is also true in a similar sense
of the relation of parents to children: the excellence of parents
consists in the " correspondence of their parenthood to God's being and action " (274) , or more exactly, in the " Fatherhood of
God revealed " in Jesus Christ " and in man being a child of God "
(278) . It signifies at the same time that all human fatherhood has
a derivative character; that the Fifth Commandment is under the
First; and that parental authority possesses a domestic as well as a
symbolic function. But it means — since commandment and freedom also belong together here — that precisely in this limitation
of parental authority and honor there is to be found, not their abolition to be sure, but rather their legitimate establishment.

As, however, along with the question about marriage Barth also
raised the question about celibacy resting perhaps on God's calling, so also, in the relation of parents and children, he is concerned (which is easily understandable after what has been said
above) about the question of a possible childlessness. Barth believes that to think that an unintentional childless marriage is not
a " normal, full marriage," as Brunner does, is an " abstract, Old
Testament " judgment (299) . Childless couples, especially, should
know that " *the* Child, who is the only one that matters, has also
been born for them " (299) . The propagation of the human race
post Christum natum is no longer an unconditional commandment (301) , and hence the lack of a child is not an absolute defect.
Indeed, Barth goes still farther. If the procreation of a child is an

act " of a simple, courageous trust in life " (305) , the lack of which
is the cause of earnest questions with so many people today, then,
at least in a borderline case, it must be admitted that the muster-
ing of this trust in life cannot be supposed to be a universally
valid rule; for then faith would become " a law so to speak "
(306) . The will to have a child is actually a decision (303) ; and it
would be a mistake to equate the " course of nature " directly with
God's providence, or to accord it equal authority (304) . As surely
as the deliberate foregoing of offspring can endanger sexual intercourse, and with it the marital relationship (302 f.) , and as surely
as the foregoing of a child can be the " refusal " of a divine offer,
as little can the marital relationship be restricted to the purpose of
procreation by simply letting nature take its course. Thus in
Barth's view there is — as a borderline case — the possibility of
" birth control " (306 ff.) , provided that the decision respecting it
is made " with a free conscience " and therefore not with a " bad "
one; that it is a common decision; and that, corresponding to the
position of the husband, it becomes a greater burden for him than
for the wife. It may be said that precisely the section in which this
difficult question is handled shows us especially clearly the basis
of Barth's ethics. If anywhere, it becomes evident at this point that
he knows no other freedom than a freedom in God's commandment, and what is more, he knows God's commandment not otherwise than as a commandment of freedom.

Barth ends the section on " Freedom in Community " with a
part entitled: " Those Who Are Nigh and Those Who Are Afar
Off " [1] (321 ff.) . Here it is chiefly a matter of man's existence in a
people (as the essential meaning of " those who are nigh ") and
in mankind (the essential meaning of " those who are afar off ") .
Here we do not have to do with creation, but with God's providence, and therefore not with a commandment which is perhaps

[1] TRANSLATOR'S NOTE: " Those who are nigh and those who are afar off " is a
literal translation of the German: " *Die Nahen und die Fernen.*" Barth has evidently
taken it from Eph. 2: 13, 17. By " those who are nigh " he means those who are a
man's acquaintances or associates, and therefore that people which is any man's own
people. By " those who are afar off " is meant foreigners or strangers, and therefore
mankind in general to which every man belongs with his people. The question
Barth raises here is what significance God's commandment has for man in these
forms of community which are broader than those of marriage and the family.

especially valid at this point, but with God's dispensation (344, 349). This means at the same time that neither the language, nor the people, nor the " Fatherland " (338), is " holy," but " God alone is holy " (329, 333). However, that does not now exclude, but includes, these spheres, within which and at whose " place " God's commandment meets man, as being precisely in God's providence and dispensation — not " *ordines,*" not " orders of creation " — but " *ordinationes,*" " orderings " (341). If this, moreover, be so, then man's sanctification by God's commandment inevitably also means the sanctification of " his historical existence " and therefore it includes " his historical responsibility as a member of his people "; otherwise it could certainly not be his sanctification (333). Thus there results, it is true, a profound but, under God's commandment, a fruitful, positive, liberating relativizing of his connection with his people. And this necessarily involves that the man whom God's commandment meets is never directed into his own people alone: it is God, " the Lord of all history," who permits the nations each to go their own ways. But he has fulfilled the " history of his covenant " in the " one Man Jesus Christ," and has thereby established a center and a goal for the history of all peoples. However, he thereby of necessity ushers the man who hears his commandment out of the " narrow confines " of his own people into the " spaciousness " of the one people of God, and to that extent into " mankind " (335). With that the main outlines have been indicated within which Barth, in a final, renewed debate with the theology of " orders of creation " (345 ff.) illuminates this whole field. His ultimate purpose is to show, by contrasting in particular the account of the Tower of Babel with the story of Pentecost, that opening in the restriction which, first of all still within the people of Israel, opens the way for the congregation as the new people which does not do away with the existence of the nations, but points the congregation in the direction of another all-embracing reality.

XVII

FREEDOM TO LIVE

[Volume III, 4, pp. 366–648]

THE THEME of the unusually exhaustive section (§ 55), which is also the heading for this chapter of our report, will seem immediately remarkable to many. Practically all ethics teach that God's commandment — we think of the Decalogue — forbids murder and so protects the life of another person against our encroaching upon it. But can it be said that there is a commandment which commands us to live? Only if there is such a commandment, can we then indeed speak of freedom in accordance with Barth's presuppositions. An ethics stemming from idealism has no use for anything that could be connected with the " right to live," because the right to live is purely natural and therefore " prior to morality " (369). But could there not also be theological considerations of another source which referred us strictly to the " vertical," to that familiar " perpendicular from above," and which did not want to know anything about a " horizontal "? And could not such a reference acquire importance in view of the circumstance that as a rule we exist, in fact, on an all too " horizontal " level and therefore we did not first need the divine commandment in order to " live " and for an " affirmation of life " (established in one way or another) ? We can understand why Barth covers a good deal of ground and why he takes special pains to be sure of his approach before he advances here to particular statements. Our understanding of him hitherto must have been very poor indeed if we were to expect him to assert that theology has no interest whatever in that " horizontal plane." (We need only to think of what he was able to say about " people " and " mankind.") And, what is more, our knowledge of modern man would be very slight indeed if we were to assume that he still had that unruffled (and precisely therein extremely unchristian) " affirmation of life " of a bygone day, and if we were not inclined to ask whether at bottom both that unruffled " affirmation of life " and the (no less unchristian)

negation of life and fear of life, so common today, were not due to
the fact that in this matter modern man knows nothing about the
commandment and therefore does not know about the freedom to
live either.

Barth begins with what he calls a " reverence for life " (366–
453) . With this idea he consciously associates himself with Albert
Schweitzer, without, of course, substituting life for God's commandment (367) . For Barth life is not, so to speak, " the highest
good," but a " loan." Yet just for that reason the " sphere of the
natural and the human " does not constitute an " ethical vacuum "
(368) . As theological ethics does not make life to be an absolute
value, so neither on the other hand does it countenance a " rigor-
ism " which regards life as being prior to morality since it is something purely " natural " (369) .

How is life a " loan "? How is it that I, who am " destined to be
free before God " and so pointed in a " vertical direction " (375) ,
am nevertheless also at the same time referred to a " horizontal "
direction? In answering this question Barth first of all refers back
(III, 2) to his doctrine of the creature (that is, of man) . Man actually " exists " distinct from God (370) . Through God addressing him he is acknowledged to be a homogeneous creature which,
as such, " exists in an indestructible order . . . as a soul of a
body " (371) . He is a " particular person " and has a " life of his
own " (372) . He lives " in time," yet as a creature which " is identical with itself " in the flux of time (372) and whose life has " a
certain originality of its own " — a " free subject of his life." For
God speaks to him; he does not decree about him wordlessly (373) .
Thus we are again confronted by that " vertical " which determines man. However, it is still only the one determinant to which
another then corresponds, namely, that man is destined to live in
a " solidarity " with his fellow man on a " horizontal " plane
(375 ff.) . That, then, is the man about whose life we are here
speaking. His life is seen from the way in which it has been determined, and it is recognized as a loan just in that fact.

However, this " loan " as such is not and cannot be neutral. On
the contrary, through God's commandment man receives the
" freedom to live." He receives the freedom to accept this life,
" and the life like his of all other men," not only as a " dispensa-

tion of providence," yes, as a " blessing," [1] but — in the light of
the fact that " in Jesus Christ " God did not become identical
" with the universe but with man " and " sides with man " — so
that he may honor the " trust God reposed in him " in granting
him this gift by his own spontaneous " management " of such a
loan (382).

From this it becomes clear how we are to speak about a " reverence for life " theologically. " The birth of Jesus Christ is, as such,
the revelation of the commandment as a command to reverence
life " (384)! The incarnation points to ethics! Therefore a reverence for life is not merely a " theoretical and aesthetic admira-
tion " of life, even though it means that I must " keep my distance " and have a respect for the mystery of my own life (386).
Rather, it is of a practical nature. It can never simply have my own
life in view but always the life of another person together with
one's own (387 f.). Since this life of mine is nevertheless a creaturely life and thus " not a second God " (388), and since it has
been granted in virtue of an eternal life and is therefore eschatologically determined, a reverence for life always includes an
" awareness of its limitation " as well — provided that the relativity of life thereby posited can never mean that man is discharged
from reverence. On the contrary, in reality it simply establishes a
limited restriction. Man cannot and ought not to " emancipate "
himself from the freedom to live by appealing to those limitations
(389 f.).

The commandment which requires us to reverence life (within
the extent described) finds its " explicit Biblical form " in the
words, " Thou shalt not kill " (390). Barth understands the commandment first in a positive way (in order then, in a later section
on " The Protection of Life," to consider its primarily defensive
character). He points to the various spheres in which a reverence
for life is manifested — life which is limited, pressed into service,
and which has been granted to the creature as a loan! He speaks
about the will to live (392 ff.); about the relation of human life
to that of plants and animals (396 ff.); about health (404 ff.), joy
(426 ff.), self-assertion (439 ff.), and power (445 ff.). Here the
main ideas, already briefly outlined above, are further developed.

1 " Wohltat."

We can call attention to only a few particulars. That the will to
live (including sexual life) deserves only a " conditional respect "
follows from the fact, Barth teaches, that man is truly " the soul
of his body " and the physical course of life takes the form of an
event which is " guided and governed by the soul which, in turn,
is awakened by the divine pneuma " (392) — a " loose-living
man " behaves in a manner " lower than the beasts " (392) ! However, neither may man deny a conditional respect for the will to
live; he " may not abandon himself to the power of the will to live,
and neither may he want to get rid of it " (395).

In regard to the relation of man to plants and animals, Barth
refuses, of course, to draw up a conception of " life " which would
embrace man and them together, much less to build an ethics on
that basis (376 ff., 396). But on the other hand, he stresses man's
responsibility even within this sphere. Of course, at the same time
he finds a difference between plants and animals which is shown
chiefly in the fact that, while the harvest is " not a breach in the
peace of creation," yet the killing of animals certainly presupposes
that this peace is " at least threatened " (401). Here Gen., ch. 9,
as well as Isa., ch. 11, are called to mind. Prominence is given to
the peculiar significance of the animal for the Old Testament sacrifice. And the unwarranted " murdering " of an animal is challenged (403). " Actually animals may be killed only in an appeal
to God's reconciling grace! "

Barth speaks at great length about the " will to health " as the
" strength to exist as man." Following logically from the main
ideas mentioned, and in a backward glance at his doctrine of God's
providence, he contends against refusing to have a doctor (410 ff.),
as well as against any confusion of the work of a doctor with a
sacerdotal function (411). However, it is above all a matter of
stressing the reality of sickness (in an obvious debate with Christian Science). To be sure, sickness is actually an " element and a
sign of the power of the chaos threatening creation " and likewise
" of God's righteous wrath and judgment " (417). Resistance to it,
and thus the will to health, would therefore be hopeless " if God
were not God and did not live, speak, act, and make himself responsible for man, if this whole matter were not first and above
all his affair " (419). But because such happens to be the case, and

because this becomes evident in the New Testament through the connection between the Kingdom of God and the healing of the sick, a resistance to sickness is therefore legitimate and commanded. Man ought to say " No with God " to that " whole sinister realm " (418). Here again Barth's meaning becomes especially clear when he understands the commandment from the standpoint of the gospel.

It may appear particularly striking that in the conclusion of this section — " in a somewhat daring wording " — Barth allows the will to live to pass for the " will to power " as well. Naturally he knows very well that the Bible nowhere permits power to appear as a " value " (446). The power which is given to man, together with the loan of his life, cannot legitimately be the " power of a Goliath " (446). It is nothing else than the " strength God has granted to man " (448). Consequently it is always power which falls to the lot of each particular man and which is necessary precisely for him. He has as little command over its size and caliber as over his life itself; and, like that life, he is to put it into service (451). The question for a man (but also for a generation of men) is not how much power he could have but how much he " must have " at any given time (450). Accordingly modern man's technical mastery of the world, which must call forth ever-new requirements in order to expand, and must then in the end become " a technique for disorder and destruction, of war and annihilation," appears in a truly gloomy light (451).

The commandment, " Thou shalt not kill," also signifies, as we heard, a " reverence " for life. But in its — significantly negative — wording it has first and foremost a " defensive " aim. It is a matter of the " protection of life." Barth speaks about it in the second main part of our section (453–538).

The commandment, which requires the protection of life, applies " unconditionally." But the question which in particular is repeated almost constantly is this: is the life, which is protected, also an " unconditional " thing? According to Barth's statements hitherto, this question cannot be answered in the affirmative. Life is certainly " not a sort of second God " (453) ; it is rather a " relative entity " (454). From this twofold fact, the unconditionality of the commandment and the relativity of the life protected by it, there results in particular instances the possibility of a " borderline case " (that is, of a permitted or commanded killing). With this there is no intention to limit the commandment (453). However, a limitation to the value which is placed upon human life is certainly borne in mind. The case of a justifiable killing of a man, which certainly occurs often enough in the Bible, shows that there is this limitation (455). However, in view of the incarnation, in view of the " identity of the Kingdom which has come with the Son of Man," and which is realized in the incarnation, and in view of the crucifixion of this Son of Man, the " protection of human life against willful extinction," is most certainly to be considered, on the basis of the New Testament, in a wider sense than in the Old, and consequently in practice the " borderline case " mentioned has to be further postponed (456).

Barth now examines the particular possibilities of violent killing: suicide (456 ff.), common murder (471 ff.), intentional abortion (473 ff.), and taking of a so-called " worthless " life (483 ff.), " euthanasia " (484 ff.), self-defense (488 ff.), capital punishment (499 ff.), and finally war (515 ff.).

The section on suicide immediately reveals the points of view which are decisive for the whole discussion. In contrast to a possible endangering or sacrifice of one's own life manifestly required in " obedience to the Lord of life," suicide is " the taking of one's own life as practical proof of a supposed and usurped sovereignty of man over himself " (460 f.). That is " foolhardiness and a high-handed procedure "; it is " wantonness " (461). To be sure, even suicide is not an unpardonable sin (461); but " the prospect of God's forgiveness is no more an excuse here than elsewhere " (462). But — how is the objectionableness of suicide to be established? Here Barth now gives an answer which does not come as a complete surprise but confirms afresh the importance of propositions long since propounded. The sought after reason can only proceed from the fact " that the Creator, the Giver and Lord of life, is a gracious God "; it comes, therefore, " from the gospel and from faith and not from a law " (462). Not a " You ought," but a " You may," stands over man's life (463). The " You ought to live " is the very thing that can lead a man into " temptation," into a false loneliness, into the delusion of sovereignty, and in the end into a self-elected death. But here is the root of the error: in the gospel a man may hear that God is gracious to him and that he may and can live therefrom (464). In the example of suicides in the Bible, Saul, Ahithophel, and Judas, Barth seeks to show that their sin — that is, the primary decision leading in the end to suicide — is a crime against God's free grace (466). Accordingly the message of the Church today can meet the problem of suicide, as well as other problems, only by a fresh preaching of free grace. " She has the Word which calls a halt to the suicide, but she must once again learn how to speak it, if it is to be effective " (467). — At the same time Barth teaches that every instance in which a person takes his own life is not self-murder; Samson may serve as an example, and examples from the history of the martyrs in the Early Church may be added (468 ff.). God cannot be prevented — and here the " borderline case " we mentioned becomes acute — from " actually granting to a man in a particular situation the freedom, the permission, and the command to take one's life; then in that case it is not suicide " (469) ! But this most remote borderline possibility is solely and exclusively God's affair (470).

The same basic thought which we have just encountered — namely, that God's commandment issues from his grace and that man must not, but may, live from it — also governs Barth's discussion of abortion. Barth emphasizes that in every case it is a question of taking human life. But whence are we to establish the reason for registering a " No " in this instance, when one takes into consideration all the numerous counterarguments? Barth again replies: not from the " law " but solely from the gospel (476 ff.) ! " Human life is not something forced but permitted; it is freedom, it is grace " (477). If man thinks he *has* to live, he will " not have at heart a respect " for life, nor indeed will he then have a respect for his own life or that of an unborn child (476). Thus reference is once again made to the fact that what occurs here as sin is directed against God's free grace. Just in that fact lies the seriousness of the matter. Even the fact that this sin is pardonable alters nothing in regard to it: whoever truly lays hold of God's forgiveness, " he, and only he, must and will realize that the divine No inexorably opposes the sin as such . . ." (478). — But even

here there is the possibility of a borderline case, namely, where it
is life versus life (480 f.). In such a case the decision may be made
to save the mother's life as against that of the unborn child. It
need not absolutely be so; in any case, however, the decision will
bear the character of an *ultima ratio*. Concerning the (in Switzerland as in other lands) legally established circumstances under
which an interruption of pregnancy is indicated, Barth states that
" by no means all that might be admissible and exempt from punishment, even in a strict . . . interpretation of these regulations,
is therefore also ethical, and permitted and commanded from the
standpoint of God's commandment " (481). Here — as also elsewhere — civil legislation does not relieve the individual of the
necessity of making a decision.

If in the two questions discussed so far Barth could speak, with
reason, of the legitimate possibility of a " borderline case," such
does not apply — in what follows — to the taking of a so-called
worthless life. It is to be regarded " simply as murder, that is, as
an outrageous usurpation of God's sovereign prerogative over life
and death " (483). And the same is true of " euthanasia." Whence
would anyone really know that an ever so painfully tormented
life " has ceased to be that blessing God intended for this man "
(486)? Is it not always an " arrogant, and therefore by no means
an auspicious, presumption," on the strength of which one here
imagines he is able to act (486)?

Barth sees " self-defense " and capital punishment in the same
category insofar as he looks upon capital punishment as the trans-
ference to a politically constituted society of the accepted right of
an individual (or of kinfolk) to defend himself. Hence on the
whole the ethical judgment runs parallel. In regard to " self-defense " Barth finds it worth considering that in and for itself it
arises from the natural instinct for self-preservation, which, however, as a natural instinct, is not by any means " holy " but needs
" to be sanctified by the commandment " (490). But what about
this? Do not passages like I Cor. 6:1–11 and Rom. 12:17–20, as
well as the Sermon on the Mount, point in a quite different direction? Barth answers this in the affirmative: the Kingdom of God
which has come, and its " salvation," sets a new commandment
over against instinct, and Barth is of the opinion that in this con-

nection Tolstoy or Gandhi had come very much nearer to the
truth than the attempt " to dull the edge " of such a commandment with the aid of the doctrine of the two realms (491) . Does
not a man in the act of self-defense act as if life, his life, were the
highest possession? And does he not have to have a reverence for
the other man's life, for the life of the assailant? Is not God, and
what is more, God in the grace in which he establishes a solidarity
between the attacker and the one attacked (492) , is he not completely eliminated in this act? Does not the man who acts in this
way insolently set himself up as the Judge? And yet — as clear as
the commandment is in this instance, as little is it a " law." It is
rather an " instruction, concerning the tenor of which the One
who commands . . . may not be forgotten " (495) . Tolstoy's or
Gandhi's mistake was not in having taken the instruction more seriously than a " Bible-centered Christendom " but in having made
a " law " out of it (495) . Let us note: Barth's whole concern is
once again to see that God's freedom is not in any way impaired,
and that it not be allowed to be lost even in the letter of the Biblical word. On the " outermost edge of the horizon " (493) he sees
the possibility of God's commissioning a man to offer active resistance on behalf of a neighbor who is threatened or for the sake of
law and order which has been attacked. Then such a man acts " in
the service of the divine resistance to evil " (498) , and his action is
not murder but an action that has been commanded.

Barth's train of thought in regard to capital punishment is similar. He finds the familiar theories for the justification of the death
sentence to be altogether unconvincing. Punishment as correction? Yes; but in capital punishment society quite arbitrarily sur-
renders the " obligation which it too has in relation to the crimi-
nal "! Capital punishment as a testimony to God's retributive
righteousness? Yes; that may apply to all other kinds of punishment. But precisely the death sentence, in which men effect something final and irrevocable, lacks the " humility " which men
ought to have in bearing witness to the righteousness of God
(505) . And above all it lacks — in view of the effect of God's righteousness which was finally accomplished in Jesus Christ — the necessary, simultaneous reference to forgiveness (506 f.) ! Capital
punishment for the purpose of safeguarding society and as a de-

terrent? Yes; but is punishment by death really the only means of safeguarding it? And in the countries which no longer have it, is there any evidence of an increase in the most serious crimes? Is it not above all a self-contradiction, into which society gets itself involved by inflicting this punishment? Does it not, in fact, inflict something that is irrevocable and unchangeable, whereas in keeping with the true nature of justice its action ought to possess the character of that which is always provisional and changeable? All these counterarguments lead Barth to demand the abolition of capital punishment (509). Of course, even here there can be a borderline case. According to Barth there can be something like a self-defense for the body politic. When the " existence " and no longer merely the " well-being " of the state is at stake, then it may be necessary — in this completely abnormal situation — for the state to deal with certain men forthwith " as its enemies " and to put them to death (511). Such a case can occur in connection with high treason during war (512 f.). It can likewise occur in what has been called " tyrannicide " (513 ff.). — Barth calls to mind July 20, 1944,[2] and statements by Thomas Aquinas, Calvin, and also by the early Luther. One can never definitely foretell such a borderline situation. Whoever in this instance acts on behalf of a state which is desperately threatened must count on being utterly alone, and " whoever does not find it difficult to decide to take such action had surely better not do it at all " (514).

War! One will scarcely come upon a place in Barth's expositions where one has so many questions of his own than here, and hardly any place where it is to be more urgently desired that Barth might find, not only critical readers, but also those who are ready to listen! What he asks us to consider at the outset, " to sharpen the conscience," is really nothing but a reference to facts that should be familiar: that today war can no longer be looked upon as a private problem for " military people "; that in wars it is never a matter of a crusade but usually it is primarily a question of economic power; that war has lost the last vestige of would-be glory. One ought to know all that! Nor should it need to be said that in the main the problem of war is raised decisively during peace (*si non vis bellum, para pacem!* 517). But what takes place in war? A

---

[2] The day on which the assassination of Hitler was attempted.

killing, for which all members of the political society are summoned in one way or another; which makes every member of another state, no matter whom, its object, and in regard to whose execution " obedience to God's commandment in all its dimensions "
is then called in question (519 f.) . Can it be justified? Barth urges
that here especially the " inflexible No of pacifist ethics " be
taken with the utmost seriousness. For it " has practically everything in its favor and its position is almost overpoweringly strong "
(520) . War may not possibly " be justified as a normal . . . element of that which, according to a Christian judgment, constitutes a just state, the political order willed by God," in the way in
which Christendom, with few exceptions, has let it be counte-
nanced since the time of Constantine (522) . The normal, the
" serious thing," is peace (525) ! It is Barth's opinion that immediate tasks result from this for the Church. She has to take a stand
for peace within the nations as well as for peace among them; for
good faith; for understanding and patience; for an education of
youth in the interest of peace and not war. She must declare herself against a so-called standing army and against all " inciting
hysteria." Admittedly " the Church exists in this aeon; she is
therefore not commissioned to proclaim that war is avoidable in
principle." However, she does have " the commission, even in this
aeon, to withstand the satanic doctrine that war is unavoidable in
principle and that it is therefore justifiable in principle " (526) !
The sentences just mentioned indicate that Barth — as he has frequently demonstrated in the past — does not advocate an absolute
pacifism. He reckons with the possibility of an extreme state of
emergency (527 ff.) . This can arise " where a people has serious
grounds for not being able to assume responsibility for the surrender of its independence "; or more precisely, " where it has to defend, *within its borders,* the independence which it has serious
grounds for not surrendering " (528) . Whether such a state of
emergency actually exists becomes apparent in whether the risk involved in it is accepted irrespective of the size of one's own and
the opposing forces, that is, whether it is actually accepted unconditionally (530) . The will for such a " just war " can be " just
only when it is an act of obedience," and it can be " effective only
when it is an act of faith " (531) . The question of war in general,

moreover, is never merely the business of the State. On the contrary, it is eminently the concern of the individual. And the Church has the grave task of ever again making it a pointed question for the individual: What have you done and what are you doing . . . (533 f.)?

In concluding this section Barth enters into a further discussion of certain particular issues. He declares himself in favor of universal military service because it specifically maintains the responsibility of one and all. A refusal to take military service is, in Barth's opinion, not to be ruled out on principle. However, then it is always a question, when rightly faced, of a line of action which is at once personal and political. It dare " not have anything to do with anarchism." The person who acts in this fashion should be prepared at the same time to accept willingly and without complaint all penal consequences (536 f.). The refusal to accept military service on the ground of the " ethical absolutism of radical pacifists " would really " rest upon an error." For here too it can only be a question of a relative decision on the part of the individual; he must remain open for a commandment of God which points in the opposite direction. Nor can he dispute on principle the state's right to wage war. In actual fact it can only then be proper when the one who refuses to serve acts as he does because the particular war which is to be waged is an iniquitous thing against which he protests by his action — at the risk of being in error himself. Precisely in view of the thoroughly concrete character of the decision, a decision which can never be made on the basis of absolute principles, the counsel and direction of the Church, or of well-informed individuals within her, is here necessary (537 f.).

But for what purpose are we to live this life which we are to reverence and to protect? Barth answers by teaching that it is to be looked upon as service. In this service it is an " active life " (the third part of the section: pp. 538–648). Man's activity, however, does not possess the character of a, so to speak, neutral and irrelevant occupation, but is " to consist in a correspondence to God's actions " (543). As such it is subject to the commandment; it is sanctified. In such actions human life " shares in the freedom of all God's creatures " (547). However, in man the " mystery " of

creaturely existence becomes " manifest," since he is called out
beyond himself and into an active life by the commandment (548) .

The decisive point of view, which stands over the whole activity of the human creature, is that, little as man becomes his own
" cocreator, cosavior, and coregent in his activity, and thus a sort
of co-God " (552) , nevertheless in his actions he may correspond,
within his creaturely limits, to God's actions; and that he is " summoned to a participation in the occurrence of God's will and
work " (551) . That is not based upon a highhanded appropriation
of the " word ' God ' " (549) but upon the fact that God is concretely man's God, who has nothing whatever to do with an
" empty, sterile, and — after all is said and done — intensely boring ' transcendence.' " He is the God whose concern " in all of its
austere divinity in eternity and in its historical fulfillment is man's
concern " (550 f.) .

When one thinks about it, can it be surprising that in his discussions about the " active life " Barth does not begin with pro-
ductive work or " cultural " work but rather with the congregation? What we heard about the day of rest is here repeated. Barth
does nothing else than take seriously the fact that God is God, and
so even man's activity, when it truly corresponds to God's actions,
takes place first and foremost there where God's own actions are
acknowledged, praised, and proclaimed. " Obviously a theological
ethics cannot want to universalize something that happens to be
special " (554 f.) , and the creature's response to, and vindication
of, the divine work occurs in the congregation and not just everywhere. She is a special people among the peoples of the world.
Moreover, she is a special people because, and only because, " she
has already become aware of the coming of the Kingdom which has
already come, is present, and will once appear in glory, and because
just through this awareness, as the congregation of the last times,
she is now engaged in an active life " (558) . She is a special people. (Thus she is never essentially a " national Church," but a
Church " for " a particular people; 559.) She is not an institution.
She is the people which is " constituted " by the coming Kingdom
(560) . And exactly for that reason she is called to serve through all
her members (560) .

What, then, does it mean " to co-operate in the service of the

Christian congregation "? It means, in the first place, quite simply:
Church membership! For rightly understood it is a " public, binding espousal of a cause " (563) which can be carried out only in
faith. As such, it is an " uncommon action " — " How narrow the
gate is here, how small the way "! (564) . Secondly, such co-operation means to be assembled together and thereby to be engaged in
the " building up " of the congregation (565 ff.) . There everyone
is called upon to be on guard against the dangers of schism and
heresy; to take part in the life and order of the whole; to share
in the theological work with which the congregation is charged
(" theology " being, " in principle, the business of every Christian "; 570) ; and to serve in love. Thirdly, such co-operation also
means to participate in the ministry of the congregation " outside
in the world " (574 ff.) . The congregation can " be only for the
world," if she is to proclaim God's actions at all, and " not against
it " (575) . Of course, she herself cannot supply " what men really
need," namely, the " freedom of the Spirit "; she can only " bear
witness " to it. But she cannot deliver this witness without " loving " (576) . Hence her turning toward the world is first of all simply " missions," the attempt " to summon non-Christians to a
knowledge of their calling and so to faith, to obedience, . . . to a
co-operation in the service of the congregation " (577) . She " is
a missionary congregation or she is not a Christian congregation "
(578) . This, however, directly applies to every Christian; every
Christian is, " as such, a missionary " (579) . Yet the fundamental
meaning of all missionary seeking and wooing is simply the accomplishment of the " opus proprium " of the congregation: the
proclamation of the gospel. The Church has neither a program nor
a law to offer (like perhaps the synagogue, Freemasonry, or Moral
Rearmament; 580) . She is " to announce the Kingdom of God."
She does not have to bear witness to a " new-improved Christian
and human Yea " but to " the divine Yea " (581) which, to be
sure, also includes the No of judgment. And here too every individual is called upon. Lastly, the co-operation is related to the
" prophetic ministry " of the congregation, to the ever concrete, altogether temporal witness in regard to particular " circumstances
and events " in this world. As a human witness, it too is admittedly
always " fallible." But it is " free " in relation to all human stand-

points (585). A "timeless gospel" would "certainly not be the pure gospel" (587)! However, the prophetic word of the congregation in its temporal character is not to be guaranteed by the Church appealing to "some sacred quality" about it. Rather it carries weight simply because it "actually hits the mark" (588). Also to this ministry everyone is called — even though it can never become the "private undertaking" of certain individuals (589).

God's action in and upon the world is related to his action in and upon his congregation as a "circumference" is to the "center" (592). God is "the King of the universe" (592). On the strength of that "center," of the Kingdom, and of the congregation which proclaims it, God's "decree," his "Fatherly providence," rules over the entire creaturely realm (592). Man's work is now to be seen as corresponding to this way in which God acts; it too is "not the center" of his activity but its "circumference" (593). "The meaning of the work that is required of man is that he is to exist in order to be able to be a Christian" (593).

Consequently, in obedience to God's commandment, work is always merely something incidental, a "secondary work." (Hence it may never become the whole of life; 632.) Nevertheless, as such it is necessary. As God in his providence "keeps faith" with the creature, so man's work signifies that he too "keeps faith with God and with himself as God's human creature" by "actively affirming" his own existence (596). He is never himself the end and aim of his work, and "culture" is not man's "self-expression" in which he rises above himself. (That is "sheer mythology"; 598.) As "something secondary," it is rather a "duty to be performed when in service" (599). For God has taken man into his service "beforehand" — every man. However, only the Christian knows, through a knowledge of divine providence, about the larger context into which God places man's work.

Work, as we heard, is never the center but the circumference. Its purpose is to enable man to "exist." That does not appear to be much. Yet Barth is frankly able to make his contention even more pointed: the purpose of work is in order that man "has enough to live by" (602). But he does not think that man has any occasion to be "ashamed" of this narrowing of what is left for

him to do. God in his providence has allowed him scope for his
" independence " and commands him to provide for his life within
this very scope. Barth alludes to the very unromantic motivation
for work in I Thess. 4:11 f.; II Thess. 3:10 f.; and Eph. 4:28. The
laboring man does " nothing extraordinary." But his work is nevertheless, as an " active affirmation of existence," an action in
which he, as God's creature, fulfills his human existence within
the scope granted to him. It is a " specifically human " action
(604). Can a man claim more for himself?

Barth then inquires in detail about the " criteria " of proper
work and enumerates the following:

1. The criterion of " having an objective in mind " [3]: work is a
work-righteous action,[4] a conduct in which we " stick to the matter
at hand."

2. The criterion of " dignity ": in work it is a matter of the
" creation " of the " conditions . . . of human existence " (607).
It is to be simply " honest toil " (608). Barth here raises the question whether what is demanded today, especially of industrial
workers, corresponds as yet to the criterion of dignity; whether,
for example, it is " politically possible and permissible to let " the
so-called economic life " be administered " in the, for the most
part, still prevailing " freedom, or rather, feebleness " (610) — a
question which in one way or another is addressed to employers
and employees, to state and to society.

3. The criterion of " humanity ": what is involved is that man's
work should be done " beside one another and with one another "
(615). In actual fact, however, it takes place " without one another and against one another " (615) ! Actually a struggle rages,
a competitive struggle which is illegitimate because it has become
an end in itself (619), and which is ruinous because the division
of labor is converted into a class struggle in an unwarranted exploitation of one side by the other (621 ff.). As appropriate as
competition and the division of labor could be, so surely has the

---

[3] " *Das Kriterium der ' Sachlichkeit.'* " To render this as " objectivity " would
be misleading.

[4] TRANSLATOR'S NOTE: Barth admits that the concept of " work-righteousness,"
which is otherwise in disrepute in theology, is legitimate here. Work is righteous
when it is done with a purpose and to the best of one's ability, whereas the work
of a dabbler or dilettante is not true work. See *Dogmatik*, III, 4, p. 606.

former degenerated into downright folly and the latter into exploitation. And God's commandment, which regards man in his work as a human being, signifies just as surely a " call for a countermovement " (624). For Western Christendom it means that she has " to bear to the ' left ' " in opposition to the champions of disorder (625) ; that is, she has to make the cause of " those who are wronged " by this disorder her own. However, in doing so she will " very wisely refrain " from identifying herself with the " platforms " of the " countermovements " that arise (625). For even state socialism is " not the remedy for social sickness " it " was once held to be " (625). The trouble is deeper seated than even the countermovements imagine. It lies in the lack of cohumanity in work (616 f., 625) and in man's unreasoning failure to limit himself in his demands upon " life " (617, 625). As long as no change takes place in this respect, " his work must be characterized by rivalry as well as by exploitation, and by an open class struggle with a capitalistic stamp or in a socialist garb." That both of them do not bear an even much worse appearance is to be ascribed solely to the patience of God (625). Of course, the Christian congregation may and must, in accordance with the situation, take the side " of this or that form of social progress or even of socialism." But this is not her " primary word "; it is rather the " proclamation of God's revolution against all the ' ungodliness and unrighteousness of men ' " (Rom. 1:18), that is, the proclamation " of his Kingdom which has come and is coming " (626).

4. The criterion of " reflectivity ": man is a " person " in his work, never merely an " effectual tool." Consequently, he needs " for his work the discipline of concentration which itself is intensely active " (626 f.). So along with outward work necessarily goes an " inward " activity; in fact, in an extreme case (e.g., in the case of the sick and aged) a man's activity may be altogether restricted to this " inward " work (630).

5. The criterion of " limitation ": work may not become " all-inclusive "; otherwise it is not a human work; otherwise man no longer has any freedom in his work. " Man's work requires . . . relaxation " (633) ; that is, man needs to be liberated from working in " self-exaltation and in a forgetfulness of God " (634). In fact, his work even needs " diversion," properly understood (636).

It needs " to expand into other directions and spheres " different from a man's usual work (637). Since man, even in his work, has been emancipated by God, his work will also include the necessary "hygiene" (635) — and that cannot but be good for it. (Barth illustrates in individual cases: it is good even for the work of a feverish diplomacy and of a supercharged, bustling church!) But above all man needs for his work — not, it is true, a mistaken contemplativeness [5] (627), but certainly — "contemplation or consideration" (643): he must be prepared to see himself and stand his ground (645). However, he will be able to do that only when he hears God's Word. " An active affirmation of human existence, the Subject of which is God, becomes manifest when he speaks to man and when man . . . is permitted to hear God " (647). In this " active receiving," the " rest that remaineth for the people of God — the real relaxation from his work — is announced to man " (648). With this sentence we are led to what Barth had to say about an active life at the start, and back again to that with which the entire ethics began: to the day of rest.

[5] TRANSLATOR'S NOTE: That is to say, a man does not need a mystical contemplation of God for his work — God being one thing man cannot contemplate! But he does need to contemplate the work that lies before him before he sets about to do it. This is a legitimate connection between the *vita contemplativa* and the *vita activa*. See *Dogmatik*, III, 4, 643.

XVIII

FREEDOM WITHIN LIMITATIONS

[*Volume III, 4, pp. 648–789*]

As is well known, Calvin in his *Institutes* allowed the much-discussed chapter " Meditating on the Future Life " (*meditatio futurae vitae*) to follow directly after a basic exposition of an ethics of faith (*Inst.* III, 6–8) and thereby placed ethics in the light of eschatological expectation. Barth follows the same course. We are not surprised that he does so when we think back upon what he said about the " fixed span of time " which is given to man (III, 2), and upon what afterward recurs many times in his doctrine of God's providence (III, 3). Man has his earthly life — so Barth begins a new section: " Freedom Within Limitations " (§ 56) — as a " once-and-for-all opportunity." He comes to know God's commandment as a creature to whom God has set his boundaries. And now it is a matter of a question about what God's commandment means for man in this relation. Barth makes it even more pointed. When we speak of the bounds God has set to man, it is a question of God's " special " relation to man precisely within these bounds (648).

What is the significance of this divine circumscribing of man? It is not a despotic act but an action of God in his wisdom and righteousness, just as God's commandment in all its forms does not overtake man accidentally but addresses him as one whom God has " actually disposed to be pleased with his commandment " (650). Thus even in his limiting of man, God is one who gives. The limitation which befalls man is not a curse and not something grievous. It is not a " negation but something extremely positive " (651). It is a " blessing "; for man is man " precisely in his limitations " (664). Consequently, in the light of the commandment man cannot acknowledge his limitedness in a " melancholy-cheerful " spirit nor by protesting strenuously, but only obediently. For the decisive thing is not that " God is his *boundary* " (as surely as this is also true) but that " *God* is his boundary " (666).

Why is that so? Why may man within these his limitations nevertheless be confident of his freedom? Because God himself has become man just in the same once-and-for-allness, unrepeatability, and temporality (655)! For this reason man has a "center" whence he comes and toward which he exists. However, he can have this center only when he exists, not in an "indefinite" or "infinite" time, but in an actual, limited span of time (657).

We should like to ask, as we have frequently had to do in our discussion of Barth's work: Does that apply to "the" man? Barth himself asks the same question. If God's covenant of grace is the center from which and toward which our life in its temporal limitedness wants to be understood, yes, to which it is "disposed" even when so limited (660), and to which, in view of the historical character of that covenant, it directly "corresponds" (661), then, in fact, it must be asked whether that applies to every man. Barth replies: No, it "cannot be said that he (man) in and with this limitation of his existence is without further ado also one who has been called by God, a partner in his covenant . . . that he is thereby also ' in Christ ' " (660 f.). One cannot say that all men " are ' in Christ ' " (663). But according to Barth they are all, in fact, " elected " to that end (663). The whole of their fleeting existence is " related " to God's " *opus proprium* " and, indeed, because " Jesus Christ is the fellow man of every existing and transitory man in time " (662). In virtue of this fact by which the destiny of every man has been affected from the side of God, the limitations actually render freedom possible. And for us the purport of God's commandment is to the effect that we " should recognize, take seriously, and occupy this place [1] as our own and as the one that has been assigned to us " (665). Here it is perfectly clear that the commandment issues from the gospel. Only then can that which it requires be understood at the same time as an offer of freedom.

Barth again presents several " criteria " by which a proper recognition and observance of the limits set to man, and thus the obedience to the commandment which meets him within these limits, may be perceived. He who lives in this obedience will simultaneously manifest a high degree of " openness " and " reso-

[1] TRANSLATOR'S NOTE: That is, our place in the cosmos and in history.

luteness " (671) : while he will live as an individual in his time, he will nevertheless live within the " We," yet not according to an indefinite and irresolute " third person." [2] (Here, as throughout this part, Barth's tacit debate with existential philosophy shines through, whose concepts he employs in part.) Such a man, in view of the fact that his time is coming to an end, will have " no time to lose," though it is true he will " know how to make time and to take time " (673). Therefore in proportioning his time he will be governed by an " obedient selection " (674). Above all he will " always " remember that he will die, yet " never " be afraid of dying (675). Right at this point it is now apparent that " without God " it is not possible to stand firm in the face of one's own limitation (677). The pseudosolutions (the philosophical idea of immortality; pacifying one's own mind with the thought that after all one is not yet dead; a contemplative immersion in " one's own translation and approaching departure ") are in truth " typical ideas inspired by fear " which arise from man's not being able to stand his ground in the face of the limitation of his human existence and instead raises himself, so to speak, into infinity or else puts on blinkers (678). The Yes to approaching death is possible only when I know that " the Lord is the barrier toward which I am going, and that he awaits me there " (680). Then the *memento mori* is not a terrifying word, but gives to my life a " qualified importance: in my uniqueness I have to do this one time with the only One, in relation to whom everything in regard to this present existence of mine . . . is conclusively decided for me here and now " (679).

" God's commandment calls everyone into freedom within the limitations of the once-and-for-all opportunity of the temporal existence allotted to him " (744). That has been discussed in the foregoing. God's commandment, moreover, calls everyone " into freedom within the limitations of his vocation, that is, of the sta-

[2] Translator's Note: " *Er wird, als er selber-in-seiner-Zeit, dennoch innerhalb des ' Wir,' aber nicht aus dem allgemeinen, unentschlossenen ' Man' leben.*" The meaning of this " criterion " appears to be that the individual will live in obedience to God's commandment in company with his fellow men, open to their advice and correction. Yet in the last analysis he will have to take the risk of his own decisions alone. He will not simply drift with the crowd.

tion in life at which each one happens to find himself, the historical situation assigned to him, his personal capability, his special
field of activity " (744 f.) . That is the subject of the second part
of our section (683 ff.) .

A moment ago we outlined what Barth understands by " vocation." It becomes still clearer when we learn that he makes a sharp
distinction between " calling " and " vocation." " Calling " is a
specifically eventful happening. It is " the imperious revelation
and publication of the special, electing and differentiating will of
God in his . . . Word and commandment " (686) . " Vocation,"
on the other hand, is " the sum total of what has taken place hitherto," and therefore of that which at all times already presupposes
God's " calling." " Calling " and " vocation " are thus related to
each other as " election " and " providence." Consequently they
must also be just as carefully distinguished from each other. But
then in this way " vocation " is also understood much more comprehensively than is usually done: by it is not meant merely some
" vocational work " (688) , but the " whole " of man's existence
presupposed by God's " calling " (689) . Barth explains his concept of " vocation " in a discussion of the view of vocation which
appears particularly in Luther (according to Karl Holl's understanding of it) . In the New Testament " klēsis " is " calling " in
the specific sense (as it is in I Cor. 7:20) . Then in the Middle Ages
the idea became restricted particularly to the calling to a monastic
life. In opposition to this " blatant corruption " Luther then com-
mitted the opposite error of understanding " klēsis " quite generally as the " induction " of each man into his particular " sphere of
work." Then, above all in K. Holl's understanding of the matter,
God's call was thought of in conjunction with, and as interpreting,
the " voice of ' things themselves and their laws ' " (692) . In
Barth's opinion this contradicts the New Testament. And yet Luther, as well as Holl, was not entirely wrong: not because God's
call is " not a glass bulb " which, " sealed up in itself, comes to
dangle over man without touching him and without being tangi-
ble to him " (692) , but because Jesus Christ, " as true Son of
God," is " also true man," and because God's calling reaches man
in his human-historical place, each as a particular individual (the
" hekastos " of I Cor. 7:20) . Barth understands the apostolic in-

junction of I Cor. 7:20 to mean: " Let every man be obedient to
the calling which has been assigned to him, as it has been given to
him. . . . Let him be and remain faithful — not to his profession
as such, but rather to the calling which has come to him now just
in this profession, here, as this man, with this origin and history "
(695). Let us note that the distinction between calling and vocation signifies at the same time their co-ordination. But vocation
does not become a law or a commandment (696 f.). It is the
" place " of man's responsibility. Man, however, is not responsible
to it but to God (696).

Here, too, Barth limits himself in particular to mentioning the
" criteria " which result at any time from the " chief character-
istics " of the " limitations " within which " God's calling and commandment are intended for and applied to man " (724). To these
belong first of all a man's particular age, and in such a way that
God's commandment meets man at every stage of his life as one
who exists in a state of development and transition: every " Now,"
as a Now of decision, is open for the future. From this starting
point Barth then examines the particularity yet also " secret but
real homogeneity " of the various age periods. The presentation
again becomes a theological paraenesis (exhortation), such as we
have already come upon in different places, in which theological
clarity and pastoral wisdom are intimately combined. A second
" criterion " follows from a man's special historical situation. Coming from the theology of a past day the danger of confusing the
course of history with divine " necessity " lies especially close at
hand here. In opposition to it Barth's doctrine of providence (III,
3) rings out afresh at this point. There is no fatalism, no determination, no irresistible leading. Nevertheless there is a divine leading which, as such, " in wisdom and loving-kindness aims at guar-
anteeing for every single man his time, a particular place for him
to live in, the place of his freedom " (714). Therefore the particular historical situation is man's " preparatory position for his calling," but not his " determination " (714). Consequently a man
ought not simply " to put up " with it but " come to terms with
it " (715). " In obedience to God's commandment " he should
" take " . . . the " opportunity " presented to him " into his own
hands " (715). Basically the same is true of the criterion which is

derived from each man's special " ability." A man can do nothing
more perverted than to rely on his own idea of his ability. Indeed,
the truth is he does not know it at all. In no case can he apply the
familiar *ultra posse nemo obligatur* in the sense that he would
know in advance where the " *ultra* " of his ability might actually
lie. It could very easily result in man's claiming to be his " own
Creator and Lord " (723) .

The last criterion is the most difficult; it follows from the fact
that in his vocation man always has a definite " field of activity."
The special thing in this instance is that this field of activity (in
distinction to that which we just mentioned) is chosen as a rule by
man himself (725, 729) . It is therefore a matter of the " choice of
a vocation," and one may well say that here, as in few other points,
the doctrine of God's providence finds — or does not find — practical application. But just for that reason the point here, according
to Barth, is not that in such a decision a man pays attention exclusively to all the inner and outer data, which of course have their
great importance, but hearkens to God's " own Word calling "
him (732) . When it occurs in this way, man is then able to prove
faithful even in the sphere which, " in spite of all human confusion," is now the sphere of activity allotted to him just in virtue
of divine providence (735) . Here the Lutheran ethics of vocation
has its place (741 f.) as a defense against all " downhearted or all
too lighthearted extravagance " (741) , in which a man wants to
put aside his particular vocation and instead wants to encroach
upon the field of responsibility of others. However, we must not
now make vocation into a law again; the monastic law of a former
day must not become the law of deified " orders " (742) ! From
that standpoint we can then understand what Barth says about the
possibility of changing jobs. The position itself is not permanent.
" The abiding thing is the calling itself " (743) . And a man can
be perfectly obedient when he moves into another sphere of activity from a former one which need not be regarded as having been
definitely fixed (743) .

Finally, in Barth's exposition honor belongs to that which man
also receives precisely within the " limitations " of his creaturely

existence. The last part of our section and of the whole book deals
with it (744 ff.) .

Here, too, the train of thought is determined by a distinction
which corresponds to that between " calling " and " vocation." A
distinction must be made between the honor which belongs to
man as the creature God has created and that which God grants to
him by his " calling " (751, 748) . The former is only a " correspondence " (!) and " preliminary advertisement " of the latter
(748) , merely a " reflex " of the real honor which God pays man
by calling him and thereby making him free (746) . But as God's
commandment is " not something like a meteor falling into man's
life " (cf. the figure of the self-enclosed glass bulb above; 692) ,
so when God does man the " real honor " of calling him, he also
has recourse " to this initial honor," " which he *has* already shown
him " (748 f.) , which, of course, is " buried " and " obscured " in
sinful man but yet does not cease to be a " *character indelebilis* of
his human existence " (749 f.) . Let us again notice how much
Barth is concerned that the necessary distinctions do not become a
rigid and static vis-à-vis of two magnitudes. Creaturely honor is not
the honor of his calling, yet it is a genuine honoring of the creature by the Creator. It is also so little removed by sin that it rather
constitutes its presupposition. Man is able to sin, and thus to bury
that creaturely honor, only because God is unchangeable, even in
that honoring of the creature. " Man can be godless. But God —
and this is decisive — is not without man. . . . There is no ontological godlessness. Even the most rabid atheist cannot accomplish
such a thing either theoretically or practically " (750) !

Since the honor which has been granted to man as a creature is
not entirely the one that " properly belongs to him " (750) , but is
merely a reflex of the real honor which has been bestowed upon
man in God's calling, so also the " criteria," by which an action
corresponding to that initial honor, and hence an " honorable " action, is to be recognized, become apparent by that new, real honor
being first kept in view. If the latter consists in the service into
which God places the man he has called, then it also applies to creaturely honor (757) . Of course, it must again be said that it becomes knowable only there where man is " illumined by that second, higher honoring through God's Word and commandment "

(757). However, it is actually also true of creaturely honor that only in service is it properly put into practice; it is therefore an honorable action in such a way that it is always necessarily the action of one who is eager to serve and to obey (759). A second criterion results from the fact that the honor of the calling, as well as creaturely honor, is peculiar to man only as " God's free gift." Consequently, man can act " honorably " in the one or in the other sense only by being " modest " (766). Accordingly he can truly have his honor only in " gratitude," " humility," and — " humor " (764 ff.). If in this way man's honor is to be understood only as coming from God and only on the strength of his service, then a third thing is also already clear, namely, that God alone " decides " about the " form " of the honor falling to man (769 ff.). Of course, from time to time there are particular valid conceptions of honor. And there is also a need for them; for without their acceptation " a man could not exist either for himself or together with other men " (770). Looked at from a Christian point of view, something of that " *character indelebilis* " can plainly be recognized in them (770). These conceptions, however, never become a law; they never have " more than a heuristic significance " (771). God is free of our conceptions of honor (773), and the honor which he does man in calling him can place him far below his " former standard of honor " (775); it can assume the form of " humiliation " and public contempt. With this is also connected the fact that in the congregation the " little ones " have their value. The " crown," in the sense of Rev. 2:10, by no means always needs to be a " victor's or a martyr's crown " (779) !

The final question concerns the safeguarding, the preservation, of honor (780 ff.). After all that has just been reported, it must be immediately evident that the man who is certainly not the possessor of his honor has every reason to accept even a threat to this honor with an " ultimate, extreme indifference " (780). Faith here affords a " marvelous immunity " (782). And yet — even here there is a borderline case, namely, where an " interference " or " hindering " of the service with which a man is charged is connected with the threat to his honor (782 ff.). But everything a man may do here (including in a most extreme case an appeal to " the political organs protecting society "; 786) presupposes even then in reality that ultimate indifference; it presupposes that the service is effectively endangered; and it presupposes a " demonstration of the Spirit and of power " which has previously or simultaneously taken place (786). It can be proper only when I bear in mind that even the other man in question has received his honor. Accordingly in the New Testament we are never summoned to a direct defense of our own honor, though we are certainly called upon to respect the honor of others (788).

The work about which we have reported could be called an ethics in the light of free grace — that free grace of God which in Jesus Christ permits man to live even in his creatureliness, which sets him free and honors him. Man does not have any other life, any other freedom, any other honor. All his riches lie in his being richly endowed. And the commandment of the Creator is his complete freedom.